★ SECOND EDITION ★

★ REVISED, ★
UPDATED, AND
SPRING-CLEANED!

FINALLY

········· A LOCALLY PRODUCED ·········

GUIDEBOOK TO ST. LOUIS

BY AND FOR ST. LOUISANS

NEIGHBORHOOD BY NEIGHBORHOOD

AMANDA E. DOYLE
-WITH- **KERRI BONASCH** -AND- **DON KORTE**
FOREWORD BY JOE EDWARDS

Reedy Press
PO Box 5131
St. Louis, MO 63139
www.reedypress.com

Library of Congress Control Number: 2014940810

ISBN: 978-1-935806-69-1

Please note that websites, phone numbers, addresses, and company names are subject to change or cancellation. We did our best to relay the most accurate information available, but due to circumstances beyond our control, please do not hold us liable for misinformation. When exploring new neighborhoods or suburbs, please do your homework before you go.

Design by Jill Halpin
Map by Jill Halpin

Photography in the book provided by Kerri Bonasch, Crestwood-Sunset Hills Rotary Club, Thomas Crone, Samantha Couchoud, Amanda E. Doyle, Jill Halpin, Matt Heidenry, Don Korte, David Lancaster, Library of Congress (116, 117), Brian Marston, Kris Rattini, and individual companies and institutions listed in the book. Thank you to everyone who assisted with the book's illustrations.

For more information, upcoming author events and booksignings, and even more insider stuff from St. Louis neighborhoods, please visit www.STLGuidebook.com, and find us on Facebook and Twitter.

Printed in the United States of America
14 15 16 17 18   5 4 3 2 1

CONTENTS

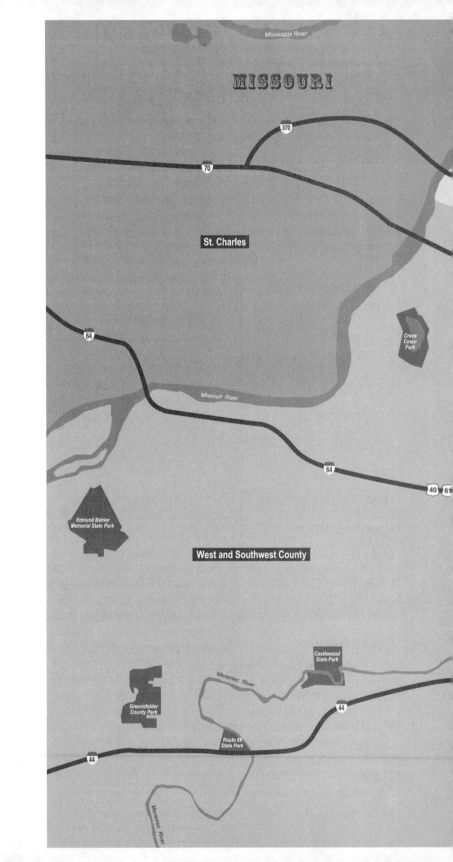

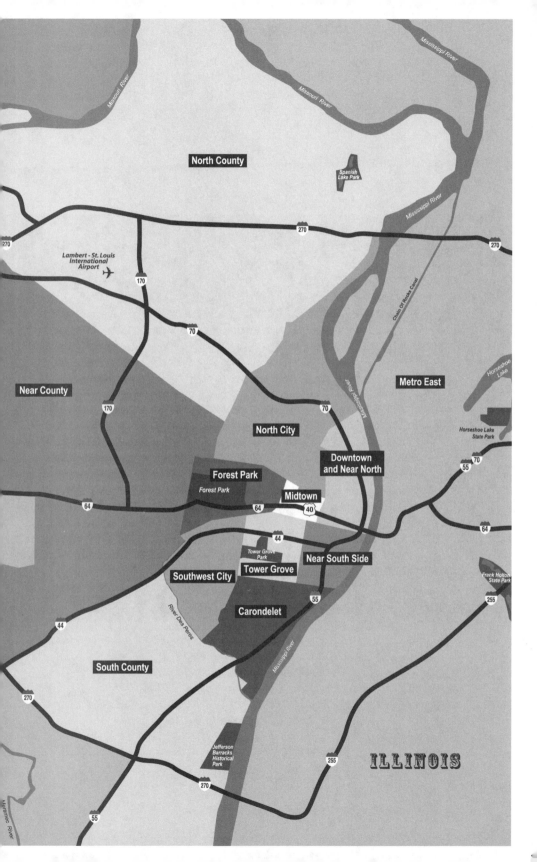

FOREWORD

Beer! Baseball! Blues! Bricks! St. Louis may be renowned for many things, but its heart is in its neighborhoods. The dynamic history and current vitality of the region are reflected in these colorful enclaves, and perhaps no better example of this exists than in my home neighborhood of the Delmar Loop.

In 1972 I opened Blueberry Hill, a restaurant and music club, in the Delmar Loop. For decades, the Loop had been a high fashion shopping district built up around a streetcar system, but the trolleys stopped running in the 1960s and the area was in decline like many areas of its kind around the country. I hoped that by programming the jukebox with an ever-changing selection of great tunes and displaying my collections of pop-culture memorabilia visitors would feel comfortable and enjoy the atmosphere as much as the food and drinks. What started out as two storefronts is now a St. Louis landmark that electrifies the whole block.

The groundwork for the gradual turnaround of the Loop was laid in the early 1970s with legislation that limited occupancy of first-floor storefronts to retail shops, galleries, and restaurants to attract more pedestrians. Sidewalks were widened to encourage outside cafes. Blueberry Hill became the first of a new era of unique owner-operated businesses.

In 1980 several businesses formed a committee to address challenges regarding lighting and cleanliness, and to create special events. In 1988 I founded the not-for-profit St. Louis Walk of Fame as a unifying educational attraction for the area. Now more than 140 stars and informative plaques are embedded in the sidewalks, providing an illuminating and engaging self-tour to pedestrians.

During the 1990s the Delmar Loop MetroLink stop opened, allowing visitors to take a clean, quick light-rail train right to the Loop and begin their visit by walking west. The once-elegant Tivoli movie theatre was beautifully restored, and many new gift shops, clothing boutiques, and restaurants with a wide variety of cuisines opened. Expansion continued in the 2000s with the grand opening of the Pageant, a 2,000-plus-capacity concert nightclub that has featured myriad artists such as Bob Dylan, Green Day, Dolly Parton, and Nelly. The unique and boutique Moonrise Hotel features the world's largest man-made revolving moon, an indoor/outdoor rooftop terrace featuring great views of the city, and display cases filled with rare space program items along with lunar toy figurines. The Loop has become a true 24/7 neighborhood with the new Peacock Diner.

In addition to the Walk of Fame, exciting attractions include the Loop Planet Walk (along which one can take a three-billion-mile walk across a scale model of the solar system), an eight-foot bronze statue of Rock and Roll Hall of Fame legend Chuck Berry, and the Centennial Greenway Bicycle Path. In 2015 streetcars will return to the area: A new fixed-track historic trolley system will connect the Loop with two MetroLink stations and Forest Park attractions.

This capsulized history of the Loop shows some of the involvement I've had in helping revitalize an historic street along with the intense dedication of countless other people, culminating in the Delmar Loop being designated one of the "Ten Great Streets in America" by the American Planning Association. The importance of such unique neighborhoods in St. Louis cannot be overstated. Other local areas are also experiencing rebirth as each community builds on its distinct characteristics.

Some of our wonderfully novel or ethnic areas are located downtown, others in Midtown, South City, North City, and the county. All of these elements are critical because they add to the quality of life for those who live across the metropolitan area, and they add to the quality of the travel experience for visitors as they discover various neighborhoods' warmth and charm. I hope you enjoy these pockets of culture, the corner bars, churches, parks, arts centers, universities, confectioneries, antique stores, historic buildings, boutiques, and more.

In this guidebook, you'll find many must-see places that make our city like no other. Amanda Doyle has taken the insider approach in the pages of this book by digging up the hidden treasures in dozens of neighborhoods across the area and providing the kind of tour recommendations you'd hope to get from a good friend. When I have friends visit St. Louis, or touring musicians perform at Blueberry Hill or the Pageant, I often recommend they check out the Museum of Transportation, get engrossed in the ever-changing exhibits at the Missouri History Museum, or make a day of exploring Washington Avenue by having lunch at the Dubliner, crawling all over the City Museum, and then ending up at Flamingo Bowl for cocktails and a few frames. Of course, we have an excellent live music scene: Two of my favorite venues are Off Broadway and, for live local music almost every night, BB's Jazz, Blues and Soups. And I always remind them as they visit different neighborhoods to marvel at the distinctive architecture.

The more you get into our local scene, the more I think you'll see what I see: St. Louis is a wonderful patchwork of old and new, of classical styles and whimsical styles. It's a city with a rich heritage of music and arts in general. It's a city of exciting sports and entertainment. It's as good a restaurant city as any in the United States. It's a fascinating city to explore, whether you've lived here since birth or made it your home last week. Maybe I'll run into you soon, checking out some of the spots in these pages.

—Joe Edwards

PREFACE (TO THE SECOND EDITION)

I have to be honest: merely typing those words you see above thrills me to no end. When this project was born—when the St. Louis neighborhoods guidebook was just a twinkle in the eye of a few of us—the thought that it would be so roundly embraced by the book-buying public was beyond my biggest dream. We are a proud lot, we St. Louisans, and it turns out if you give us a chance to celebrate the treasures, large and small, that make us who and what we are, we respond. In droves.

The first edition of *Finally!* sold out its first print run easily. Then, it sold out its hastily ordered second print run. When orders began piling up in numbers that exceeded the dwindling pile of remaining copies on the shelves at Reedy Press, we looked at each other and realized it was time for a thorough spring cleaning of the text . . . because we were going to be off to the printer again. The completely revised, updated, and expanded product is what you hold in your hands now.

Thanks for putting your trust in us to show you some of the best of this town. We hope you have as much fun exploring as we still do! And we'll leave you with the words of the preface to the first edition, because they still explain an enduring love of this place.

This is a love letter to St. Louis, one I've been working on now for more than a decade.

When I moved here in 1997, newly married to an almost-native, I remember distinctly that we drove from our apartment in Lafayette Square to Creve Coeur (where my husband grew up) to buy batteries, because we didn't know any better and were unsure of our local options. My, how the times have changed. I didn't know then what I know now: that we live in one of America's great cities, that neighborhoods from west to east are teeming with activity, hotspots, and hidden gems. A year later, my horizons had been broadened to the point that, when a tall, thin gentleman wearing nothing but briefs, boots, and a cowboy hat loped across the street at Spring and Juniata while we were house-hunting, I turned to my husband and said, "Oh, yeah, now this is what I'm talking about!" That, and the proximity of MoKaBe's coffeehouse and Tower Grove Park, were deal closers. That may not be your particular cup of tea, but luckily, there's probably a pocket of town that's perfectly aligned with your vibe, too.

What you'll find in these pages is a unique take on the elements that make many of the pockets of this metropolitan area such an appealing one in which to live. If you came to my house on a Saturday morning, I'd want to take you to the farmers' market, then hit the coffeeshop, walk the shops and restaurants of South Grand and Morgan Ford, and maybe get in the car to go check out an art show on Cherokee. What would you want to show off in your neck of the woods? This book began as that conversation, and I hope you'll find some of your favorites in its pages, but even more, I hope you'll find places you didn't even know were here. Neighborhoods and municipalities are grouped (and named) here in ways that may be a bit different than you're used to seeing, in the hope of reflecting how we actually talk about them. Information in each chapter may be arranged slightly differently, according to the most important features in each area. National chains have been largely avoided, because they usually have less influence on the character of a place than the one-offs and the independents. And good gracious, this book is by no means an attempt to be comprehensive in its scope. How could it be? Instead, take our suggestions as a starting point for your own further explorations.

The good and the bad of living in a thriving metropolis is the constant of change. Let's just assume up front that something in these pages (perhaps several somethings!) will have opened, closed, or otherwise morphed in the time since I wrote. Although we've done our best to make sure all information is current and accurate, *things change*, and it's always worth a phone call to make sure you know what you're getting into. Have fun, and viva St. Louis!

—Amanda E. Doyle, May 2014

ACKNOWLEDGMENTS

The success of this book—and its enthusiastic reception among hometowners who love to explore, residents who want to guide their visiting friends with it, innkeepers who stock it for their guests, realtors who give it as a client closing gift, families who use it to plan excursions, and so many more—makes it so much fun to revisit. My deepest thanks for their continued and unwavering support to the fine folks at Reedy Press, and to coauthors Kerri Bonasch and Don Korte for their nonstop drive to get it right.

To the many retailers who hand this book over to customers with no more than a, "Trust me. You will not do better than this," I offer my humble appreciation. We're writing for no one if you don't help us find our readers, and we authors are all in your debt. To my colleagues at my day job at *Where Magazine*, thanks for the constant challenge of keeping up with the nonstop evolution of this great city of ours. And thanks, once again, to the unflagging and enthusiastic Joe Edwards, who provided the foreword to the guidebook and continues to inspire me and plenty of other folks with his practical civic pride.

Lastly, to my family and friends who provide daily examples of how to dig into the place where you are and make a life for yourself there: thanks for walking the walk. I want to visit all of you in your cities, again and again. And I want you to visit me here in mine! To my husband, Brian Marston, and our kiddos, Milo and Molly: I love the life we create together every day here. Wanna go do something?

DOWNTOWN & NEAR NORTH

DOWNTOWN ★ HYDE PARK ★ OLD NORTH ST. LOUIS ★ ST. LOUIS PLACE

HISTORY

The portal to past and present St. Louis begins at the world-famous St. Louis Gateway Arch, and the hard-charging CityArchRiver 2015 project to transform the areas in and around the monument will provide even more opportunities to engage. In 1764, Laclede's village, which would become St. Louis, was established on the present-day arch grounds. Two more legacies of the past are nearby: the Old Cathedral and the Old Courthouse, site of the Dred Scott case. Revel in the present at Busch Stadium—aka Baseball Heaven—and don't miss the City Museum and its MonstroCity, a monumental montage of monkey bars masquerading as airplane fuselages, a fire truck, and a castle turret. Vintage architectural gems have found a place in the present as urban lofts and condominiums, trendy boutiques, restaurants, and clubs. Downtown living offers a walkable quality of life, which has brought an influx of residents into the neighborhood.

OLD NORTH ST. LOUIS

Crown Candy Kitchen has been serving St. Louisans in Old North St. Louis since 1913. Lines extend out the door for the handcrafted Christmas and Easter candy. Their ice cream is created and blended on site in an antique copper candy kettle. Try a World's Fair sundae or make it a Newport with whipped cream and pecans.

North City experienced population and ethnic changes beginning in the 1950s. After a period of disinvestment, revitalization returned. Today you will see rehabilitated historic homes in harmony with newer homes built in keeping with the neighborhood's character. The weekly farmers' market and the 13th Street Community Garden next door promote sustainable farming practices. You'll find straight-from-the-garden produce in season between June and October at the farmers' market. Crown Square, the revitalized and reopened 14th Street Mall, joins its neighbor, Crown Candy, as a classic example of melding old and new. Affectionately dubbed "Old North" by residents, this urban village is truly one to watch as an up-and-coming area.

HYDE PARK

The German-speaking enclave of New Bremen joined the city of St. Louis in 1855 and became known as Hyde Park. Designated as a local historic district, Hyde Park is architecturally rich. The Bissell Mansion, built in 1823, is one of the oldest homes in St. Louis. Nearby, both the Grand and Bissell Point Water Towers, along with Holy Trinity Catholic Church, continue to withstand the tests and challenges of time.

ST. LOUIS PLACE

Also designated an historic district, St. Louis Place is finally beginning to receive some well-deserved TLC. Columbia Brewery, former producer of once local favorite Alpenbrau, has found new life as the Brewery Apartments. There are other historically significant buildings, such as Zion Lutheran and St. Liborius, still waiting for redemption. Brick huggers and preservationists still hold out hope for the rehabilitation of the 140-year-old Clemens House, once owned by a close relative of Samuel Clemens (Mark Twain). The famed author spent time here in his early days. The Clemens home has become the poster child of decay of St. Louis's north side.

DOWNTOWN

There's more than just the Gateway Arch in downtown. A wealth of history, hipness, and fun awaits visitors. City Hall was architecturally inspired by the Hotel de Ville, Paris's city hall; the Civil Courts Building was inspired by the Mausoleum of Maussollos; and the fortress-like Old Post Office is a must-see. These are just a few of the dozens of downtown's historic landmarks. For cyclists there's the Riverfront Trail, which takes bikers on an eleven-mile trek along the Mississippi. Citygarden is a recent and successful downtown addition. Hailed as a national design model, Citygarden is a favorite spot for workers and tourists alike, with its lush landscape and internationally renowned sculptures. Washington Avenue is filled with street cafés, nightlife, and cool lofts. Holidays like Thanksgiving, St. Patrick's Day, and the Fourth of July bring some of the best parades around, with marching bands, floats, and balloons, which rival anything you'll see at the Macy's Parade. St. Louis Rams football plays at the Edward Jones Dome. St. Louis Blues hockey fans "bleed blue" in season, at the Scottrade Center. One word that definitely describes the energy in downtown is *progress*.

The long-anticipated Ballpark Village project, though changed from its first blueprints, is finally open next to Busch Stadium. The "Stan Span" bridge across the Mississippi is open too, and plans to radically transform the grounds underneath the Arch are well under way.

FOOD AND DRINK

From haute cuisine to tourist traps, you'll find it all downtown; some spots cater to office workers (read here: roll up the sidewalks at 5 and on weekends), but a burgeoning full-time population has brought more and better restaurants than ever back to the core. Up north, a handful of favorites draw from their immediate neighborhoods and way beyond.

A BITE TO EAT

AL'S
1200 N. 1st St.
314-421-6399
alsrestaurant.net
Old-school steakhouse

ALUMNI
200 N. 13th St.
314-241-5888
alumnistl.com/
A celebration of St. Louis, from the menu (Famous-Barr's French onion soup, Mayfair salad) to the décor

BAILEY'S RANGE
920 Olive St.
314-241-8121
baileysrange.com
Fancified burger/fries/milk-shake joint, with choices from bison and lamb to veggie Match Meat

BLONDIE'S
1301 Washington Ave.
314-241-6100
blondiesstl.com
Breakfast/lunch/dinner/brunch, plus coffee and wine; don't miss the popovers

BROADWAY OYSTER BAR
736 S. Broadway
314-621-8811
broadwayoysterbar.com
N'awlins come north, craw-fish, gumbo, and all

CARMINE'S
20 S. 4th St.
314-241-1631
lombardosrestaurants.com
Contemporary Italian steakhouse

{ HIGHER POWER LUNCH }

Rub shoulders with politicos and parishioners, plus hungry downtowners, at **St. Raymond's Maronite Cathedral**'s regular Wednesday cafeteria-line lunch of homemade Lebanese food. Kibbe, spinach pies, chicken and dumplings, and lentils and rice are on the menu; baklava and, for the hard-boiled, Lebanese coffee (think motor oil) for dessert. Mayor Slay is among the regulars here (931 Lebanon Dr., 314-621-0056, straymonds.net).

{ KID ZONE }

Crown Candy Kitchen (1401 St. Louis Ave., 314-621-9650, crowncandykitchen.net) will charm every generation in your party, but kids especially will enjoy the throwback soda fountain that packs 'em in for egg salad sandwiches, heart-stoppingly large BLTs, chili dogs, and oh, yes, handmade chocolates, candies, and ice cream concoctions. Small booths mean families are gonna get squished together, but that makes sharing a chocolate malt that much easier! Bring change for the jukebox to pass the time if there's a wait.

CHARLIE GITTO'S
207 N. 6th St.
314-436-2828
charliegittosdowntown.com
Classic Italian stalwart

CLARK STREET GRILL
811 Spruce St.
314-552-5850
clarkstreetgrill.com
Contemporary
American cuisine

DRUNKEN FISH
612 N. 2nd St.
314-241-9595
drunkenfish.com
Sushi and Japanese
cuisine

EAT-RITE DINER
622 Chouteau Ave.
314-621-9621
Greasy menu, semi-
greasy ambience; the
slinger is king.

GELATERIA TAVOLINI
1327 Washington Ave.
314-621-8838
gelateriatavolini.com
Gelato and coffee drinks

HIRO ASIAN KITCHEN
1405 Washington Ave.
314-241-4476
hiroasiankitchen.com
Contemporary setting
for real-deal ramen, gua

bao, and other East Asian
dishes

**LOMBARDO'S
TRATTORIA**
201 S. 20th
(in the Drury Inn)
314-621-0666
lombardosrestaurants.com
Fancy Italian standards,
great homemade toasted
ravioli

LUCAS PARK GRILLE
1234 Washington Ave.
314-241-7770
lucasparkgrille.com
Modern American cuisine,
great patio

MANGO
1101 Lucas Ave.
314-621-9993
mangoperu.com
Peruvian cuisine with an
elegant touch

MARSHA'S, LTD.
3501 Kossuth Ave.
314-371-0188
Soul food upstairs
(bar downstairs)

MAURIZIO'S PIZZA
220 S. Tucker Blvd.
314-621-1997
mauriziospizzastlouis.com
Pizza, pasta, and a
buffet til 4 A.M. (Th–Sa)

PI
610 Washington Ave.
314-588-7600
restaurantpi.com
Famed local pizzeria's
downtown outpost

PICKLES DELI
701 Olive St.
314-241-2255
picklesdelistl.com
Corned beef, egg salad,
a great Cuban sandwich,
and more deli faves

ROBUST
635 Washington Ave.
314-287-6300
robustwinebar.com
Small plates and ap-
proachable wine tastings

{ IF YOU BUILD IT }

Will they come? The year 2014 saw the long-anticipated opening of at least some version of **Ballpark Village**, a sports-themed entertainment plex adjacent to Busch Stadium. Those who remember early iterations of the plan still grumble about the elements that aren't there (a residential component, for one), but tourists and even the folks who only make it inside the Inner Belt for sporting events will likely flock to the Budweiser Brew House, the Fox Sports Midwest Live! venue, satellite locations of Ted Drewes and Drunken Fish, and PBR St. Louis (yep, there's a mechanical bull). The St. Louis Cardinals Hall of Fame and Museum, on the second floor of Cardinals Nation, satiates the most die-hard of fans ... perhaps while they wait to take their game-day stadium seats on levels 3 and 4 (601 Clark Ave., 314-345-9481).

Several spots, ranging from haute to homely, deal in gourmet goodies for your next dinner party. **Culinaria** (a fancy name for a boutique Schnucks grocery) has grocery staples plus their own line of pastas and sauces, and a nicely stocked upstairs wine department (315 N. 9th St., 314-436-7694, culinariaschnucks.com). **Grande Petite Market**'s (2017 Chouteau Ave., 314-241-7799, grandpetitemarket.com) inventory is a bit more expansive, covering spices, wines, olives, vinegars, rubs and dips, plus fine cookware, kitchen linens, and gadgetry. Hit **Piekutowski's** (4100 N. Florissant Ave., 314-534-6256) for an old-school butcher shop experience, where the fresh Polish sausage, kielbasa, brats, and pickles were sought out by Pope John Paul II on his 1999 visit to the city.

ROOSTER
1104 Locust St.
314-241-8118
roosterstl.com
Crepes, sandwiches, breakfast

ROSALITA'S CANTINA
1235 Washington Ave.
314-621-2700
rosalitascantina.com
Mexican classics and a few inventive extras, plus margaritas

SAUCE ON THE SIDE
903 Pine St.
314-241-5667
eatcalzones.com
Fresh calzones rule the menu, and the Smokehouse Salad is a winner.

SEN THAI
1221 Locust St., #104
314-436-3456
senthaibistro.com
Thai cuisine

Missouri's first documented site on the Underground Railroad lies along the Riverfront Trail. **The Mary Meachum Freedom Crossing** (on the riverfront, just north of the Merchants Bridge) was named for the free woman of color who accompanied a group of would-be runaway slaves as they embarked from the point in 1855, seeking an escape through Illinois. A colorful mural and historical marker tell the story.

{ SPORT SET }

Soak in Cardinals team spirit in memorabilia-laden dining rooms at **Mike Shannon's** (fancy, glassed-in steak and seafood house; 620 Market St., 314-421-1540, shannonsteak.com) and **Joe Buck's** (casually hip spot great for pre-game eats, 1000 Clark Ave., 314-436-0394, jbucks.com).

....

SMOKI O'S
1545 N. Broadway
314-621-8180
smokiosbbq.com
BBQ done right, they like to say; home of some of our town's most lauded snoots

STEFANO'S
504 N. 10th St.
314-241-7722
stefanos10thst.com
Modest, tasty Italian (in a parking garage's shadow), and for novelty, breakfast pizza

THE TAP ROOM
2100 Locust St.
314-241-BEER
schlafly.com
Microbrewery for Schlafly beer, pub grub with locavore leanings

TONY'S
410 Market St.
314-231-7007
saucecafe.com/tonys
Bucket-list gourmet Italian

WASABI
1228 Washington Ave.
314-421-3500
wasabistl.com
Sushi and Japanese cuisine

YUMMIE'S SOUL FOOD
2800 Olive St.
314-696-2444
yummiesrestaurant.com
Soul/Southern food

{ ROOMS WITH A VIEW }

Need to be inspired by the skyline or cultural amenities of our fair city? Book a table, sit back, and enjoy the panorama before you at **Harry's** (popular patio facing downtown, 2144 Market St., 314-421-6969, harrysrestaurantandbar.com); **Cielo** (Arch-side on the 8th floor of the **Four Seasons Hotel**, 999 North 2nd Street, 314-881-5800); **Kemoll's** (40th floor of Met Square, kemolls.com, 314-421-0555); and **Three Sixty** (named one of the top hotel rooftop bars in the world by Frommer's, atop Hilton at the Ballpark, One S. Broadway, 314-241-8439, 360-stl.com).

The spotlight (and news camera) has been trained often on the parish of **St. Stanislaus Kostka** (1413 N. 20th St., 314-421-5948, saintstan.org), just below Cass Ave. in North St. Louis. Much of the recent attention has focused on the church's separation from the archdiocese (due to disputes over property rights, finances, lay control, and especially the controversial leadership and vision of its pastor, Marek Bozek), but the church has soldiered on, with an influx of new congregants replacing some of the disgruntled who've departed. Historically designated the city's Polish parish, the church continues to offer a weekly Polish mass (Sunday at 11 A.M.) and annual Polka Mass/Fall Festival.

SOMETHING TO DRINK

ALPHA BREWING
1409 Washington Ave.
314-621-2337
alphabrewingcompany.com
Microbrewery popular for its "Firkin Fridays," when one-off cask ales are poured fresh.

BEALE ON BROADWAY
701 S. Broadway
314-621-7880
bealonbroadway.com
Live blues nightly from local and national luminaries, til 3 A.M.

BIG DADDY'S—LANDING
118 Morgan St.
314-621-6700
bigdaddystl.com
Hot-girl bartenders and drinking games

BLOOD & SAND
1500 St. Charles St.
314-241-7263
bloodandsandstl.com
Membership-only cocktail/wine/small plates bar

BRIDGE TAP HOUSE & WINE BAR
1004 Locust St.
314-241-8141
thebridgestl.com
Vast and worldly selection by tap, bottle, and glass

COPIA URBAN WINERY & MARKET
1122 Washington Ave.
314-241-9463
copiaurbanwinery.com
Pretty patio, pretty
people

DUBLINER PUB
1025 Washington
Ave.
314-421-4300
dublinerstl.com
Pints and pub ambience

FOUR HANDS BREWING CO.
1220 S. 8th St.
314-436-1559
4handsbrewery.com
Craft brewer making full use of wild
yeasts, fruit, spices, and other surprises.

LOLA
500 N. 14th St.
314-621-7277
welovelola.com
Ambitious cocktails and absinthe bar

**MISSISSIPPI MUD COFFEE
ROASTERS CAFÉ**
1223 Pine St.
314-369-0432
mississippimudcoffee.com
Locally roasted coffee available by drink
or bag

MISSOURI BAR & GRILLE
701 N. Tucker
314-231-2234
Basic beer and mixed drinks with non-
hipster crowd; former newspapermen
hangout

MORGAN STREET BREWERY
721 N. 2nd St.
314-231-9970
morganstreetbrewery.
com
Microbrewer of award-
winning varieties

**OVER/UNDER BAR
& GRILL**
911 Washington Ave.
314-621-8881
overunderstl.com
Upscale sports bar

THE PEPPER LOUNGE
2005 Locust St.
314-241-2005
thepepperlounge.com
Tiki and 'tinis in true loungey atmosphere

THE POUR HOUSE
1933 Washington Ave.
314-241-5999
stlpourhouse.com
Games, karaoke, drinks, grub

ROB'S PLACE
1428 Benton St.
314-588-7627
Unpretentious neighborhood gathering
spot good for a stiff drink and a round of
darts

SIDEBAR
1317 Washington Ave.
314-621-7376
thesidebarstl.com
Handsome wooden bar, good basics
(food and drink)

{ TRAILBLAZERS FOR EQUALITY }

The importance of **Dred and Harriet Scott** in the long, unfinished march to equal rights for all is (or should be) well known to everyone from schoolchildren on up; now, the couple is honored with a bronze statue on the south lawn of the Old Courthouse. Their 1846 legal case ultimately ended in defeat (at the U.S. Supreme Court), but set into motion social forces that could not be stopped.

THAXTON SPEAKEASY
1009 Olive St.
314-241-3279
thaxtonspeakeasy.com
Th–Sa only, utter the password
(found on the website) and gain
access to "Art Deco meets the DJ."

WASHINGTON AVENUE POST
1315 Washington Ave.
314-588-0545
washingtonavepost.com
Coffee, smoothie bar

{ ARCHITECTURAL ODDITY }

What is that odd ball atop the glazed white **Terra Cotta Lofts** (at 15th and Locust Streets)? Take off your tinfoil hat and relax: the Weather Ball started its life as a clever advertising gimmick. The General American Life Insurance Company that called the building home in the early decades of the 1900s built the eight-foot-diameter ball in 1956 and installed it on a fifty-foot rotating tower, utilizing a color-coded lighting system to alert folks as far as ten miles away as to the weather forecast for the immediate future. Didn't hurt, of course, that when the meteorologically curious took an upward glance, the company's logo, in twenty-foot neon letters, was in the line of sight, too.

RECREATION

Downtown St. Louis serves, naturally, as the public face of our town, both to ourselves and to the larger world. It's only fitting, then, that many of the longest-running parades, festivals, and civic celebrations have their home here. Additionally, the influx of residents in recent years has significantly increased feet on the streets, and both attention and investment in amenities (witness the newest, Citygarden) have followed. Former mayor Clarence Harmon used to say that he would know that downtown had turned a corner when he saw "people walking their dogs on downtown streets at any hour of day or night"; his dream has come true, and thanks to the law of unintended consequences, copious canine companions recently required a campaign to remind downtowners to pick up the resulting poop.

The near North Side neighborhoods, within sight of the Gateway Arch, have to some extent fallen prey to decades of disinvestment and disintegration of social capital—they don't house the same density of population or businesses as many of their South Side counterparts. Still, for those willing to look beyond the surface, the architecture and community resources (like parks, elite residential streets, and churches) are worth discovering, and pockets of interesting neighborhoods, restaurants, bars, and shops hold some treasures.

FESTIVITIES

ANNIE MALONE MAY DAY PARADE
Mid-May
Marching bands, floats, drill teams, and tricked-out cars compete in this annual fundraiser for a long-standing children's charity founded by a female African American entrepreneur from the early 1900s.

BIG MUDDY BLUES FESTIVAL
Labor Day weekend
Free, family-friendly outdoor music festival attracts big-name and up-and-coming blues, soul, and R&B acts.

ST. LOUIS CARDINALS OPENING DAY
Early April
A street party attended by hooky-playing office workers and schoolkids alike, with music, contests, and a lot of red.

DR. MARTIN LUTHER KING JR. HOLIDAY CELEBRATION
On the Monday holiday
A program at the Old Courthouse and a chilly but uplifting march through downtown to Powell Hall

FAT TUESDAY PARADE
Saturday prior to Ash Wednesday
Official end of Mardi Gras season lights up the night streets of downtown.

HOLIDAY MAGIC
December
In the dead of winter, this gathering of shopping, carnival rides, ice skating, and holiday music (plus indoor beer/wine garden!) promises families a reprieve from cabin fever. Inside the confines of America's Center, at 8th and Washington.

LABOR DAY PARADE
On the Monday holiday
Need a reminder of the role of union organizing in our Midwestern burg? Workingmen and women march, wave, and ride in comically small cars to show strength in numbers.

MOONLIGHT RAMBLE
August
Leisurely nighttime bicycle ride draws cyclists of all ages for fun and games, then a midnight kickoff for cruising the streets of downtown and beyond with tens of thousands of compatriots, all to raise money for the Gateway Chapter of Hostelling International.

POLISH FESTIVAL
September
Polish pride (and food, beer, music, and polka dancing!) abounds at this annual celebration, with newcomers welcome among those who've attended for generations; inside and on grounds of the Polish Falcons Nest 45, 2013 St. Louis Ave.

PRIDEFEST
June
314-772-8888
pridestl.org
Parade, information booths, food/drink/entertainment celebrating the gay/lesbian/bisexual/transgender community.

ST. PATRICK'S DAY PARADE
Saturday prior to St. Patrick's Day
When all of St. Louis is Irish and green.

THANKSGIVING DAY PARADE
November
Giant balloons, floats, and holiday cheer—plus the arrival of the man in red himself.

{ STAN SPAN }

OK, officially it's the **Stan Musial Veterans Memorial Bridge**, but it's hard to resist the rhymey shorthand. Whatever you call it, the fifteen-hundred-foot cable-stayed bridge just north of downtown (the third-longest of such design in the country) should spell relief to the expected forty-thousand daily users driving between St. Louis and Illinois.

A civic success story, **Citygarden** (801 Market St., citygardenstl.org) has garnered international attention and acclaim since it opened in 2009. National art publications fawn over the world-class sculptures amassed on the two-square-block site, and locals love the unprecedented access—the public has thus far been allowed to touch, climb on, swim in, and generally interact with the art, landscaping, and water features. St. Louisans' propensity to treat it as their own backyard swimming pool can lead to some odd encounters between well-heeled patrons of the restaurant and bikini-clad tweens, but isn't that what urban spaces are supposed to foster?

{ PUTTIN' UP PAINT }

On probably zero brochures produced by local tourism entities, the couple-of-mile stretch of **floodwall south of the Arch**—known as the graffiti wall or the floodwall or some hybrid thereof—is nonetheless an excellent spot for anyone to catch a bit of the flavor of our town, albeit from a scene few regularly inhabit. Over the years, the wall has been the site of graffiti painting both sanctioned (Paint Louis events) and not (the ever-evolving images are testament to that). It's a fascinating drive/walk: just head east on Chouteau until you can't go any further. Viewer discretion advised.

EXERCISE

FLAMINGO BOWL
1117 Washington Ave.
314-436-6666
flamingobowl.net
Roll a few frames and toss back a
mai tai on twelve lanes.

RIVERFRONT TRAIL
Eleven paved miles for your cycling/
running/walking/equestrian pleasure,
along the Mississippi River, including
some amazing juxtapositions of the wild
and the urban; easily accessed from the
Laclede Power Center from the south
or the Old Chain of Rocks Bridge from
the north.

UPPER LIMITS
ROCK CLIMBING GYM
326 S. 21st St.
314-241-7625
upperlimits.com
Quit bitching about our lack of an ocean
or mountains, and instead take out your
frustrations on the ten-thousand square
feet of climbable sculpted surface in this
downtown gym. Equipment rentals and
lessons make it easy to get started.

ARTS, ENTERTAINMENT, & EDUCATION

ART ST. LOUIS
1223 Pine St.
314-241-4810
artstlouis.org
Regional promoter of visual arts
mounts great group shows at its
downtown gallery space.

BB'S JAZZ, BLUES, & SOUPS
700 S. Broadway
314-436-5222
bbsjazzbluessoups.com
Sip and sup to live music.

CITY MUSEUM
701 N. 15th St.
314-231-CITY
citymuseum.org
If Willie Wonka dropped acid, inherited a
former factory building, and designed a
fantastical play scape for kids and adults,
well, it couldn't compare to this. Highlights
include the architectural museum, resident
circus, and everything on the building's roof.

GRIOT MUSEUM
2505 St. Louis Ave.
314-241-7057
thegriotmuseum.com
Small but serious collection of artifacts
and wax figurines of important African
American historical figures, all with ties to
St. Louis, make for an eye-opening afternoon of racial and social history lessons.

MX MOVIES
618 Washington Ave.
314-222-2994
mxstlmovies.com
Downtown's only first-run movie theater
offers three screens, full bar, appetizers,
and from-your-seat ordering.

SHOPPORTUNITIES

AIA BOOKSTORE
911 Washington Ave.,
#100
314-231-4252
aia-stlouis.org
Architecture-themed
books, toys, and gifts

**BEVERLY'S HILL/
BOXERS**
1309 Washington Ave.
314-621-1633
123underwear.com

1305 Washington Ave.
314-454-0209
mensunderwearstore.com
Fancy undies and lingerie
for guys and gals

COLLECTIVE AT MX
626 Washington Ave.
314-241-5420
collectivemx.com
Micro- to mini-boutiques
from lots of local retail
favorites (K. Hall, Adam
Foster jewelry, and more)
under one co-op roof

HAMMER & HAND
415 Olive St.
314-932-1313
hammerandhandimports.
com/
Refurbished antique
Indian furniture;
appointment only
shopping

LEVINE HATS
1416 Washington Ave.
314-231-3359
levinehat.com/
More than one-hundred
years in the lid business
has made this spot
an institution: stellar
customer service and
selection.

**MACROSUN
INTERNATIONAL**
1310 Washington Ave.
314-421-6400
macrosun.com
Asian textiles, clothing,
art, jewelry

MAKABOO
609 N. 13th St.
314-553-9555
makaboo.com
Personalizable, coo-coo
cute baby blankets, kid
clothes

MARX HARDWARE
2501 N. 14th St.
314-231-8435
135 years selling
hardware and paint to
North Siders

NICHE
300 N. Broadway
314-621-8131
nichestl.com
Retail arm of interior
design shop sells Knoll,
Herman Miller, and other
modern stuff.

{ BIG-TIME BUILDINGS }

Among the scores of significant structures, some of the more noteworthy include **City Hall** (1200 Market St., 314-622-4000; completed in 1904, constructed of Missouri pink granite and brick, and based on a design inspired by the City Hall of Paris); **Soldier's Memorial Military Museum** (1315 Chestnut St., 314-622-4550, stlsoldiersmemorial.

org; completed in 1938 to honor World War I veterans and dedicated by President Franklin D. Roosevelt); **Central Library** (pictured above, 1301 Olive St., 314-241-2288, slpl.org; completed in 1912, designed by architect Cass Gilbert and renovated from stem to stern in late 2012 in time to celebrate its centennial, receiving international acclaim and upwards of a dozen architectural and other awards for the finished product. The more than forty-thousand monthly visitors enjoy extensive technological resources, gloriously restored lighting/flooring/shelving/painted embellishments, and a performance venue carved from the building's former coal bin.); **Union Station** (1820 Market St., 314-421-6655, stlouisunionstation.com; opened in 1894; once the largest and busiest train station in the world, it ended rail service in 1978); **Peabody Opera House** (1400 Market St., peabodyoperahouse.com; completed in 1934; former Kiel Opera House reopened as the Peabody in fall 2011, after extensive renovation); **Old Post Office** (9th and Locust; completed in 1884, in French Second Empire style, and now home to a library branch, campus of Webster University, and offices); **Wainwright Building** (705 Chestnut St., completed in 1891, internationally known as the first skyscraper at ten stories high, and designed by architect Louis Sullivan); and **Mullanphy Emigrant Home** (built in 1867 as a welcoming haven for the immigrants arriving to settle in St. Louis or points westward, currently partially collapsed).

SPA AT FOUR SEASONS
999 N. 2nd St.
314-881-5800
fourseasons.com/stlouis/spa
Decadent spa experience
overlooking Mississippi River

STANLEY CIGAR COMPANY AND LOUNGE
1000 Washington Ave.
314-436-3500
stanleycigarco.com/
Fully stocked humidor and adjacent
swanky (smoker-friendly) lounge

TROVA GIFTS
550 N. 7th St.
314-588-8098
trovagifts.com/
Just-so gifts, from unique jewelry to
tabletop goodies to intricate wooden
vases

{ NORTHERN RENAISSANCE }

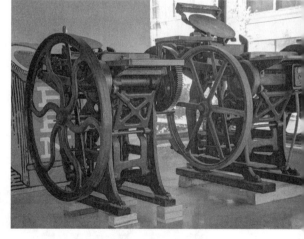

Downtown's neighbor to the north, Old North St. Louis, is rising, phoenix-like, from decades of physical and social disarray. The most noticeable turnaround? The complete rehabilitation, renovation, and rebirth of an attractive, viable neighborhood business district along the former 14th Street Mall (a 1970s urban-planning fiasco). Now known as **Crown Square**, the mixed-use storefront and apartment buildings houses a clothing boutique, the neighborhood association, law offices, and other retail and service options. It's also the site of a thriving weekly farmers' market, and adjacent to Crown Candy Kitchen, and **La Mancha Coffeehouse** (2800 N. 14th St., 314-932-5581), a community gathering spot that serves a tasty gazpacho. **Firecracker Press** (pictured above), the letterpress revolutionaries of Cherokee Street, has taken on a large space on the strip as well. It's given them room to house several of the behemoth antique presses they employ, as well as space to branch out with a nonprofit arm, Central Print, which aims to host workshops, offer after-school programming, and foster entrepreneurial growth in the area (2612 N. 14th St., 314-241-7272).

{ HISTORIC HOMES }

Two historic home museums merit a visit, for a refresher on your Missouri history. **The Eugene Field House** (634 S. Broadway, 314-421-4689, eugenefieldhouse.org) was the boyhood home of the popular "children's poet" (home also to his father, Roswell, the local lawyer who took the Dred Scott case to federal court). Along with various early Victoriana, it boasts an impressive Toy Museum with collectibles dating back to the 1700s. Further west, the **Campbell House** (1508 Locust St., 314-421-0325, campbellhousemuseum.org) recently underwent a significant restoration and is now among the best high-Victorian-era mansions in the country. Campbell family possessions populate the rooms, and the tales of fur trader Robert Campbell (who underwent a remarkable transformation from rough-and-tumble to domesticated pillar of society, and along the way acquired a strong-minded wife who challenged conventions of her era) bring local history to colorful life.

MIDTOWN

GRAND CENTER ★ MIDTOWN ALLEY ★ SAINT LOUIS UNIVERSITY

HISTORY

The Jesuit-founded Saint Louis University, at almost two centuries old, is partially located on the site of Camp Jackson, a Civil War Confederate encampment that was quickly seized by a Union force. Future Union generals Grant and Sherman were on hand as civilians. The eastern half of SLU is known as Frost Campus, in honor of a Confederate general at Camp Jackson. A statue of General Nathaniel Lyon—leader of Union forces at the affair—was quietly relocated from this part of campus to Soulard. SLU's Pius XII Memorial Library holds the only reliquary of Vatican documents outside Vatican City in their entirety. SLU gives its part of Midtown a Gothic flair, with the recognizable Gothic arches and stylized fleur de lis—as well as the extraordinary St. Francis Xavier Church. SLU has played a major role in the renovation of Midtown, purchasing more than forty acres and thirty buildings.

St. Louis's theatre district—Grand Center—rests just north of SLU. The long-gone Princess, the first vaudeville theatre in St. Louis, opened Grand Center's life as the theatre district, followed by the Rialto, a repurposed Knights of Columbus building with the same Gothic bent as many of the university's structures. The Fabulous Fox was decorated in the Siamese Byzantine style, a striking approach that still dazzles attendees today. The 1929 interior has been fully and authentically restored, from the unique carpet to the chandelier.

Vandeventer Place attracted the wealthy and prestigious with its emphasis on privacy, security, and gentility. The neighborhood, with its million-dollar mansions, was dotted with fountains and small parks. However, Vandeventer Place, like the rest of Grand Center, found new purpose in a new time, as it is now occupied by a veterans hospital, built after the end of World War II.

19

FOOD AND DRINK

A surprisingly small concentration of restaurants and bar options occupy the district, given the sheer number of people that pass through for college classes or matinée culture. The upside? You often get to see worlds colliding in these establishments. (Think mink coats and pearls en route to the **Fabulous Fox**, queued up at the **Best Steak House**.)

A BITE TO EAT

CITY DINER
541 N. Grand Blvd.
314-533-7500
saucemagazine.com/
citydiner
Retro-cool comfort food

DIABLITO'S
3761 Laclede Ave.
314-644-4430
diablitoscantina.com
Day-of-the-Dead décor
and a fresh salsa bar are
among the highlights

HAMBURGER MARY'S
3037 Olive St.
314-533-6279

hamburgermarys.com/
stlouis
National chain, yet locally
beloved for LGBT-friendli-
ness and drag shows

NADOZ
3701 Lindell Blvd.
314-446-6800
nadozcafe.com
Sandwich/crêpe/
dessert café

PAPPY'S SMOKEHOUSE
3106 Olive St.
314-535-4340
pappyssmokehouse.com
Moan-inducing BBQ,
Memphis-style

SMALL BATCH
3001 Locust St.
314-380-2040
smallbatchstl.com
Upscale vegetarian cuisine
and scads of whiskey

TRIUMPH GRILL
3419 Olive St.
314-446-1801
www.triumphgrill.com
Vintage motorcycle décor,
vast eclectic menu

VITO'S
3515 Lindell Blvd.
314-534-8486
vitosstl.com
Pizza and the best of Sicily

{ SPIKED SHAKES }

At **The Fountain on Locust** (3037 Locust, 314-535-7800, fountainonlocust.com), ice cream martinis make a great nightcap.

{ RADIO REVOLUTION }

Longtime local institution **KDHX-88.1 FM** continues to evolve, with a big move to a huge, renovated space known as the Larry J. Weir Center for Independent Media (3524 Washington Ave., 314-664-3955, kdhx.org). Still rockin' (and folkin', and hip-hoppin', and space-trippin') the radio airwaves, for sure, but now the organization can move forward on many more fronts, from teaching media literacy and production to hosting shows in its very own venue (the Stage), sating hungry/ thirsty concert-goers at the on-site Magnolia Café, and in general serving as a hub for local musicians and community-loving types. Just down the street, their Folk School (3323 Washington Ave., 314-441-6062, folkschoolstl.org) offers lessons in traditional music for banjo, harmonica, fiddle, and more, along with events like square dances.

SOMETHING TO DRINK

EXO
3146 Locust St.
314-707-8709
exostl.com
Upscale and urban lounge

CHRONICLE COFFEE
1235 Blumeyer St.
314-534-0524
chroniclecoffee.com
Northwest coffee, tasty sandwiches/breakfast, and a community gathering spot

THE DARK ROOM
615 N. Grand Ave.
314-531-3416
thedarkroomstl.com
Wine/craft beer, small plates, and ever-changing photography exhibits

{ JOIN THE HERD }

Take your place in line at the **Best Steak House** (516 N. Grand Blvd., 314-535-6033, beststeakstl.com), squint to make out the lettering on the menu board, and above all, be ready! When you hear "Next!" from the line cooks, a moment's hesitation will get you a look. And then another, more insistent, "NEXT!" Glamorous it's not, but high theatre in its own right, just down the way from some of our town's poshest performance venues. As for the food, it's cafeteria service and budget prices: 16-oz Porterhouse dinner (with all trimmings) will set you back under $20, and the Texas toast and fried okra are scrumptious.

{ FAITH IN ART }

If you have preconceptions of "religious art," prepare to have them challenged at SLU's **Museum of Contemporary Religious Art** (MOCRA) (3700 W. Pine Blvd., 314-977-7170, mocra.slu.edu). As the first institution of its kind in the world, MOCRA spotlights contemporary art with an interfaith focus, in past exhibits like "Andy Warhol: Silver Clouds" and "Consecrations: The Spiritual in Art in the Time of AIDS." Free admission.

HUMPHREY'S
3700 Laclede Ave.
314-535-0700
humphreysstl.com
Penny pitcher nights
and an endless supply of
SLU kids

SIX ROW BREWING
3690 Forest Park Ave.
314-531-5600
sixrowbrewco.com/
Low-key brewpub on the
site of the historic Falstaff
brewery; try the Whale Ale

**URBAN CHESTNUT
BREWING COMPANY**
3229 Washington Avenue
314-222-0143
urbanchestnut.com
UCBC made a big splash
on the brewing scene
(witness expansion to a
second location, in the
Grove); the expansive
tasting room showcases
their "reverence and revolution" approach to beer

{ KID ZONE }

Outside (and even inside, despite a massive new a/c system), it's often hot as blazes, and you're there for a while with the crush of unwashed humanity spilling snow cones on your feet . . . but when the lights go down and the band starts up, **Circus Flora** (on the parking lot behind Powell Hall, 718 N. Grand Blvd., 314-289-4040, circusflora.org) becomes a tent full of pure magic. Funny (and humane) animal acts, stunning acrobatics, and gut-busting clowning, all within a few feet of your seat. Few cities are blessed with such memory-making entertainment.

RECREATION

Culture vultures, art lovers, and urban revivalists converge on the institutions and upstart efforts in Midtown: many of our well-known venues, including the **Fabulous Fox Theatre** (527 N. Grand Blvd., 314-534-1111, fabulousfox.com), **Powell Hall** (718 N. Grand Blvd., 314-533-2500, stlsymphony.org/powell/index.htm), and **The Sheldon** (3648 Washington Blvd., 314-533-9900, sheldonconcerthall.org) are here, but take some time before sprinting to your car post-performance and discover that there's plenty going on beyond the brightest lights, too.

FESTIVITIES

FIRST NIGHT
New Year's Eve
grandcenter.org/firstnight
Alcohol-free, family-friendly street party (with plenty of indoor fun, too!) of live entertainment, costumes, participatory art, and fireworks

MIDTOWN ALLEY STREET FEST
Late summer
midtownalley.com
Bands, beer, and food vendors; check the website for current info

EXERCISE

MOOLAH LANES
3821 Lindell Blvd.
314-446-6866
moolahlanes.com
Roll thunder til 3 A.M. nightly, and fuel your amazing athleticism with food and drink from the full menu and bar

{ HINT OF HISTORY }

On his way to becoming "the King of Ragtime," composer and pianist Scott Joplin made his way from Texas (by way of Sedalia, Mo.) to a second-floor flat in St. Louis in 1900, today the **Scott Joplin House State Historic Site** (2658A Delmar Blvd., 314-340-5790, mostateparks.com/scottjoplin.htm). For three years, Joplin and his wife lived here and he composed some of his most famous works, including "Elite Syncopations" and "The Entertainer."

{ KID ZONE }

Wondering how to transform your offspring from wild heathens to cultured citizens? You could start, about an hour at a time, with the **Family Concerts** offered by the St. Louis Symphony at Powell Hall (718 N. Grand Blvd., 314-533-2500, stlsymphony.org). The occasional Sunday matinées feature programs like Prokofiev's *Peter and the Wolf* to grab the attention of youngsters and their chaperones. A little squirming and stage whispering is accepted, and parent-of-the-year types can use online program notes and activities to keep the discussion going at home or in the car.

ARTS, ENTERTAINMENT, & EDUCATION

THE BLACK REP
3101 Laclede Ave.
314-534-3810
theblackrep.org
The nation's largest professional African American theatre company performs theatrical and dance works in its new home, the Emerson Performance Center at Harris-Stowe State University.

BRUNO DAVID GALLERY
3721 Washington Blvd.
314-531-3030
brunodavidgallery.com
Nimble gallery showing emerging local and national/international contemporary artists, quite active in promoting the STL arts scene

CINEMA ST. LOUIS
3547 Olive St.
314-289-4150
cinemastlouis.org
Portal to all things film in town, including screenwriting competitions, Oscar-night parties, free community movie screenings, and local film showcases

CONTEMPORARY ART MUSEUM
3750 Washington Blvd.
314-535-4660
camstl.org
Non-collecting institutional gallery housed in striking minimalist building, building bridges between international art world and local artists and collectors

{ SACRED SPACE }

Now known as the **Spring Avenue Church**, the shell at 688 N. Spring Ave. was originally built by a Baptist splinter congregation in 1884 and underwent a succession of denominational and demographic changes (lastly as a Church of God in Christ Church) before being gutted by fire in 2001. Schemes for its revitalization as an urban sculpture garden have yet to materialize, but the remaining bones of the building were the backdrop for a recent installation of colorful lamps commissioned by the Pulitzer Foundation for the Arts.

{ LANDMARK }

Sharing its era of provenance with other significant Art Deco skyscrapers like the Empire State Building and the Chrysler Building, the **Continental Life Building** (3615 Olive St., 314-652-3615, continentallifeapartments.com) provides one of the most striking points on the mid-city skyline. When built in the late 1920s, it was elaborately decorated inside and out and featured modern miracles like air conditioning and a basement parking garage. The Depression, mismanagement, and other problems marred its early days, and although it remained a prestigious business address for decades, the building was emptied and boarded up in the late 1970s. Vandalized and element-weathered, it became an albatross that was too expensive to renovate and too expensive to raze. Developers rose to the considerable challenge, and after meticulous research and restoration, the building reopened in 2002 as an apartment high-rise.

CUPPLES HOUSE
3673 West Pine Mall
314-977-2666
cupples.slu.edu
On campus of SLU, mash-up of Romanesque Revival mansion, with a straightforward Arts and Crafts interior sensibility, sets the scene for an ongoing display of Tiffany and Steuben glass, Western Jesuit Mission oil paintings, and more.

DANTE'S
3221 Olive St.
314-696-2029
clubdantes.com
Weekend-only hotspot for Latin dance, reggaeton, salsa, and Spanish-tinged rock music and shows

FIREBIRD
2706 Olive St.
314-535-0353
firebirdstl.com
Smallish, largely ambience-free room still packs in crowds for local rock and indie touring acts

FUBAR
3108 Locust St.
314-289-9050
fubarstl.com
Rock/punk vibe at this frenetic, all-ages club featuring local and traveling acts

GYA COMMUNITY GALLERY & FINE CRAFT SHOP
2700 Locust St.
314-226-9899
Co-op exhibit and store space for the creations and events of a collective of woman artists and interested community members

INTERNATIONAL PHOTOGRAPHY HALL OF FAME AND MUSEUM

3415 Olive St.
314-535-1999
iphf.org
It's been a cross-country journey for this institution (pictured above) dedicated to preserving and promoting the history of photography, and having arrived here, the IPHF presents exhibitions of both photographic hardware and output. Recent exhibitions have included contemporary street photography and nature photography.

JAZZ AT THE BISTRO

3536 Washington Ave.
314-534-3663
jazzstl.org/jazz-at-the-bistro
Reverent listening-room atmosphere for sophisticated sets from local, national, and international jazz luminaries

KRANZBERG ARTS CENTER

501 N. Grand Blvd.
314-533-0367
Black-box and studio spaces host cabaret and theatre groups

MOOLAH THEATRE

3821 Lindell Blvd.
314-446-6868
stlouiscinemas.com/moolah
Gigantic single-screen theatre shows first-run movies with sofa seating and cocktails

PLUSH

3224 Locust St.
314-535-2686
plushstl.com
Multitasking multiplex is a two-story mishmash of restaurant (especially yummy homemade breakfast dishes), bar, and a double-decker concert venue for that mid-sized crowd of about eight hundred. Eclectic in design and programming.

PULITZER FOUNDATION FOR THE ARTS

3716 Washington Blvd.
314-754-1850
pulitzerarts.org
Space by renowned architect Tadao Ando is the backdrop for temporary exhibits, pieces from the collection, and fascinating interactions of artistic disciplines

SAINT LOUIS UNIVERSITY BILLIKENS BASKETBALL

1 S. Compton Ave.
314-977-5000
slubillikens.com
Played at Chaifetz Arena; the Atlantic 10 Conference SLU team turns out a respectable, engaged crowd for home games

SAINT LOUIS UNIVERSITY MUSEUM OF ART

3663 Lindell Blvd.
314-977-3399
slu.edu/sluma.xml
On-campus and exhibiting the university's collections, including Asian art and work from the Western Jesuit Missions

VAUGHN CULTURAL CENTER

3701 Grandel Sq.
314-615-3624
ulstl.org
Art shows, concerts, and discussions related to African American history and culture; at the Urban League

SHOPPORTUNITIES

Midtown is no shopaholics' paradise: head to the nearby Central West End for better boutiquing. Here, a smattering to explore.

··

GRAND WIG HOUSE
2911 Washington Ave.
314-533-6699
Yep, it's a wig store, for serious tress-seekers and costume-hunters alike

PRESTON ART GLASS
2651 Chouteau Ave.
314-772-2611
prestonartglass.com
Stained, leaded, beveled, and more: they can sell it, repair it, and even teach you how to make it

{ FLORIST ROW }

A concentration of flower, plant, and nursery product purveyors occupy a few blocks of LaSalle St. near Jefferson, in an otherwise light-industrial area off Chouteau. Though some are wholesale only, a handful of retail operations can net you bargains on cut flowers, plant baskets, floral arrangement supplies, glassware, and much more.

{ DIY }

Craft Alliance (6640 Delmar Blvd., 314-725-1177, craftalliance.org), long a staple in the Loop, has expanded to Grand Center. In addition to its gallery space, they offer a wide variety of adult and kids' classes and workshops, from handmade zines to metal cast jewelry.

{ GET YOUR MOTO RUNNING }

Need somewhere new to take dad for a field trip? Tool up to the **Moto Museum** (3441 Olive St., 314-446-1805, themotomuseum.com), a collection of rare and vintage mostly European motorcycles, dating from 1900 to 1975, give or take. Lovingly restored and displayed at eye level, it'll give you a new appreciation for the machines, and the minds that built them. Monday–Friday, 11–4, free admission. Private guided tours also available by reservation.

{ THE SHELDON'S OTHER SIDE }

Pretty sure we're contractually obligated to reference the concert hall's perfect acoustics, but here's something about **The Sheldon** (3648 Washington Blvd., 314-533-9900, thesheldon.org) you may not know: just to the west of the auditorium, several art galleries exhibit photography, the history of jazz, children's art, architecture, and other compelling subjects. Well worth a visit on their own, or before your show.

FOREST PARK

**CENTRAL WEST END ★ DEMUN ★ DOGTOWN ★ FOREST PARK
SOUTHEAST ★ THE GROVE ★ SKINKER-DEBALIVIERE**

HISTORY

Forest Park occupies a special place in St. Louis's history. It was the site of the 1904 World's Fair, where many foods we take for granted were introduced or made popular. Hamburgers, hot dogs, lemonade, peanut butter, cotton candy, the debut of Dr. Pepper, the ice cream waffle cone, iced tea, as well as the first utterance of the axiom, "An apple a day keeps the doctor away," all have a connection with the fair. Forest Park and Washington University also played host to the first American-sponsored Olympic Games. The fair brought in business from over sixty nations and forty-three of the forty-five states.

Many exhibits from the 1904 World's Fair remain an integral part of Forest Park. The Palace of Fine Arts evolved into the St. Louis Art Museum, built to resemble the Baths of Caracalla in Rome. The Smithsonian Institution commissioned the Flight Cage for the fair, intending to move it to the National Zoo in Washington, D.C. St. Louisans rallied to keep the Flight Cage intact, and the city of St. Louis purchased it for $3,500 (the structure had originally cost $17,500 to construct). The cage served as the impetus for St. Louis to develop a full-fledged zoo—the first municipally supported zoo in the world and one of two U.S. zoos where admission is free.

The first memorial to honor Thomas Jefferson now serves as the headquarters of the Missouri History Museum, which has the largest collection of Lewis and Clark artifacts in the world. In 1936, one of the most iconic structures in St. Louis was built—a cantilevered, glass-and-wood, Art Deco treasure known to St. Louisans as the Jewel Box. Originally designed to display native Missouri plants, it today is a destination for weddings and other events.

Forest Park Forever, a private, nonprofit organization, was founded in 1986 to restore, maintain, and sustain Forest Park as one of America's great urban public parks. Over $94 million has been invested in the restoration of this community treasure in the past decade, restoring the park to its full-fledged glory.

Few vestiges remain in Forest Park Southeast of the formerly hopping **Laclede Race Course**, built in 1865 from then-vacant common fields that lay far outside the city limits. The horse race track operated until 1869, when the area was parceled up for housing, in one of the first real subdivisions in town. Keep your eyes peeled for Race Course Avenue.

The Central West End was developed during the time leading up to the 1904 World's Fair. St. Louis anticipated the influx of visitors and guests. Many of the wealthy were moving westward, away from older city neighborhoods, and resettling in the Central West End. Thus many of the avenues and boulevards in the area, designed as part of the Renaissance Revival and the Romanesque movements, possess a grandeur and elegance only achieved through great expense. One of the most dominant features of this neighborhood is the Cathedral Basilica. The Central West End, which has long prized heritage, tradition, and social responsibility, was home to the artistic set—including T. S. Eliot and Tennessee Williams (who set *The Glass Menagerie* here) and many early proponents of women's suffrage, including Kate Chopin, author of *The Awakening*.

Today, visitors and residents can stroll through the stately avenues and enjoy the culture and history—a communal habit of awareness of the present combined with preparation for the future.

FOOD AND DRINK

There's some serious eating, drinking, and clubbing to be had in this part of town, from nationally lauded chefs and envelope-pushing culinary trends to down-home goodness on a cafeteria tray. The concentration of restaurants in the Central West End makes it an easy place to just park the car and wander until you find something to your liking. Manchester Avenue in the Grove is tailor-made for a bar crawl with your dedicated party people, with many bars open until 3 A.M. In DeMun, experience a pocket neighborhood of establishments so charming you may just want to rent an apartment and stay.

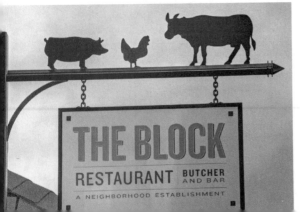

A BITE TO EAT

ATLAS
5513 Pershing Ave.
314-367-6800
atlasrestaurantstl.com
Solid, under-the-radar
neighborhood bistro

BAR ITALIA
13 Maryland Pl.
314-361-7010
baritaliastl.com
Italian, not overly
Americanized

BIXBY'S
Missouri History Museum,
2nd Floor
5700 Lindell Blvd.
314-361-7313
bixbys-mohistory.com
Great views of the park,
great plates of local food

THE BLOCK
33 N. Sarah St.
314-535-5100
theblockrestaurant.com
Butcher-happy, casual
spot for homemade pork
rinds, burgers, chops, and
addictive garlic herb fries

BOBO NOODLE HOUSE
278 N. Skinker Blvd.
314-863-7373
bobonoodle.com
Sleek, chic pan-Asian
dishes

BRASSERIE BY NICHE
4580 Laclede Ave.
314-454-0600
brasseriebyniche.com
Unfussy French, from
sweetbreads to coq au vin

CAFÉ OSAGE
4605 Olive St.
314-454-6868
bowoodfarms.com
Homey breakfast, lunch,
or afternoon tea, seasonal
and simple

CENTRAL TABLE FOOD HALL
23 S. Euclid Ave.
314-932-5595
centraltablestl.com
Brought the buzz upon its
2013 opening, with the
food-court setup drawing
comparisons to Chicago's
Eataly, among others. Su-
shi, pizza, deli, and other
stations during the day,
and seated dinner service
at night.

CRÊPES ETC.
52 Maryland Pl.
314-367-2200
crepesstl.com
Savory or sweet,
always a treat

CUCINA PAZZO
392 N. Euclid Ave.
314-696-8400
oghospitality.com
Italian classics (linguini
and clams, caprese salad,
chicken parmigiana)
and riffs upon the same
(flaming pizelle waffle
and chicken saltimbocca
Benedict at brunch)

CULPEPPER'S
300 N. Euclid Ave.
314-361-2828
www.culpeppers.com
Wings are the thing,
plus pizza, beer, and
people watching

DRESSEL'S
419 N. Euclid Ave.
314-361-1060
dresselspublichouse.com
Cozy, woody room for
Guinness and warming
pub grub

{ KID ZONE }

Give them a concrete example of what you mean
with your archaic phrases like "a kid in a candy store"
at **Oh Lolli Lolli** (802 DeMun Ave., 314-721-9600),
a tiny retro candy shop with a bonanza of bins of
licorice, gummies, sours, chocolates, and more. It's
right next door to a pint-sized playground, where they
can burn off that sugar high.

{ IT'S ALL AT THE CHASE }

Storied luxury hotel, exquisite dining, entertainment (dancing or piano bar, anyone?), elegant lobby bars, in-house multiscreen cinema: it's hard to imagine why you'd ever need to leave the posh confines of the historic **Chase Park Plaza Hotel** (212 N. Kingshighway Blvd., 314-633-3000, chaseparkplaza. com). Impressive for date night, brunch with the out-of-towners, and just about any other occasion. Dining includes the swanky Tenderloin Room, buzzy Eau Café, and quietly elegant Eau Bistro.

DRUNKEN FISH
1 Maryland Pl.
314-367-4222
drunkenfish.com
Sushi, cocktails, and scene-making, not necessarily in that order

EVANGELINE'S BISTRO AND MUSIC HOUSE
512 N. Euclid Ave.
314-367-3644
evangelinesstl.com
Cajun/Creole cuisine on the menu, live jazz/blues/ etc. on the stage

GRINGO
398 N. Euclid Ave.
314-449-1212
gringo-stl.com
Street tacos, craft beer and lip-smackin' cocktails in an enviable corner perch

EVEREST CAFÉ
4145 Manchester Ave.
314-531-4800
everestcafeandbar.com
Nepalese and Korean, popular lunch buffet

HERBIE'S VINTAGE 72
405 N. Euclid Ave.
314-769-9595
herbies.com
Refreshed room for a revered, upscale bistro

{ SHOWPLACE }

The **Cathedral Basilica** (4431 Lindell Blvd., 314-373-8200, cathedralstl.org), aka the "New Cathedral," completed in 1914, boasts among other treasures the largest indoor collection of mosaic art in the world . . . a fact mentioned with just a trace of envy by tour guides at St. Mark's Basilica in Venice, Italy (itself home to an impressive mosaic assemblage).

JIMMY'S CAFÉ ON THE PARK
706 DeMun Ave.
314-725-8585
jimmyscafe.com
St. Louis's Sardi's, with local celeb caricatures on the walls

JUNIPER
360 N. Boyle Ave.
314-329-7696
junipereats.com
Chef/owner John Perkins brought the underground restaurant phenom to town, and now he's gone all legit with this fixed-location joint specializing in Southern cuisine and bar wizardry.

KALDI'S
700 DeMun Ave.
314-727-9955
kaldiscoffee.com
Veg-heaven menu from local coffee-roasting empire

KAYAK'S
270 N. Skinker Blvd.
314-862-4447
Student-heavy coffee-shop, tabletop s'mores

THE KITCHEN SINK
255 Union Blvd.
314-454-1551
letseat.at/thekitchensink
NOLA-inspired grub like oysters Rockefeller, andouille and sautéed shrimp, jerk chicken, and more

KOPPERMAN'S DELI
386 N. Euclid Ave.
314-361-0100
saucemagazine.com/koppermans
Deli-market . . . and some regrettable sandwich names ("Ike and Tina Tuna," anyone?)

LATITUDE 26
6407 Clayton Ave.
314-932-5600
latitude26texmex.com
Tex-Mex cuisine

{ COMFORT, CAFETERIA-STYLE }

For old-school, down-home, gut-busting home cookin', get in line and don't ask too many questions at **Sweetie Pie's** (4270 Manchester Ave., 314-371-0304). You'll get a tray and a walk in front of some of the most mouthwatering veggies, meats, and desserts this side of the South. The everyman appeal also makes these likely rooms in which to spot politicians, business leaders, and other Big Deals.

{ SWEET SPOTS }

You almost don't want to know about Pie Fridays at **Sugaree Baking** (1242 Tamm Ave., 314-645-5496, sugareebaking.com): once you are aware of the wedding cake specialist's open hours, once you've tasted the whoopie pies and triple-berry pie and realized it's not just Friday but Saturday, too . . . well, it's the kind of place you'll fake other errands to "just happen to be in the neighborhood" for. At **The Cup** (28 Maryland Pl. Rear, 314-367-6111, cravethecup.com), the humble cupcake reigns supreme, in varieties like confetti and peanut butter cup, but a cakewich (born in an attempt to use up errant scrap ends from custom-ordered wedding cakes) deserves your attention as well. **Bissingers** (32 Maryland Pl., 314-367-7750, bissingers.com), a full-on chocolate lounge experience, stays open late on weekends for you to drown yourself in decadent desserts, paired with your wine of choice. **Amy's Corner Bakeshop** serves a lovely breakfast and lunch, but let's be real: the tiramisu, cupcakes, scones, and pies are what you're here for (4476 Chouteau Ave., 314-371-2253, amysbakerystlouis.com).

LAYLA LEBANESE RESTAURANT
4317 Manchester Ave.
314-553-9252
laylastl.com
They're mixing it up with standards like baba ganoush, stuffed grape leaves, and the like, and throwing in "pitzas" (on pita), a wide array of burgers . . . and Mediterranean-flavored shakes

LITTLE SAIGON
10 N. Euclid Ave.
314-361-8881
littlesaigoncafe.com
Fresh, light Vietnamese

LLYWELYN'S
4747 McPherson Ave.
314-361-3003
llywelynspub.com
Celtic pub, family-friendly food

MICHAEL'S BAR & GRILL
7101 Manchester Ave.
314-644-2240
Longtime favorite/institution for Mediterranean fare; the lamb shanks, gyro salad, lemon soup, and chicken wings are favorites.

{ ALL-IN-ONE EVENING }

Like to park your car once and make an evening of it? Consider stopping by the **West End Grill and Pub/Gaslight Theatre** (354 N. Boyle Ave., 314-531-4607, westendgrillandpub.com) complex, where you can enjoy cocktails in the undeniably sensual bar, plus tasty appetizers or dinner, then scoot next door for a great theatrical production by resident company **St. Louis Actors' Studio** (stlas.org) . . . and head back to the restaurant side for post-show discussion and dessert! Win-win-win . . . win. That's four wins.

NATHALIE'S

4356 Lindell Blvd.
314-533-1580
nathaliesstl.com
Farm-to-table . . . from
her very own farm!
Nathalie Pettus, who also
co-owns Overlook Farm
in Clarksville, MO, is the
latest restaurateur to
take on this impressive
space. Frequent live
entertainment.

NICK'S PUB

6001 Manchester Ave.
314-781-7806
nickspub.info
Wings, beer, darts, and
pool

NORTHWEST COFFEE
ROASTING CO.

4251 Laclede Ave.
314-371-4600
northwestcoffee.com
Beans-to-go, brewed
to drink

OLYMPIA KEBOB
HOUSE & TAVERNA

1543 McCausland Ave.
314-781-1299
Greek; be sure to try the
saganaki (flaming
cheese); *Opa*!

OR SMOOTHIE & CAFÉ

3 N. Euclid Ave.
314-367-8883
orsmoothieandcafe.com
Super-healthy choices for
carnivores to vegans

PI

400 N. Euclid Ave.
314-367-4300
restaurantpi.com
Cornmeal-crusted pizza-
of-the-moment

PICCADILLY
AT MANHATTAN

7201 Piccadilly Ave.
314-646-0016
thepiccadilly.com
Family owned and
operated for three
generations; comfort food
menu and casual decor

PURAVEGAN

307 Belt Ave.
314-932-5144
puravegan.com
All-vegan, gluten-free,
mostly raw menu: mari-
nated kale salad, pasta
"rawfredo," tropical tacos.
Also a hub for juicing,
yoga, and other organic
lifestyle needs.

RACANELLI'S

12 S. Euclid Ave.
314-367-7866
racanellis.com
New York–style pizza

RASOI

25 N. Euclid Ave.
314-361-6911
rasoi.com
Indian flavors, eye-
popping décor

SAMEEM AFGHAN
RESTAURANT

4341 Manchester Rd.
314-534-9500
kabob-palace.com
Kabobs, plus lamb, chick-
en, stews, rice dishes and
other traditional Afghan
delights.

SCAPE

48 Maryland Pl.
314-361-7227
scapestl.com
Date-night bistro

THE SCOTTISH ARMS

8 S. Sarah St.
314-535-0551
thescottisharms.com
Haggis, smoked salmon,
and plenty of whiskey

{ 24/7 PEOPLE-WATCHING PERCH }

Nothing attracts a crowd like a crowd . . . well, that and maybe coffee. From
WiFi squatters to dog walkers, **Coffee Cartel**'s (2 Maryland Pl., 314-454-0000,
thecoffeecartel.com) prime location on the Central West End's most prominent
corner provides an amazing window on the neighborhood. Sit outside when it's
clement, inside when it's not; either way, you'll never lack for street theatre.

SEAMUS MCDANIEL'S
1208 Tamm Ave.
314-645-6337
seamusmcdaniels.net
Irish bar, great burgers

SEEDZ
6344 S. Rosebury Ave.
314-725-7333
seedzcafe.com
Raw, organic, vegan food in small café
space: tempeh Reuben, housemade
miso soup, fresh juices

SUBZERO VODKA BAR
308 N. Euclid Ave.
314-367-1200
More than twenty varieties, plus toppings
like eel and fried egg

THAI 202
235 N. Euclid Ave.
314-367-2002
thai202.com
Quick turnaround Thai, from tom yum
soup and pad Thai to curries and stir-
fried dishes

TOM'S BAR AND GRILL
20 S. Euclid Ave.
314-367-4900
tomsbarandgrill.com
CWE staple for more than four decades,
serving burgers, fish & chips, and cold
beer. Blue cheese chips are delish.

TORTILLARIA
8 S. Euclid Ave.
314-361-4443
tortillaria.net
Homemade salsa bar, fresh guac, and
savory street corn are among the Mexican favorites in this homey spot.

WILD FLOWER CAFÉ
4590 Laclede Ave.
314-367-9888
wildflowerdining.com
Whimsical, casual
American food

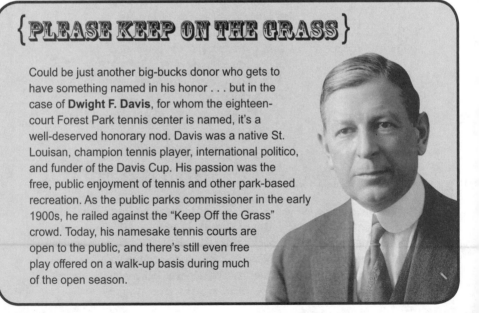

{ PLEASE KEEP ON THE GRASS }

Could be just another big-bucks donor who gets to have something named in his honor . . . but in the case of **Dwight F. Davis**, for whom the eighteen-court Forest Park tennis center is named, it's a well-deserved honorary nod. Davis was a native St. Louisan, champion tennis player, international politico, and funder of the Davis Cup. His passion was the free, public enjoyment of tennis and other park-based recreation. As the public parks commissioner in the early 1900s, he railed against the "Keep Off the Grass" crowd. Today, his namesake tennis courts are open to the public, and there's still even free play offered on a walk-up basis during much of the open season.

{ FORGET THE EGGS }

Instead, spend your Easter Sunday scoping out the immaculately restored/maintained classic cars entered in the Horseless Carriage Club of Missouri's **Easter Concours d'Elegance**: the car show is a more than fifty-year tradition, drawing thousands to Forest Park (314-991-HONK, hccmo.com). The St. Louis Street Rod Association hosts a simultaneous car show nearby, with about five-hundred display cars (314-315-1712, stlstreetrods.com)

SOMETHING TO DRINK

34 CLUB
34 N. Euclid Ave.
314-367-6674
Basic booze, divey digs

ATTITUDES
4100 Manchester Ave.
314-534-0044
LGBT-welcoming as long as you dance, dance, dance!

BIG MOE'S
1072 Tower Grove Ave.
314-324-8697
Drink specials and freestyle rap nights

BRENNAN'S/ MARYLAND HOUSE
4659 Maryland Ave.
314-497-4449
Wine and cigar sales downstairs, oddly subdivided apartment rooms for drinks upstairs

COMET COFFEE
5708 Oakland Ave.
314-932-7770
cometcoffeestl.com
Serious coffee and espresso from a handful of roasters, plus brewed-to-order tea and gourmet baked goods (Lithuanian bacon bun, anyone?)

ERNEY'S 32
4200 Manchester Ave.
314-652-7195
Vodka and video dancing for LGBT crowd

FELIX'S
6335 Clayton Ave.
314-645-6565
felixspizzapub.com
Martinis and live music

GAMLIN WHISKEY HOUSE
236 N. Euclid Ave.
314-875-9500
gamlinwhiskeyhouse.com
Yes, it's a full-service, steak-centric restaurant,

too . . . but the whiskey, bourbon, and scotch are the stars, both behind the bar and in the décor.

HANDLEBAR
4127 Manchester Ave.
314-652-2212
handlebarstl.com
Bike-themed watering hole

JUST JOHN
4112 Manchester Ave.
314-371-1333
justjohnsclub.com
LGBT-friendly, bingo, dance, and karaoke

MANDARIN LOUNGE
44 Maryland Pl.
314-367-4447
mandarinlounge.net
Asian motifs, rooftop patio

REHAB
4054 Chouteau Ave.
314-652-3700
LGBT-welcoming party corner

SOMETHING TO DRINK

RISE COFFEE HOUSE
4180 Manchester Ave.
314-769-9535
risecoffeestl.com
Blueprint and Intelligentsia coffee, Whisk baked goods, brown-bag lunches and a super-friendly (and kid-welcoming) vibe

ROSIE'S PLACE
4573 Laclede Ave.
314-361-6423
Cheap drinks,
no pretensions

SANCTUARIA
4198 Manchester Ave.
314-535-9700
sanctuariastl.com
Inventive cocktails and tapas

SASHA'S WINE BAR
706 DeMun Ave.
314-863-7274
sashaswinebar.com
Wines, cheeses, and noshes

SUBZERO VODKA BAR
306 N. Euclid Ave.
314-367-1200
subzerovodkabar.com
Three-hundred vodkas, twenty-five-foot ice bar

TAHA'A TWISTED TIKI
4199 Manchester Ave.
314-202-8300
tahaatiki.com
Tropical-themed food (ceviche, meat skewers, and the like) and tiki drinks from Zombies to the Pineapple Punisher

URBAN CHESTNUT GROVE BREWERY AND BIERHALL
4465 Manchester Ave.
314-222-0143
urbanchestnut.com
Second, and larger, location for the popular craft brewer; this one boasts a full kitchen and expansive room for tastings

THE WINE PRESS
4436 Olive St.
314-289-9463
stlwinepress.com
Wine, beer, apps, acoustic music

{ ENTERTAINMENT & ECLETICA }

The scene at **Joe's Café and Gallery** on a Thursday evening is often magical, always lively, and occasionally indescribable (6014 Kingsbury Ave., Skinker-DeBaliviere, 314-862-2541, Facebook.com/ArsPopuliGallery). The two adjacent spaces offer, on the café side, energetic musical entertainment for a 30+ crowd, BYOEverything, and the wildly random décor from the mind/collection of proprietor (and artist) Bill Christmas. Next door, he curates gallery shows also open on Thursday nights. Just when you think you've seen it all, step outside into the tiki garden for more encounters with random stuff.

RECREATION

It's the eight-hundred-pound gorilla of recreational opportunities (to say nothing of culture and attractions; sorry, everywhere else!): Forest Park lies at the heart of these neighborhoods, and, really, is the heart of the entire region. At around thirteen-hundred acres (five-hundred more than New York's Central Park, not that we're bragging), this verdant oasis offers myriad outdoor amenities, including almost six miles of dual-surface trails given a nonstop workout by runners, walkers, cyclists, and bladers; hiking trails throughout the park's interior; fishing in the lakes and lagoons; two golf courses; eighteen-thousand trees for arborists and avid birders; and an unbeatable smorgasbord of humankind.

FESTIVITIES

ANCIENT ORDER OF HIBERNIANS ST. PATRICK'S DAY PARADE
Dogtown
stlhibernians.com
March 17
It's as Irish as it gets, and you should bundle up and experience it at least once in your St. Louis tenure.

FAIR ST. LOUIS VEILED PROPHET PARADE
Weekend prior to July 4
Free lineup of concerts, air shows, and fireworks, relocated for 2014 to Forest Park; VP Parade is among the nation's oldest continuous parades, at 130+ years, and has the distinction of having been dreamt up by a group of businessmen in 1878 who imagined that the appearance of a mysterious "Veiled Prophet" could capture the public's imagination.

GREAT FOREST PARK BALLOON RACE
Forest Park
greatforestparkballoonrace.com
September
Most hot air in town outside of political campaigning season, with many folks

advocating the night-before-the-race "balloon glow" as the must-do

GREEK FESTIVAL
4967 Forest Park Blvd.
sngoc.org
Labor Day weekend
St. Nicholas Greek Orthodox Church, where you can stuff your face with phyllo and catch some folk dancing

GROVEFEST
October
Art, music, and general neighborhood mayhem draw big crowds to one of the city's latest hot districts.

HALLOWEEN IN THE CWE
Central West End
314-367-2220
thecwe.org
Halloween weekend
A nod to the kiddos with a morning parade and costume contest, but this is really all about grown-ups getting dressed up and getting drinks.

CITY CYCLING TOURS

Forest Park Visitor Center
314-616-5724
citycyclingtours.com
Bike, helmet, and water, along with
expert narration, included on this three-
hour tour of Forest Park (ignore fateful
Gilligan theme in the back of your head)

HANDBALL & RACQUETBALL IN
FOREST PARK

fphcbigblue.com
Four wooden and four concrete courts
are perfect for pick-up ball, just north
of the visitor center

THE HIGHLANDS GOLF
& TENNIS CENTER

5163 Clayton Rd.
314-531-7773
highlandsgolfandtennis.com
Nine holes, state-of-the-art driving range,
and clay tennis courts in Forest Park

IPOD WALKING TOURS
OF FOREST PARK

Check out a free player pre-loaded with
four narrated tours from the visitor center,
or visit forestparkforever.org to download
the mp3s to your own player.

NORMAN K. PROBSTEIN
GOLF COURSE

6141 Lagoon Dr.
314-367-1337
forestparkgc.com
Three 9-hole courses, all par 35, can be
split up or played together, with equipment
and pro shop on-site in Forest Park.

STEINBERG SKATING RINK

400 Jefferson Dr.
314-367-7465
steinbergskatingrink.com
Practice your Rockefeller Center spins
without big-city prices (or big-city credit
card acceptance). Open Nov–March,
weather permitting.

{ FUNPLEX DUPLEX }

At **Atomic Cowboy** (4140 Manchester Rd.,
314-775-0775, atomiccowboystl.com), you're
as likely to see Mr. Leather 2010 tossing back
shots at the bar as you are to find a suburban
family with little kids munching chips and salsa
at a booth on the patio . . . and that's just an
average afternoon. Then come the burlesque
shows, the cycling-themed poster art shows,
raucous concerts, bonfire parties, and just about
anything else you can think of. It's a cacophony
that somehow works. And the burritos are tasty,
too. Far more sedate, but equally multipurpose, **Café Ventana** (3919 West
Pine Blvd., 314-531-7500, cafeventana.com) steams from early morning til late
at night on a crowd-pleasing mix of coffee, beignets, absinthe, bagels, and a
Sunday jazz brunch, with a healthy dose of SLU students studying through it all.

{ KID ZONE }

Sure, **Forest Park** has many of the major attractions you know by heart. But if you're looking for fresh inspiration, here are some seasonal locations for you and your family. Climb to your heart's content at **Turtle Park**, designed by artist Robert Cassilly. Or you can explore the **Variety Wonderland Playground**, with its fun-for-all-ages design. Pop into **Nora's** for picnic victuals, then spread a blanket out on the lawn of the **Missouri History Museum** for an outdoor concert. The **Boathouse** offers refreshments to fuel your afternoon boating, as well as paddle or rowboat rentals. In colder weather, visit **Art Hill**, one of the best sledding spots in St. Louis, then head to the **visitor center** where a café can whip up some hot chocolate to warm those cold fingers. Too hot or too cold or too . . . whatever to be outdoors? It seems counterintuitive, but head to the **Saint Louis Zoo**. Start with indoor films and hands-on fun in the Living World building. From there, a short walk will get you to the fascinating **Insectarium**: you'll know it by the giant beetle sculpture outside. Finally, push on up the hill and duck into the **Bird House**, where you can get really close to hornbills, owls, roadrunners, and all manner of fowl.

TURTLE PARK
Clayton Ave. at Art Hill Pl.

NORA'S
1136 Tamm Ave.
314-645-2705
norasindogtown.com

THE BOATHOUSE
6101 Government Dr.
314-367-2224

MISSOURI HISTORY MUSEUM
5700 Lindell Blvd.
314-746-4599
mohistory.org

VARIETY WONDERLAND PLAYGROUND
5595 Grand Dr.
314-877-1309

VISITOR CENTER
5595 Grand Dr.
314-367-7275

ST. LOUIS ART MUSEUM
1 Fine Arts Dr.
314-721-0072

SAINT LOUIS ZOO
1 Government Dr.
314-781-0900

ARTS, ENTERTAINMENT, & EDUCATION

CHESS CLUB & SCHOLASTIC CENTER OF SAINT LOUIS
4657 Maryland Ave.
314-361-2437
saintlouischessclub.org
Attractive storefront home for casual games, big-time tournaments, lessons, and more, all in the interest of promoting chess in the community

CLUB VIVA
408 N. Euclid Ave.
314-361-0322
clubvivastl.com
High-energy dance floor hosts reggae, world, and wildly popular salsa nights for 21+.

THE CHAPEL
6238 Alexander Dr.
314-721-0943
chapelvenue.com
Literal "sanctuary for the arts" in converted Gothic chapel offers free space for bands, musicians, poets and other artists to present work in lovely, intimate setting.

{ ARCHITECTURAL ODDITY }

Where Kingshighway meets Washington, position yourself to admire **Holy Corners**, a designated National Register Historic District that encompasses six houses of worship, built between 1902 and 1908, concentrated at the intersection. It's also perhaps the only corner in the city from which you can test your knowledge on this point: Can you spot the three distinct architectural column styles? You're looking for Corinthian, Doric, and Ionic.

THE GRAMOPHONE
4243 Manchester Ave.
314-531-5700
thegramophonelive.com
Small live music venue with a bit of a loungey vibe, hosting everything from local blues to DJ spins to touring Americana bands, plus a comfy bar, 21+

HI-POINTE THEATRE
1005 McCausland Ave.
314-995-6273
hi-pointetheatre.com
Single-screen movie theatre, built in 1922 but upgraded charmingly over the years, is a spectacular place to catch a flick (with five hundred of your closest friends).

KEMPER ART MUSEUM
One Brookings Dr.
314-935-4523
kemperartmuseum.wustl.edu/
On the Washington University campus and showcasing the university's nineteenth- to twenty-first-century American and European treasures

MISSOURI HISTORY MUSEUM LIBRARY AND RESEARCH CENTER
225 S. Skinker Blvd.
314-746-4500
mohistory.org
Archives (documents, photographs, objects) about St. Louis, the state, the Louisiana Purchase Territory, and regional river valleys, open to the public Tu–Sa (call for specific collection access requirements)

{ GALLERY WALK }

Immerse yourself in culture at some of the Central West End's art galleries. **Atrium Gallery** (4814 Washington Ave., 314-367-1076, atriumgallery.net; sculpture, mixed-media and large-scale work), **Duane Reed Gallery** (4729 McPherson Ave., 314-361-4100, duanereedgallery.com; glass, painting, photography, and fiber art), **Philip Slein Gallery** (1319 Washington Ave., 314-621-4634, philipsleingallery.com), and **William Shearburn Gallery** (665 S. Skinker Blvd., 314-367-8020, shearburngallery.com; sculpture, painting, and mixed-media) have established themselves as homes for the most promising and engaging regional and international artists.

{ DRINK IT IN }

Some people frequent art openings strictly to score a few plastic cups of Costco wine. Why not upgrade to a more legit scene? At the **Vino Gallery** (4701 McPherson Ave., 314-932-5665, thevinogallery.com), the wine is front and center (and it's good stuff, too, with a concentration on small-production artisan wines), but local art hangs on the walls, giving you a chance to stretch those mental muscles a little.

THE MUNY
1 Theatre Dr.
314-361-1900
muny.org
Come sweat it out at the nation's oldest and largest outdoor theatre, which mounts crowd faves like *Annie*, *Roman Holiday*, and *West Side Story* each summer from June to August; 1,500 free seats for each show fill up fast, so line up early if you're averse to paying.

ST. LOUIS SHAKESPEARE
314-361-5664
stlshakespeare.org
The long-running theatre company has nearly thirty years under its cloak, presenting the entire canon of the Bard. (In answer to your question: they'll complete the canon in 2015.) Their longtime association with their former home theater has ended, so now you'll find them practicing their trade at venues including DeSmet Jesuit High School, The Regional Arts Commission, Florissant Civic Center, and other local stages.

TAVERN OF FINE ARTS
313 Belt Ave.
314-367-7549

tavern-of-fine-arts.blogspot.com
Local art on the walls, chamber music and cabaret on the bill; plus wine bar, café, desserts

THIRD DEGREE GLASS FACTORY
5200 Delmar Blvd.
314-367-4527
thirddegreeglassfactory.com
Glass studio and gallery space most known for fun "Third Friday Open House," with free glassblowing demos, live entertainment, and food/drink for sale

UNION AVENUE OPERA
733 Union Blvd.
314-361-2881
unionavenueopera.org
Professional opera sung in their original languages, by composers from Bizet to Verdi

WHITE FLAG PROJECTS
4568 Manchester Ave.
314-531-3442
whiteflagprojects.org
Nonprofit, cutting-edge gallery space exhibits local and national art, and recently garnered a grant from the Andy Warhol Foundation.

SHOPPORTUNITIES

10DENZA
44 Maryland Plaza
314-361-1010
10denza.com
"Lifestyle boutique" caters to the clothing, accessory, and pop culture needs of the fashionable young St. Louisan.

BOWOOD FARMS
4605 Olive St.
314-454-6868
bowoodfarms.com
Locally supplied plant nursery with eclectic gift shop, too

CENTRO MODERN FURNISHINGS
4727 McPherson Ave.
314-454-0111
centro-inc.com
Sleek furniture and accessories from Herman Miller, Alessi, and more

CITY BOUTIQUE
4300 Manchester Ave.
314-657-0125
ilovecityboutique.com
Trendy clothes for sassy young things, in a wide array of sizes: formal wear, hot dresses, statement tees, and a stellar steppin' out shoe selection

DOT DOT DASH
6334 N. Rosebury Ave.
314-862-1962
dotdotdashboutique.com
Comfy classic clothes for moms and tots, many Euro lines

{ MADE TO ORDER }

No mass merch will do for you: unique or nothing, right? Extend your sensibilities to your scent by mixing up your own custom fragrance at **Cassie's Fragrance Boutique and Scent Bar** (316 N. Euclid Ave., 314-454-1010, cassiesscents.com). More than four-thousand possibilities await your discerning sniff, and the result can be used to blend everything from spray perfumes to bath oils, aftershave to hair spray.

{ DECOR DIG }

If your idea of nesting is less Restoration Hardware and more "clambering around piles of—who knows what?—to find that perfect finial," **Fellenz Antiques** (439 N. Euclid Ave., 314-367-0214) might be your idea of hoarder heaven: vintage and salvage items from wood doors and wrought-iron gates to odd-sized doorknobs, escutcheon plates, and much more are piled willy-nilly (and seemingly priced that way, too) for your perusal. The hours and service might best be described as erratic, so don't expect a lot of hand-holding. Just across the street, **Art Glass Unlimited** (412 N. Euclid Ave., 314-361-0474, artglassunlimited.com) offers a more serene experience, with custom stained-glass work, and high-quality repair for the glass in your home (or church).

GOLDEN GROCER
335 N. Euclid Ave.
314-367-0405
goldengrocer.com
Natural health foods and supplements in a crunchy ambience

IVY HILL
304 N. Euclid Ave.
314-367-7004
ivyhillboutique.com
Stylish women's boutique for cute, current clothes and gifts

LIBBY'S
4742 McPherson Ave.
314-454-3003
Colorful cruise wear, separates and evening wear for gals of a certain age

NEW MARKET HARDWARE
4064 Laclede Ave.
314-371-1720
newmarkethardware.com
Old-school dry goods for every nook and cranny of your aging house

ST. LOUIS STRINGS
6331 Clayton Ave.
314-644-6999
stlstrings.com
Violin, cello, and bass manufacture, repair, sales, and rental

THE SILVER LADY
4736 McPherson Ave.
314-367-7587
thesilver-lady.com
Stunning sterling silver jewelry for men and women, great customer service and advice

A TASTE OF LUXURIE
364 N. Boyle Ave.
314-534-3800
atasteofluxurie.com
Of-the-moment designer trends for ladies

WOLFGANG'S PET STOP
328 N. Euclid Ave.
314-367-8088
wolfgangspetstop.com
Treats, toys, grooming, and necessities for the furry set

{ DELIBERATELY LITERATE }

The Central West End enjoys a reputation as a literati locus, with stalwarts of the scene set conveniently along Euclid Avenue. From **Left Bank Books** (399 N. Euclid Ave., 314-367-6731, left-bank.com) to **Big Sleep Books** (239 N.

Euclid Ave., 314-361-6100, bigsleepbooks.com; hole-in-the-wall devoted to mysteries) to the newish **Schlafly branch of the St. Louis Public Library** (225 N. Euclid Ave., 314-367-4120, slpl.org), it's the kind of place you could bring your notebook (paper or digital), get a corner table, and get crackin' on the great American novel. Before long, your own sculpted author bust might be added to the installations at **Writers' Corner** (Euclid at McPherson), joining Tennessee Williams and T. S. Eliot.

{ KID ZONE }

In an old house in the West End that was covered in vines . . . well, okay, it's not quite *Madeline*, but there is something otherworldly, and old-fashioned, and thoroughly enchanting about the longtime home of **Bob Kramer Marionettes** (4143 Laclede Ave., Central West End, 314-531-3313, kramersmarionnettes.com). Kramer and his puppeting partner Dug Feltch are dedicated to the point of fanatical about the magic of puppets. Together they handcraft each character that appears in their shows, a process that can take fifteen hundred hours from start to finish. They're evangelists for the importance of unplugged entertainment, and with generations of St. Louis kids (and adults) having passed through their doors, they're clearly doing something right. Reservations are required for shows, which take place at 10 A.M. and 1 P.M. Monday–Saturday, and 1 P.M. Sunday.

TOWER GROVE

BOTANICAL HEIGHTS ★ COMPTON HEIGHTS ★ OAK HILL ★ SHAW ★ SOUTHWEST GARDEN ★ TOWER GROVE EAST ★ TOWER GROVE SOUTH

HISTORY

This collection of neighborhoods is home to the world-class Missouri Botanical Garden, aka Shaw's Garden, after founder Henry Shaw. Tower Grove Park, with its Victorian-era pavilions, is another of Henry Shaw's legacies that continues to delight locals and visitors alike. Homes were built to attract a range of incomes, making the area accessible for working people as well as professionals. The developer also offered long-term financing to attract potential buyers—something new to St. Louis. Diversity of housing stock and residents is a case study of neighborhood stability through the years.

Truly a neighborhood of neighborhoods, Tower Grove—with its architecture, landscape of tree-lined streets, walkable shopping on South Grand, and beauty of the Missouri Botanical Garden and Tower Grove Park—is a wonderful place to be throughout the year.

COMPTON HEIGHTS

This magnificent neighborhood is also a National Historic District of about two hundred homes, planned in 1889 with the view that nature was a neighbor. Wide setbacks and curving streets were designed to create beautiful views. Compton Hill Reservoir Park with its historic water tower greets you at the neighborhood's Grand Blvd. entrance. This engineering marvel, completed in 1896, is one of just seven remaining in the United States, three of which are in St. Louis City. Also located at the park is a controversial statue called *The Naked Truth*. Unveiled in 1914 it was considered quite daring for the times, so much so that a jury requested the image be in bronze versus white marble to hide some of the "nakedness."

SHAW

Named for Missouri Botanical Garden founder and philanthropist Henry Shaw, Shaw is one of the oldest and most intact neighborhoods of St. Louis City's fourteen historic districts. There are beautiful grand homes on Flora and Shaw Places as well as spacious multifamily dwellings. In a recent *New York Times* travel piece, the Shaw neighborhood was depicted as "the leafy neighborhood where stately architecture mixes with hip spots." Naturally, the locals knew all along this was right on the money.

SOUTHWEST GARDEN

Within the Southwest Garden neighborhood, you'll find a colorful historic collection of turn-of-the-century frame and brick homes, storybook bungalows, two- and four-family flats, and an area of newer single-family homes. Brick became the building material of choice after a fire destroyed fifteen city blocks in 1849, and frame construction was officially banned. Clay deposits found west of Kingshighway helped to create a flourishing brick industry. German, Irish, and Italian immigrant factory workers and African Americans working the railroad settled this area in the 1890s.

TOWER GROVE EAST

The location of four major streetcar lines made the neighborhood prime for institutional, cultural, and entertainment uses. The 7th District Police Station (check out the cool ironwork), Messiah Lutheran Church, and the Strassberger Music Conservatory (you can still see the composers' faces on the sides of the building) are some of the places that created the neighborhood's character. Tower Grove East's eclectic fabric has contributed to its continuity through time. Be sure to drive down Halliday and Crittenden.

TOWER GROVE HEIGHTS

Tower Grove Heights is a mini-neighborhood—its boundaries are Utah (south), Gustine (west), Arsenal (north), and Grand (east)—built out as nearly a single piece between 1905 and 1908. It was required that all residential structures be constructed of brick or stone, two-and-a-half stories high, and set back from the street at a uniform distance. Hartford and Juniata were designated as single-family streets while Arsenal, Connecticut, Wyoming, and Humphrey were "two-family" streets. Tucked away in Tower Grove Heights you'll find coffeehouses and neighborhood pizza places, which are widely considered metro-area eating destinations. Check out the homes on Utah.

TOWER GROVE SOUTH

The city of St. Louis calls this area Tower Grove South. Another name used through the years is Oak Hill, the name given the area by the early landowner. Official boundaries are a bit flexible. Everyone agrees on the Gustine (east) and Arsenal (north) boundaries. City agencies have made Chippewa the southern boundary and Kingshighway the western border. Most residents, however, see the neighborhood's southern boundary as Humphrey and the western boundary as Morgan Ford.

Is it Morganford or Morgan Ford? In typical St. Louis fashion, there seems to be more than one spelling. Residents seem to prefer Morganford; city officials use Morgan Ford. Either way, there is a spirited rebirth of the neighborhood's main street well under way. More local and intimate than Grand Blvd., this resurging district has become both a hangout for the locals and a destination for metro-area residents.

FOOD AND DRINK

The neighborhoods surrounding the park are home to a wide range of ethnic eateries (at some of the region's most reasonable prices), from Moroccan dishes like spicy harira soup at **Baida**, to the rare, chopped beef kitfo sopped up with sour injera bread at **Meskerem Ethiopian Cuisine**. Other global cuisines represented include Middle Eastern, Japanese, Chinese, Thai, Vietnamese, and Italian and plenty of good ol' American food when you're craving familiarity. This variety makes the choices here especially friendly for vegetarian/vegan diners, and the health- and environment-conscious will feel right at home in the burgeoning locavore paradise along Morgan Ford Rd.

A BITE TO EAT

BAIDA
3191 S. Grand Blvd.
314-932-7950
Moroccan delights from savory stuffed pastries (m'lwee) to tasty tajines; belly dancing first Saturdays

BASIL SPICE
3183 S. Grand Blvd.
314-776-1530
basilspicethai.com
Thai cuisine

BLACK THORN PUB
3735 Wyoming St.
314-776-0534
Excellent pizza in grungy digs

CAFÉ MOCHI
3221 S. Grand Blvd.
314-773-5000
cafemochistl.com
Sushi/Japanese cuisine

CAFÉ NATASHA
3200 S. Grand Blvd.
314-771-3411
cafenatasha.com
Middle Eastern; kabobs

THE DAM
3173 Morgan Ford Rd.
314-771-3173
thedamstl.com
Specialty burgers, dressed-up dogs, and Belgian fries

DINER'S DELIGHT
1504 S. Compton Ave.
314-776-9570
dinersdelightstl.com
Cash only, cafeteria-style soul food

KING AND I
3157 S. Grand Blvd.
314-771-1777
kingandistl.com
Thai cuisine; a mainstay

LA PATISSERIE CHOUQUETTE
1626 Tower Grove Ave.
314-932-7935
simonefaure.com
A serious, French-style pastry shop serving macaroons, éclairs, and other treats, plus intricately

{24-HOUR EATS}

Working late, done drinking for the night, or just need a 3 A.M. stack of pancakes? Get your wee hours grub on at **Courtesy Diner** (3153 S. Kingshighway, 314-776-9059), **Uncle Bill's** (3427 S. Kingshighway, 314-832-1973), **The Buttery** (Tuesday thru Saturday only; 3659 S. Grand Blvd., 314-771-4443, cash only), and **City Diner** (Friday morning thru Sunday night only; 3139 S. Grand Blvd., 314-772-6100, citydiner.us).

{ KID ZONE }

A popular neighborhood hangout in its own right, **Hartford Coffee Company** (3974 Hartford, 314-771-5282, hartfordcoffee.com) has really earned its fame among the sleep-deprived, caffeine-seeking parents of Tower Grove South and beyond—with a large, somewhat sequestered children's play area featuring a train table, play kitchen, chalkboard, stocked bookshelves, and most importantly, other little kids. It's a welcoming spot for people whose party includes members of the shorter set. The staff whips up a mean chocolate milk, plus there's a kids' menu and plenty of grab-and-go cups of snacks like Goldfish crackers and Cheerios. At 5 P.M. on the first Wednesday of the month, there's a kid-centered concert; even the non-breeders here are reasonably tolerant. Bring your own Purell, if you're germ-averse, because there's no telling how many times a day those train pieces get chewed.

designed cakes (mock Chanel purses and shoes are among the most popular).

LEMONGRASS
3161 S. Grand Blvd.
314-664-6702
lemongrass-rest.com
Vietnamese cuisine

MAMA JOSEPHINE'S
4000 Shaw Ave.
314-771-4001
mamajosephines.net
Southern home cooking to fill belly and soul

MANGIA ITALIANO
3145 S. Grand Blvd.
314-664-8585
dineatmangia.com
Homemade pasta

{ SOMETHING SWEET }

Let's get straight to the good stuff: For a sweet tooth, a trio of worthy stops includes **World's Fair Donuts** (old-school, with your blueberry cake, plain glazed, or long johns dropped in white paper sacks, drip coffee in Styrofoam cups, and counter staff doing the math by hand, in pencil, on the back of a donut box; 1904 S. Vandeventer Ave., 314-776-9975, cash only), **SweetArt Bakeshop and Art Studio** (homemade sugary goodness centered on cute-as-pie cupcakes, such as Come Hither Carrot, The Fauxst-ess, and Red Velvet, including vegan baked yummies; 2203 S. 39th St., 314-771-4278, sweetartstl.com), and rich, creamy gelato served in the handsome surroundings of **Gelateria del Leone** (3197 S. Grand Blvd., 314-776-3500, thegelateria.com).

MEKONG RESTAURANT
3131 S. Grand Blvd.
314-773-3100
Vietnamese cuisine

MESKEREM
3210 S. Grand Blvd.
314-772-4442
meskeremstl.com
Ethiopian cuisine

MOKABE'S
3606 Arsenal St.
314-865-2009
mokabes.com
LGBT-friendly coffeehouse,
veg-friendly Sunday
brunch

OLIO & ELAIA
OLIO
1634 Tower Grove Ave.
314-932-1088
oliostl.com

ELAIA
1634 Tower Grove Ave.
314-932-1088
elaiastl.com
Adjacent restaurants (one
in a reborn gas station, the

other in a retrofitted home)
have attracted great buzz,
both for their food/drink
and for their role in kicking
up the "it" factor of the surrounding Botanical Heights
neighborhood.

PHO GRAND
3195 S. Grand Blvd.
314-664-7435
phogrand.com
Vietnamese cuisine

THE PURPLE MARTIN
2800 Shenandoah Ave.
314-898-0011
thepurplemartinstl.com
Neighborhood corner spot
for cocktails and Mediterranean eats

SEKISUI SUSHI BISTRO
3024 S. Grand Blvd.
314-772-0002
sekisuiusa.com
Japanese cuisine; sushi

THE SHAVED DUCK
2900 Virginia Ave.
314-776-1407
theshavedduck.com
BBQ ribs/beef/pork/
chicken/duck

THREE MONKEYS
3153 Morgan Ford Rd.
314-772-9800
3monkeysstl.com
Cajun-influenced bar food
and pizza

THURMAN GRILL
4069 Shenandoah Ave.
314-772-8484
thurmangrill.com
Seafood gumbo, sand-
wiches

TREE HOUSE
3177 S. Grand Blvd.
314-696-2100
treehousestl.com
Vegetarian and vegan
cuisine with foodie flair;
impressive bar

THE VINE
3171 S. Grand Blvd.
314-776-0991
thevinestl.com
Middle Eastern cuisine

WEI HONG
3175 S. Grand Blvd.
314-773-8318
weihongrestaurant.com
Cantonese cuisine

How can you not have a soft spot for a bar that, in its early days, functioned as a de facto meeting hall for the local Catholic church? Fast forward eight decades, and **Friendly's Sports Bar and Grill** (3503 Roger Pl., 314-771-2040, friendlyssportsbar.com) is still going strong, thanks to its homemade fried chicken, cold beer, numerous TVs and, for the athletic set, pool, darts, Skee-Ball, shuffleboard, and patio games out back in the beer garden.

SOMETHING TO DRINK

Plenty of corner taverns and neighborhood watering holes have crowds of regulars, but you'll find most are welcoming to the first-timer, too; this being the ancestral home of the south St. Louis brewery worker, expect to find a lot of Anheuser-Busch products crossing the bar, and sometimes a game of washers or cornhole out back.

ABSOLUTLI GOOSED
3196 S. Grand Blvd.
314-771-9300
absolutligoosed.com
LGBT-friendly martini bar, appetizers

AMSTERDAM TAVERN
3175 Morgan Ford Rd.
314-772-8224
amsterdamtavern.com
Nonsmoking, soccer-mad

CBGB
3163 S. Grand Blvd.
314-776-3756
Smoky dive, big patio, live music

LONDON TEA ROOM
3128 Morgan Ford Rd.
314-241-6556
thelondontearoom.com
A most proper cuppa and baked goods/quiches/soups for sustenance; small Brit-tastic merchandise selection, too

O'CONNELL'S PUB
4652 Shaw Ave.
314-773-6600
Award-winning burgers, house-made Mayfair dressing, and historical ties to Gaslight Square make this dark-interiored pub appealing.

RILEY'S PUB
3458 Arsenal St.
314-664-7474
Cozy booths, cheap pizza, and pints

THE ROYALE
3132 S. Kingshighway Blvd.
314-772-3600
theroyale.com
Top-notch hip cocktails and food

When former wine bar owner Jake Hafner returned from a European walkabout to open a microbrewery, few had any doubt he'd make it a raging success. And lo, his tested formula of quality over quantity, excellent customer service, and a major emphasis on building community (instead of just maximizing the bottom line) has quickly established **The Civil Life Brewing Company** (3714 Holt Ave., thecivillife.com; no phone) as one of the city's friendliest watering holes. A handsome interior is home to scrumptious brews from the American brown ale to milk stout, great accompaniments to the sandwiches, and apps produced in a micro-kitchen adjacent to the bar. Upstairs, tall-walled booths provide great space for intimate conversation, board games, or flipping through the pages of a book from the bar's own curated library. Outside,

picnic tables and pea gravel serve as unofficial play space for the smart South Side families who've figured out that their (well-behaved) kids are welcome. Bring cash, don't bring the bachelorette bus, and you'll be greeted with open arms.

SASHA'S ON SHAW
4069 Shaw Blvd.
314-771-7274
sashaswinebar.com
Wine bar and cheese/crepes/full menu

TOWER PUB
3234 Morgan Ford Rd.
314-771-7979
Pool table, loud music, plenty of beer

VAN GOGHZ
3200 Shenandoah Ave.
314-865-3345
vangoghz.com
Arty martini bar, full menu, breakfast

RECREATION

These neighborhoods and their community life are centered on the twin institutions of Tower Grove Park and the Missouri Botanical Garden, providing a green oasis amid the bricks and bustle of the city streets. It's a community of dog walkers, softball players, stroller pushers, and blanket liers, from every age group, national heritage, and cultural demographic imaginable. And the park and surrounding streets (architecturally impressive) also provide a backdrop for the numerous public **festivals** and **house tours** that happen every year.

FESTIVITIES

FESTIVAL OF NATIONS
August
314-773-9090
festivalofnationsstl.org
The world comes to Tower Grove Park at this massive international celebration of food, music, dance, arts, crafts, and culture.

GRAND SOUTH GRAND HOUSE AND GARDEN TOUR
mid-April
Tour the majestic homes that surround Tower Grove Park

THE HISTORIC SHAW ART FAIR
October
314-773-3935
Juried show of art and fine craft from across the country, set along an elegant residential street

PAGAN PICNIC
June, Tower Grove Park
314-398-2992
paganpicnic.org
Rituals, workshops, and entertainment for Pagan families and interested others

{ DRINKS AND DRAG }

At the **Grey Fox Pub** (3503 S. Spring Ave., 314-772-2150, greyfoxstl.com) you can get a drink, but the real attraction of this gay-friendly corner bar is the drag shows that take over the stage several nights a week. More seasoned performers strut their stuff for "La Cage aux Foxes" on Friday and Saturday nights, but it's hard to beat the sheer entertainment value of the aspiring dancers, singers, lip-synchers, jugglers, and more who get their turn under the lights at the Sunday night variety show.

The **Missouri Botanical Garden** (4344 Shaw Blvd., 314-577-5100, mobot. org) enjoys a stellar international reputation for research and facilities and is locally beloved for its visitor amenities, providing the backdrop for generations of family memories created at what old-timers still call "Shaw's Garden," after founder and benefactor Henry Shaw, a prominent merchant and amateur botanist who established this oasis in the 1850s. Worth a visit any time of year, favorite highlights include the geodesic dome Climatron (indoor tropical rain forest is a winter mood-booster), the annual Best of Missouri Market (great food, arts, toys, and furniture, all from Missouri producers; first weekend in October), and the Kemper Center for Home Gardening (spot-on advice and inspiration for your yard, from volunteer master gardeners).

{ DON'T MISS }

Ye olde corner store is not just cigarettes and lottery tickets anymore: in fact, you won't find those at all at neighborhood bodega **Gustine Market** (3150 Gustine Ave., 314-932-5141, gustinemarket.com). In addition to a great supply of tasty wines and locally made snacks (often offered for sampling), you'll find a small deli case, an eensy selection of salads and other fresh produce, and that staple of life at Mizzou/CoMo -- Shakespeare's Pizza. From the freezer, and paired with a decent brew from their beer cooler, you can close you eyes and almost imagine you're within spitting distance of the columns.

At 170 feet, visible from miles around in many directions, the limestone/brick/terra cotta **Compton Hill Water Tower** (Grand Blvd. just south of I-44, 314-552-9000, watertowerfoundation.org) was built in 1898 as decorative camouflage for the water standpipe the city had designed to help regulate the flow of city water to what were then the booming edges of the metropolitan area. A lovely, landscaped park made the spot a popular gathering place for local families, visitors who wanted to climb the 198 inside steps for the view, and sightseers in town for the 1904 World's Fair. Asbestos and general deferred maintenance shut the tower in the mid-1980s, but a demolition threat in 1995 rallied local preservationists, who saw the value of keeping intact one of just a handful of towers remaining in the United States (two others are elsewhere in St. Louis). Today, $5 ($3 for kids 6–12) will get you in for a chance to make the climb yourself, from noon to 4 P.M. on the first Saturday of each month, from April through November.

ARTS, ENTERTAINMENT, & EDUCATION

STRAY DOG THEATRE IN TOWER GROVE ABBEY
2348 Tennessee Ave.
314-865-1995
straydogtheatre.org
Regular season of stage performances (*Rocky Horror Show*, *Into the Woods*, and *Our Town* recently); also serves as umbrella for other groups specializing in improv, youth workshops, and experimental theatre.

{ A WALK IN THE PARK }

Visitors will discover their own delights among the 289 acres of the stunning Victorian **Tower Grove Park**, nestled in a thoroughly urban setting. A selection of the varied diversions includes: **Café Madeleine** (Sunday brunch spot inside the Piper Palm House, a brick conservatory with numerous windows on the park, 314-575-5658); **Tower Grove Farmers' Market** (Saturdays from May to October, near the center circle, with farmers and food producers from within 150 miles of town, tgmarket.org); the **Muckerman Children's Fountain** (pop jets and wading pool, open daily throughout the summer and free of charge); twelve hard tennis courts and three grass tennis courts, available for public use (small fee, 314-771-7776); and pony and horse-drawn carriage rides, available by reservation (314-771-2679).

{ RETRO-A-GO-GO }

Prefer your fashions, furnishings, and home remedies from a decade other than our own? Clothe yourself in finery from the age of Victoria on at **The Vintage Haberdashery** (3181 Morgan Ford Rd., 314-772-1927, vintagehab.com), and deep-clean the way your great-grandma did with time-tested products from the old-school **Watkins/Avon/Fuller Brush Distributors** (3179 S. Grand Blvd., 314-776-0009, fuller.com) storefront on South Grand.

SHOPPORTUNITIES

Neighborhood retail outlets tend toward the functional (post offices, groceries, and the like), but several spots offer great gift and gourmet shopping.

BALI CARGO CO.
3203 S. Grand Ave.
314-762-0231
balicargocompany.com
Furniture, gifts, and accessories from the islands of Indonesia

THE BUG STORE
4474 Shaw Blvd.
314-773-9251
bugstore.com
Home and garden store

DUNAWAY BOOKS
3111 S. Grand Blvd.
314-771-7150
Stacks and stacks of used books

GARDEN GATE SHOP
4344 Shaw Blvd.
(at Missouri Botanical Garden)
314-577-0865
gardengateshop.org
Clothing, home décor, books, kids' toys, and plants

GROVE FURNISHINGS
3169 Morgan Ford Rd.
314-776-7898
grovefurnishings.com
Mission furnishings, vintage and vintage-inspired lighting and frames, candles, tableware, and distinctive local art
(pictured on the following page)

You can literally be a kid in a candy store: **General Candy Company** (4800 Oleatha Ave., 314-353-1133, generalcandycompany.com) wholesales goodies from Jujyfruits and Mike and Ike to candy necklaces and wax mustaches (plus popcorn, nachos, mints, candy bars, bubble gum, and more), but the public can just walk right into the warehouse, too, and pretty much go crazy. If Willie Wonka had a working warehouse, this would be the scene.

G&W BAVARIAN STYLE SAUSAGE COMPANY
4828 Parker Ave.
314-352-5066
gwsausage.com
Sausage, salsiccia, Polish, chorizo, and more, made on site, plus deer processing and free canned beer while you wait

JAY INTERNATIONAL FOODS
3172 S. Grand Blvd.
314-772-9393
Multiethnic grocery store

LITTLE SHOP AROUND THE CORNER
4474 Castleman Ave.
314-577-0891
littleshop.org
Antiques and collectibles, artwork, china

NHB KNIFEWORKS
4155 Beck Ave.
314-825-5398
nhbknifeworks.com
Custom-made knives for every kitchen application, crafted from steel and materials from burled wood to color-saturated resin. Other handmade cook-y gifts, too. Appointment only.

GRINGO JONES IMPORTS
4470 Shaw Blvd.
314-664-1666
Multiroom jumble of jewelry, home accents, pottery, garden gear

PAPERKEET

3237 Morgan Ford Rd.
314-773-1117
paperkeet.com
Bespoke stationer and awesome paper
goods supplier

PARSIMONIA

3194 S. Grand Blvd.
314-282-5201
shopparsimonia.com
Quality vintage clothing for men, women,
and kids, plus home goods

PETS IN THE CITY

1919 S. Grand Blvd., Suite 100
314-772-7387
thecitypet.com
Holistic pet supply store features food,
treats, toys, bedding, and gear.

TRX TATTOOS

3207 S. Grand Blvd.
314-664-4011
trxtattoos.com
Tattoos, piercing, erotic gifts, gay pride
merch

THE UPCYCLE EXCHANGE

3206 S. Grand Blvd.
314-282-7042
upxchange.com
Heaven on South Grand for crafty types,
this nonprofit offers all manner of maker
supplies for pay-as-you-wish prices.

{ FUN FACT }

In one of his first on-screen leading roles, actor Steve McQueen was among the
cast of emotionally damaged bank robbers in *The Great St. Louis Bank Robbery*.
This well-regarded 1958 bank heist film was based on true events in 1953 and
directed by the acclaimed Charles Guggenheim (who also directed *Monument
to the Dream* at the Gateway Arch, if you're playing St. Louis movie trivia). The
attempted robbery and the movie both went down at the real-life Southwest Bank
branch, now renamed but still firmly anchored at the corner of Kingshighway and
Southwest (you'll know it by the golden eagle rotating on
top). Other local spots making an appearance include the
pagodas of nearby Tower Grove Park, to which the gang
repairs to refine their dastardly plans. Many of the cops
and other extras in the film are St. Louisans who were
somehow involved in the events of that 1953 day.

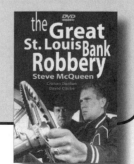

We're in the heartland, so it only makes sense that the national obsession with locally and sustainably produced foodstuffs would take hold here. The twin epicenters in town are conveniently positioned across the street from each other, forming a small but well-fed empire on Morgan Ford Rd. **Local Harvest Grocery** (3108 Morgan Ford Rd., 314-865-5260, localharvestgrocery.com) and **Local Harvest Café and Catering** (3108 Morgan Ford Rd., 314-772-8815, localharvestcafe.com) seek a minimum of 50% of their store inventory (and café ingredients) from the best farmers/producers they can find within 150 miles of St. Louis. The list is long: vegetables, sure, but also bison, lamb, eggs, milk, peanut butter, honey, herbs, coffee, chocolate, wine, beer, soap, soup, goat cheese, pizza, baked goods, and on and on. Their business practices are green, too; all in all, it's garnered numerous awards for both operations.

{ KID ZONE }

Located in a magical "cottage castle" (formerly living quarters for groundskeepers at Tower Grove Park), the **Saint Louis City Open Studio and Gallery (SCOSAG)** (4255 Arsenal St., 314-865-0060, scosag.org) has brought the wonder of the arts to kids (and now adults) through weekly open studio time, hands-on classes in disciplines from cartoon drawing to instrument making, and popular spring break and summer art camps for kids from kindergarten on up.

CARONDELET

BEVO ★ BOULEVARD HEIGHTS ★ CARONDELET ★ CHEROKEE ★ DUTCHTOWN ★ GRAVOIS PARK ★ HOLLY HILLS ★ MARINE VILLA ★ MOUNT PLEASANT ★ PATCH

HISTORY

Carondelet and its neighborhoods are the essence of what St. Louisans affectionately call the South Side. Carondelet Park is where the community gathers to play. Its lakes, picnic grounds, playgrounds, baseball diamonds, and tennis courts are in constant use. The historic and beautiful boathouse dates to 1908. On Sunday nights during the summer, lawn chairs line the grass and music fills the air with free concerts at Carondelet Park's bandstand, built in 1898. Nearby is the Bevo Mill, a working windmill; Sugarloaf Mound, one of the few surviving Indian mounds in St. Louis; and the always delicious Ted Drewes Frozen Custard stand on Grand Blvd.

CARONDELET

Until its annexation to St. Louis in 1870, Carondelet was an independent city. French explorer Clement Delore de Treget, authorized by the Spanish to create a settlement, arrived in 1767. Carondelet's early days were a model of diversity, where Creoles (those of Spanish and French heritage) lived in peaceful coexistence with Native Americans and free African Americans. A working-class community, Carondelet also earned the dubious nickname *Vide Poche*, or "empty pockets," apparently in reference to either the financial status or the gambling skills of the residents.

Des Peres School, the first public kindergarten west of the Mississippi, was founded in 1873. The Sisters of St. Joseph's Holy Family Chapel at the Carondelet Motherhouse is noted for its artifacts, hand-carved altar, and relics, said to date to the Roman Empire. The Steins Row Houses, built in the mid-nineteenth century and renovated in the twenty-first century, provide a glimpse of housing in the early Carondelet years. James Eads, of Eads Bridge fame, built Union ironclad gunboats on Carondelet's riverfront during the Civil War.

HOLLY HILLS

The name comes from combining the California city names of Hollywood and Beverly Hills. Holly Hills was marketed to buyers as "the California of St. Louis," a testament to the early twentieth century's infatuation with Hollywood. Federer Pl., Leona St., Bellerive Blvd., and Holly Hills Blvd. are part of a picturesque drive that is a must for natives and newcomers alike. The bluffs of Bellerive Park, built in 1908, offer visitors panoramic views of the Mississippi. Local legend says that 7UP was invented in a basement lab in Holly Hills. Plus, Butch O'Hare, the World War II flying ace for whom Chicago's O'Hare Airport is named, is a neighborhood native son.

DUTCHTOWN

German immigrants who settled here earned the "Scrubby Dutch" nickname for their legendary insistence on cleaning everything right down to their front steps and brick façades. The massive Romanesque towers of St. Anthony of Padua Church are an impressive presence in Dutchtown. The Feasting Fox, originally Busch's Inn, was built by August Busch Sr. in 1914 as a venue to show that beer could be served in a family establishment. The Feasting Fox is one of the few remaining places in St. Louis where German favorites such as schnitzel, sauerbraten, and strudel can regularly be found on the menu.

BEVO

No visit to the South Side is complete without a trip to Bevo Mill. This still-working replica Dutch windmill was built by August Busch in 1917. Honoring a German and Dutch tradition, the storks mounted on the chimney ensure good luck to visitors. The Mill Room, once the exclusive dining room of August Busch, features arches ending in stone-carved gnomes. Bevo Mill helped Anheuser-Busch market its popular Bevo beverage, a 1% alcohol malt beverage, during Prohibition. In its time, Bevo was an integral part of popular culture. Irving Berlin referred to Bevo in song, as does the song "Trouble" from *The Music Man*, and Sinclair Lewis mentions Bevo in *Babbitt*.

The Bevo neighborhood grew up around the Bevo Mill. Today Bevo has added the nickname of "Little Bosnia," due to a recent influx of eastern Europeans. Be sure to take the time to try a taste of the old country in one of the coffeehouses, bakeries, or restaurants of St. Louis's most recent immigrant community.

FOOD AND DRINK

A BITE TO EAT

BANH MI SO
4071 S. Grand Blvd.
314-353-0545
banhmiso1.com
Spring rolls and the
famous sandwich, that's
why you're here

BLACK BEAR BAKERY
2639 Cherokee St.
314-771-2236
blackbearbakery.org
Worker-owned collective;
lunch and brunch with a
side of anarchy

BOSNA GOLD
4601 Gravois Ave.
314-351-2058
Bosnian sausages and
cabbage rolls in
hunting-lodge ambience

CHIMICHANGA'S
5425 S. Grand Blvd.
314-352-0202
chimichangastl.com
Cheap and festive
Mexican, huge patio

FEASTING FOX
4200 S. Grand Blvd.
314-352-3500
feastingfox.com
German fare in charming
historic building

{ SPOOK PATROL }

Ghost tours—or, if you prefer, "paranormal excursions"—will take the starch out of even the most jaded participant at the historic **Lemp Mansion** (3322 DeMenil Pl., 314-664-8024, lempmansion.com). Local historians and paranormal investigators set the scene, then lead groups through the house, site of numerous suicides and unexplained deaths during the residence of the Lemp family. Feeling especially brave? Book a tour with an overnight stay. And keep your eyes on that door.

{ THE DEVIL INSIDE }

Perhaps not surprisingly, a lot of mystery and misinformation surrounds the case of a possessed young boy whose spiritual reckoning formed the basis for the movie *The Exorcist*. Are the details sufficiently murky to allow you not to shudder a bit when you pass the old **Alexian Brothers Hospital** (3933 S. Broadway) (now St. Alexius), supposed site of the casting-out?

In a Hispanic twist to the traditional Catholic fish fry, **St. Cecilia Parish** (5418 Louisiana Ave., 314-351-1318, stceciliaparishstl.org) spices up the standard fare with fish tacos, chiles rellenos, and enchiladas. Be warned: you won't be the only one thinking this is a great idea on Lenten Fridays. Get there at the opening moment or plan to wait in line . . . and perhaps walk away rellenos-less.

FERARO'S JERSEY STYLE PIZZA
7704 Ivory Ave.
314-256-0500
ferarospizza.com
East Coast pie fans, rejoice; get it delivered or enjoy the spot's bar and small music venue, too

GARDUNO'S
2737 Cherokee St.
314-776-2315
Tacos, tamales, and tasty salsas and guacamole

GRBIC
4071 Keokuk St.
314-772-3100
grbicrestaurant.com
Schnitzel, goulash, and delights of Bosnia

THE HAVEN
6625 Morgan Ford Rd.
314-352-4283
thehavenpub.com
Fried pickles, awesome meatballs, and desserts from Federhofer's Bakery

IRON BARLEY
5510 Virginia Ave.
314-351-4500
ironbarley.com
Roasted pork and chicken, smoked trout, and the famous Ballistic Elvis Sammiche

IOWA BUFFET
2727 Winnebago St.
314-776-8000
Word of mouth has this as the best burger spot in town; the promised buffet curiously never materializes. Beer, juke box, and cigarette smoke round out the scene.

LEMMONS
5800 Gravois Ave.
314-481-4812
Black Thorn pub's pizza, further south

MELT
2712 Cherokee St.
314-771-6358
Whimsical upcycled décor seems apropos backdrop for waffles (and not just the plain kind), cocktails, and pinball

THE MUD HOUSE
2101 Cherokee St.
314-776-6599
themudhousestl.com
Indie coffeeshop serves full menu, breakfast through early evening; pretty back patio

ORIGINAL CRUSOE'S
3152 Osceola St.
314-351-0620
dineocr.com
Solid American bar-comfort food, and Mayfair dressing by the jar

STACKED BURGER BAR
7637 Ivory Ave.
314-544-4900
stackedstl.com
A multitude of patty choices and something upwards of fifty toppings draw the crowds

TOWER TACOS
3147 Cherokee St.
314-256-1141
towertaco.com
Tasty Mexican, comfortable side patio

{ SWEET STUFF }

Taste the sugary South Side at **Dad's Cookies** (3854 Louisiana Ave., 314-772-3662, dadscookies.com; can't go wrong with the classic Scotch oatmeal, plus St. Louis–themed chocolates make great gifts); **Diana's Bakery** (2843 Cherokee St., 314-771-6959; Mexican churros, enormous fruit-filled pastries: just pick and point); **El Chico Bakery** (2634 Cherokee St., 314-664-2212; addictive tres leches cake and fruit empanadas); **Carondelet Bakery** (7726 Virginia Ave., 314-638-3519, carondeletbakery.com; old-school spot for elephant ears, special occasion cakes, stollen, and donuts); **I Scream Cakes** (2641 Cherokee St., 314-932-5758, iscreamcakes.com; from-scratch cakes and ice cream, in fanciful shapes from trophy deer head to launch-ready rocket); and **Whisk: A Sustainable Bakeshop** (2201 Cherokee St., 314-932-5166, whiskstl.com; all-natural, seasonal, and locally sourced treats from slurp-worthy ice pops in flavors from caramel to strawberry rhubarb to homemade pop tartlets).

. . . .

TAQUERIA EL BRONCO
2817 Cherokee St.
314-762-0691
Homey menu, tiny space, and Mexican soap operas

URBAN EATS
3301 Meramec St.
314-558-7580
urbaneatscafe.com
You call it brunch, they call it revolution: the owners are dedicated to neighborhood revitalization . . . and boozy smoothies.

LA VALLESANA
2801 Cherokee St.
314-776-4223
Authentic Mexican fare from pork-cheek tortas to fresh-made popsicles (paletas, in the parlance)

{ OH YEAH, THE RIVER }

It's just right over there: Spend an afternoon admiring it from the picnic-table perch at **Bellerive Park** (S. Broadway and Bates St.). Let Old Man River roll by, taking your cares along with him.

ART BAR
2732 Cherokee St.
314-769-9696
Booze, food, and art of every medium and description meld the essential elements of Cherokee Street.

FOAM
3359 S. Jefferson Ave.
314-772-2100
foamstl.com
Coffee, beer, music, cultural events, and funky decor

FORTUNE TELLER BAR
2635 Cherokee St.
314-776-2337
thefortunetellerbar.com
Fortunes are, indeed, on offer (weekends), along with drinks and legendary and vibrantly colored pickled eggs

HALFWAY HAUS
7900 Michigan Ave.
314-256-0101
Beer and wine bar with music on the patio

THE HEAVY ANCHOR
5226 Gravois Ave.
314-352-5226
theheavyanchor.com
Bar side and venue side, hosting movie nights, trivia, and bands

HUMMEL'S PUB
7101 S. Broadway
314-353-5080
Gay-friendly corner bar, weekend drag shows

KICKER'S CORNER
6201 S. Broadway
314-832-7935
Head down for $5 Tuesday night pizza

LOS PUNK
2709 Cherokee St.
314-932-5411
Punk rock aesthetic, local-heavy beer selection, and a mash-up of food from BBQ to tacos

LUNA LOUNGE
4561 Gravois Ave.
314-481-5862
letseat.at/Luna
Stealth restaurant-as-bar, exposed brick walls, in Bevo Mill's long shadow

PERENNIAL ARTISAN ALES
8125 Michigan Ave.
314-631-7300
perennialbeer.com
Adventurous microbrewer got national press for its Abraxas beer, and continues to produce inventive styles.

POOH'S CORNER
6023 Virginia Ave.
314-351-5313
Beers with the police . . . and fresh-laid eggs for sale

RED'S EIGHTH INNING
6412 Michigan Ave.
314-353-1084
From cops at Pooh's to firefighters (and bikers) here, plus ping-pong and a 6 A.M. open

SHOT HEAVEN
5233 Gravois Ave.
314-351-9606
shotheaven.com
Drinks, pool, darts, karaoke

THE SILVER BALLROOM
4701 Morgan Ford Rd.
314-832-9223
thesilverballroom.com
Pinball, punk rock jukebox, much-touted Australian meat pies

SLO TOM'S LOUNGE
6728 S. Broadway
314-351-0829
slotomslounge.com
Drink cheap, that's the name of this game; maybe shoot pool

SMALLS TEA AND COFFEE
2619 1/2 Cherokee St.
314-669-5698
facebook.com/smallsteaandcoffee
For real: it's tiny in here, but bursting with a sincere belief in the medicinal power of tea (jars of ingredients line the walls).

SUMP COFFEE
3700 Jefferson Ave.
917-412-5670
sumpcoffee.com
A passion for coffee, from regular brewed joe (the only thing you can get during "R&D Monday" hours) to mad-scientist-precise matching between bean and brewing method, from Chemex to a Japanese Kyoto cold-drip process

SUPER'S BUNGALOW
5623 Leona St.
314-481-8448
Imagine crochety Uncle Raymond turned his house into a beer bar, complete with a tidy backyard patio

TIM'S CHROME BAR
4736 Gravois Ave.
314-353-8138
Live music and old-timer dancing on weekends

WHISKEY RING
2651 Cherokee St.
314-769-7249
Fifty-odd choices of whiskey, local brews, wine, and cocktails on weekends

{ SHAKE A TAIL FEATHER }

On the famous floating dance floor of the **Casa Loma Ballroom** (3354 Iowa Ave., 314-664-8000, casalomaballroom.com), good folks have been coming to Charleston, jive, swing, mosh, and noodle since 1935. The stage has hosted everyone from an unknown Frank Sinatra to Count Basie, and today still draws crowds for swing dancing, Latin music nights, and rock 'n' roll shows.

{ MISSISSIPPI MOUND }

Rising up prominently on Ohio St., and with a commanding view of the river, **Sugarloaf Mound** (4420 Ohio St.) is the last surviving example of the Native American mound formations that once dotted the landscape on this side of Big Muddy and lent St. Louis the "Mound City" moniker. The site's been dated to about 1050 A.D., and ownership recently passed to the Osage Nation, which plans to restore a structure there and preserve its heritage.

RECREATION

This chapter's namesake, **Carondelet Park**, is the third largest park in the city at nearly two hundred acres. It was built to provide a closer alternative to far South Siders than Forest Park. Today it houses two stocked fishing lakes, picnic and play areas, baseball/softball/tennis facilities, bike and walking paths, and a popular summer Sunday evening concert series.

EXERCISE

The **Carondelet Park Rec Complex** (930 Holly Hills, 314-768-9622, ymcastlouis. org/carondelet-park-rec-complex) is a joint venture of the city and the YMCA, but no membership is required to visit the most attractive feature, the fancy outdoor pool. Built to rival suburban water funplexes, the pool features an interactive kiddie splash/play structure, a walk-in rec pool, a lazy river, lap lanes, and waterslides. On weekends, you'll have to glom onto a member and also pay a day usage fee, but during the week, you just pay up and walk in.

The **St. Louis Skatium** (120 E. Catalan St., 314-631-3922) is an indoor roller rink with a limited and changing public schedule; well used, though, for private parties and rentals.

FESTIVITIES

CINCO DE MAYO
May
3407 S. Jefferson Ave.
314-632-6498
cincodemayostl.com
Family-friendly free-for-all along Cherokee Street includes live entertainment (with a Main Stage and a Gringo Stage), the wildly random People's Joy Parade, tons of authentic foodstuffs and drink.

CZECH FESTIVAL
April
4690 Lansdowne Ave.
314-752-8168
acec-stl.org
Gorge on roasted meats of all sorts, kolaches, Czech beer, and more while the fleet of foot take turns on the dance floor to the musical stylings of the St. Louis Czech Express

2720

2720 Cherokee St.
314-875-0233
2720Cherokee.com
Multilevel, multipurpose concert venue
and gallery space, special emphasis
on dubstep/reggae/funk/soul bands

IVORY THEATRE

7620 Michigan Ave.
314-631-8330
theivorytheatre.com
Theatre space in a beautiful
renovated church, presenting
mostly musicals

OFF BROADWAY

3509 Lemp Ave.
314-773-3363
offbroadwaystl.com
Among the city's best concert venues;
pleasingly medium size, great series
of Sunday family matinee shows, and
crowds who (mostly) come to actually
listen to music

PHD GALLERY

2300 Cherokee St.
314-664-6644
phdstl.com
Sculptor Philip Hitchcock's clean, spare
gallery space presents challenging
work from local and international artists,
including frequent ruminations on
human sexuality.

{ KID ZONE }

Get messy and arty at the **South
Broadway Art Project** (3816
S. Broadway, 314-773-3633,
southbroadwayartproject.org),
a nonprofit studio dedicated to
giving kids (and the adults who
raise 'em) tools and means of
self-expression through the arts.
If all that sounds highfalutin, dig
on these birthday party themes
instead: Picassoesque Portraits,
Beatnik Batiks, Dada Tea Party.
Tell me you wouldn't love that
invite! Adult classes/workshops/
parties, too.

{ DIY OR DIE }

One of the most distinctive pockets of the region can be found along **Cherokee Street**, from its dusty antiquey east end clear through to the spunky, gritty arts corridor near Jefferson. A fascinating amalgam of an African American residential core, a Hispanic-anchored business district, and a burgeoning art and activism haven, this street has it all. The newest energy centers on Cherokee's art community are upstarts like **The Firecracker Press** (2838 Cherokee St., 314-776-7271, firecrackerpress.com; letterpress print shop); **Red Fox Baking** (3101 Arsenal St., redfoxbaking.com; bakers of naturally fermented breads and pastries, all from a hand-built wood-burning oven in the backyard, available at farmers' markets and by subscription at redfoxkitchen@gmail.com); **Community, Arts, and Movement Project** (3022A Cherokee St., 314-827-4730, stlcamp.org; home to communal housing, bike repair shop, indy media center, and community engagement events); **All Along Press** (2712 Cherokee St., 314-827-6185, allalongpress.com; letterpress/screenprinting co-op); and **Fort Gondo Compound for the Arts** (3151 Cherokee St., 314-313-5787, fortgondo.com; exhibits, arts instigators, and granddaddy of 'em all.)

SHOPPORTUNITIES

Among other pockets, Cherokee boasts a world-famous antiques district, worth exploring til you find your favorite.

··

HOME/GARDEN/BODY/GIFTS

APOP
2831 Cherokee St.
314-664-6575
apoprecords.com
Rare vinyl, zines, pop culture schtuff

THE ARCHIVE
3215 Cherokee St.
314-288-0712
archivescribe.com
Eclectic used bookstore

BOROUGH VINTAGE
447 N. Euclid Ave.
314-884-8436
boroughvintage.com
Best looks from the 1940s–1980s

THE CRYSTAL WIZARD
7621 S. Broadway
314-638-7721
facebook.com/pages/The-Crystal-Wizard
Billed as the Midwest's oldest occult shop, great when you're fresh out of fortune-telling supplies

FLOWERS TO THE PEOPLE
2317 Cherokee St.
314-762-0422
flowerstothepeople.biz
Sustainably sourced flowers, plus terrariums

GOOOLLL
3353 California Ave.
314-443-7668
facebook.com/pages/Gooolll
Whether you call it soccer or futbol, everything you need is here

{ CIVIC PRIDE, SOUTH SIDE }

Enter the vortex of STLphilia at two shops on Cherokee Street: the **STL Stylehouse** (3159 Cherokee St., 314-494-7763, stl-style.com; home of the awesome neighborhood-loving tees, bags, and maps from the brains and hearts of Jeff and Randy Vines, the proudest hometowners you ever did see) and the **St. Louis Curio Shoppe** (2301 Cherokee St., 314-771 6353, stlcurioshoppe.com; purveyors of everything local, from books and music to jewelry, foodstuffs, artwork, and backyard "warshers" sets). Feel the love, people!

{ MUSIC ROW }

Gear up your garage band with sales, lessons, and service from **Midwest Guitar** (2610 Cherokee St., 314-962-8822, midwestguitar.com); **Saxquest** (2114 Cherokee St., 314-664-1234, saxquest.com; also housing a saxophone museum); and **Geoffrey Seitz Violins** (4171 Loughborough Ave., 314-353-1312, seitzviolins.com). If you want to build your own violin or guitar, your luthier dreams can come true.

....

REFABULOUS
3314 Meramec St.
314-353-1144
refabulous.com
Trend-savvy women's resale

SCARLETT GARNET JEWELRY
2619 Cherokee St.
314-540-0300
scarlettgarnet.com
Modern and distinctive jewelry, in intricate lines cut onto wood, copper, brass, and other materials. Great for affordable gifting!

ANTIQUES/COLLECTIBLES

CHINA FINDERS
2125 Cherokee St.
314-566-5694
chinafinders.com
Match just about any pattern and replenish that set of china you inherited

DEAD WAX RECORDS
1959 Cherokee St.
314-913-3692
facebook.com/pages/
Dead-Wax-Records-
STL/304690572980780
Weekends-only vinyl browsers' paradise, running the gamut from rock and blues to soundtracks, plus turntables and speakers

ELDER'S LTD.
2124 Cherokee St.
314-772-1436
Always good quality and selection, reliable hours

HAMMOND'S
1939 Cherokee St.
314-776-4737
hammondsbooks.net
Vintage and antiquarian books

PANORAMA FOLK ART
1925 Cherokee St.
314-772-8007
panoramafolkart.com
Folk art and primitive crafts

RETRO 101
2303 Cherokee St.
314-762-9722
Kitsch and vintage fashion

RIVERSIDE ARCHITECTURAL ANTIQUES
1947 Cherokee St.
314-772-9177
riversideantiquesstl.com
Wrought iron, doors, decorative hardware

COMESTIBLES

COMPANION EARLY BIRD OUTLET
4555 Gustine Ave.
314-352-4770
companionstl.com
All the Companion baked goods originate here, and weekend mornings are the time to stock up at by-the-pound pricing.

EUROPA MARKET
5005 Gravois Ave.
314-481-9880
europa-market.com
Specializes in eastern European staples and other groceries

MERB'S
4000 S. Grand Ave.
314-832-7117
merbscandies.com
Bionic apples, molasses puffs

MIDWEST PASTA COMPANY
2023 Cherokee St.
314-772-7560
midwestpastaco.com
Fresh-cut/rolled/stuffed pastas, from standby spaghetti to more exotic white-truffle ricotta ravioli

{ HINT OF HISTORY }

We've barely scratched the surface of what there is to know about the area, so stop by the **Carondelet Historical Society** (6303 Michigan Ave., 314-481-6303, carondelethistoricalsociety.org) to get schooled on all the rest; among the highlights is a reproduction of the classroom of educator Susan Blow, founder of the first public kindergarten in the U.S., here in the former Des Peres School.

NEAR SOUTH SIDE

BENTON PARK ★ BENTON PARK WEST ★ FOX PARK
★ LAFAYETTE SQUARE ★ LASALLE PARK ★ MCKINLEY
HEIGHTS ★ SOULARD

HISTORY

SOULARD, BENTON PARK, AND LASALLE PARK

Soulard is one of St. Louis's earliest neighborhoods. Its heritage dates to early French landowners Antoine and Julia "Madame" Soulard. In the years leading up to the Civil War, Soulard experienced massive European immigration as well as an influx of Americans headed west. This spike in population created highly diverse architecture, with St. Louis putting its own spin on the Italianate, Federal, and Second Empire styles. The early twentieth century saw Soulard temporarily fall from grace into disrepair, but mid- to late-century urban pioneers brought revitalization with tremendous results.

Soulard celebrates its French lineage with one of the largest Mardi Gras celebrations in the United States and gives a post–July 4th nod to freedom in mid-July with its Bastille Day celebration. The French translation of *soulard* is to "make drunk," and Soulard lives up to this meaning, with its pubs and bars that are notable for their support of local musicians. If it's live music you're looking for, Soulard offers some of the best anywhere in St. Louis. Art galleries and Soulard Market (since 1779) make Soulard a cool place to hang out any time of day or year.

LaSalle Park is a historic residential neighborhood with distinctive streetlights, brick sidewalks, and two homes dating to the Civil War era. Fortunately design standards require new construction to be in the same style as the Federalist and Victorian architecture. Religious options reflect the diverse nature of LaSalle Park: you'll find the Religious Society of Friends (the Quakers), the LaSalle Baptist Church, St. John Nepomuk (the first Czech Catholic parish in the United States, founded in 1854), and St. Raymond Maronite Cathedral (founded at the turn of the twentieth century by Lebanese and Middle Eastern immigrants).

Benton Park became a haven for the early brewers. The natural limestone cave system below the neighborhood, with its cooler temperatures, was perfect for storing beer. There is also a park in Benton Park, naturally named Benton Park—a perfect and frequent setting for neighborhood festivals and events with its picturesque bridge, fishing lake, and shady picnic spots. The restoration efforts of nearby Soulard eventually flowed into Benton Park.

LAFAYETTE SQUARE

Named for the famous Frenchman, the Marquis Jean de Lafayette, after his notable American tour brought him to St. Louis, Lafayette Square became St. Louis's first suburban neighborhood. Grand Victorian homes and beautiful vistas and landscaping became the hallmark of Lafayette Square. Lafayette Park, St. Louis's oldest city park, offers a beautiful green oasis amid one of St. Louis's premiere neighborhoods. As the population continued migrating west in the early to mid-twentieth century, the luster returned to this grand neighborhood. The Victorian homes have been restored to their rightful elegance. Boutiques, restaurants, coffeehouses, and even a chocolate bar can be found along Park Avenue. If your time is short in St. Louis, put Lafayette Square high on the must-see list.

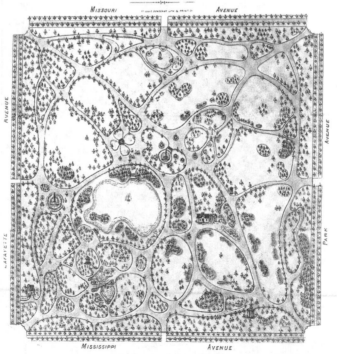

LAFAYETTE PARK
ST LOUIS, MO.

AREA, 30 ACRES.

FOX PARK AND MCKINLEY HEIGHTS

Countering the French influence in Soulard, Fox Park shows a dominant German influence. In the 1880s, German immigrants began arriving, and they took on the task of carving a neighborhood for themselves, sometimes quite literally. Many early residents were craftsmen, a trait that can still be seen today with the meticulous attention to architectural detail. Unlike Lafayette and Soulard, the booming working class built this neighborhood. Each home was affordable but gorgeous. The molding on the homes and businesses is unique and artistic, and German influences can be spotted in the gables, towers, windows, and steep rooflines. St. Louis landmark St. Francis de Sales, a German Gothic cathedral, was built and paid for by neighborhood parishioners.

McKinley Heights is nestled east of Fox Park, south of Lafayette Square, and west of Soulard. Often overlooked in the presence of its more prominent neighbors, this unique, historic neighborhood's interior is filled with an eclectic array of small to large brick residences along tree-lined streets.

FOOD AND DRINK

A wide range of dining options, from blue-collar diners to some of the city's most cutting-edge cuisine, dot these neighborhoods, with plenty of 3 A.M. bars in the Soulard area to keep it rocking all year round.

A BITE TO EAT

BILLIE'S FINE FOODS
1802 S. Broadway
314-621-0848
billies-fine-foods.com
Old-school diner serving
all-day breakfast, BBQ

CAPITALIST PIG
2727 S. 12th St.
314-772-1180
capitalistpigbbq.com
BBQ (including tempeh,
for the veg crowd) and
sides served inside Mad
Art Gallery

CHAVA'S
925 Geyer Ave.
314-241-5503
chavasmexican.com
Mexican fare (Guadala-
jara tacos recommended)
and chicken wings

ELEMENT
1419 Carroll St.
314-241-1674
elementstl.com
Atop a luxuriously reno-
vated power plant build-

ing, commanding a great
view of the downtown
skyline and serving New
American cuisine

**ELEVEN ELEVEN
MISSISSIPPI**
1111 Mississippi Ave.
314-241-9999
1111-m.com
Wine-country-inspired
bistro

{ GET GOOEY }

Among our foodstuffs of local lore, gooey butter cake seems the most self-explanatory. It's gooey. It's buttery. It's cakey. But consider the possibilities: **Park Avenue Coffee** (1919 Park Ave., 314-621-4020, parkavenuecoffee.com) sure has. In their roster of seventy-six flavors (!), a few of the more unusual include banana split, chocolate key lime, espresso chip, and cranberry orange. They rotate through 'em all, twelve to fifteen a day.

You don't need us to tell you about beads and such, but how about the ritual begging? **Twelfth Night** (314-771-5110), marking the official start of the Mardi Gras season, involves raucous "petitioning" from krewes, neighbors, and politicians demanding that Mardi Gras begin, followed by a procession unfurling the Mardi Gras flag, to firework accompaniment. Other don't-miss events include the deliriously frantic **wiener dog races**, a **Cajun/Creole cook-off** (watch chefs compete, sample culinary delights, drink hurricanes, and rock out to live music), and the **Family Winter Carnival** (with live music, crafts/art activities, children's parade)—a good intro to the event for the younger set.

EPIC PIZZA & SUBS
1711 S. 9th St.
314-436-3742
epicpizzaandsubs.com
Pizza, yes, by the slice and by the pie (try the Hot Hawaiian for something a bit different). Plus subs, a great burger, wings, and more.

FRANCO
1535 S. 8th St.
314-436-2500
eatatfranco.com
French-inspired fare, great cocktails

FRAZER'S
1811 Pestalozzi St.
314-773-8646
frazergoodeats.com
One of the city's original

"chalkboard specials" spots, serves fresh veggies, seafood, steak

FRITANGA
2208 S. Jefferson Ave.
314-664-7777
fritangastl.net
Home-style Nicaraguan food, like empanadas and carne asada

HARDSHELL CAFÉ/ GEYER HOUSE
1860 S. 9th St.
314-231-1860
1860saloon.com
Gumbo, fresh oysters, steaks and more, in two distinct rooms: Hardshell is "indoor patio" and Geyer is "historic wood-beamed."

HODAK'S
2100 Gravois Ave.
314-776-7292
hodaks.com
Famous fried chicken

JAX CAFÉ
2901 Salena St.
314-449-1995
jax-cafe.com
Satisfying comfort food from a local fixture (chef Brian Hale) in a friendly neighborhood spot

LAREDO
2001 Park Ave.
314-231-9200
laredoonlafayettesquare. com
Mexican and nouveau Mexican specialties in an environment 180 degrees from your typical sombreros-and-Cuervo joint

LLYWELYN'S PUB
1732 9th St.
314-436-3255
llywelynspub.com
Upscale sports pub atmosphere, fried pickles

LUVY DUVY'S CAFÉ
2321 Arsenal
314-776-5889
luvyduvys.com
Southern specialties and hospitality

RICARDO'S
1931 Park Ave.
314-421-4833
ricardositaliancafe.com
Italian neighborhood mainstay

RIVERBEND
701 Utah St.
314-664-8443
riverbendbar.com
Cajun/Creole goodies, like po'boys and oyster bread, plus a happy NOLA-meets-STL vibe

SIDNEY STREET CAFÉ
2000 Sidney St.
314-771-5777
sidneystreetcafe.com
Romantic spot for seasonal food

SOULARD COFFEE GARDEN
910 Geyer Ave.
314-241-1464
soulardcoffeegarden.com
Perennial weekend breakfast/brunch fave

SOULARD'S
1731 S. 7th St.
314-241-7956
soulards.com
Fireside dining, good wine list, Saturday breakfast

SPARE NO RIB
2200 Gravois Rd.
314-202-8244
sparenorib.com
Latin America meets the 'cue here: tacos, guac, ribs, and pulled pork

SQWIRES
1415 S. 18th St.
314-865-3522
sqwires.com
American cuisine in "industrial/inviting"-style décor

TRIPEL BRASSERIE
1801 Park Ave.
314-678-7787
tripelstl.com
Entry in the "best Belgian" category . . . OK, maybe the only Belgian joint, but still. European beers on draft, served in their appropriate glassware, and food from mussels to quail.

TUCKER'S PLACE
2117 S. 12th St.
314-772-5977
tuckersplacestl.com
Steaks, burgers, potatoes in dark, woody atmosphere

{ SANDWICH AND A SONG }

If primacy were determined solely on the basis of bumper sticker dominance, **Blues City Deli** (2438 McNair Ave., 314-773-8225, bluescitydeli.com) would be as ubiquitous as McDonald's: just about every contractor-driven pickup truck in town sports one of the joint's stickers. You gotta figure these guys know where the eating's good, though. Memphis-style pulled pork, NOLA-inspired muffaletta, Chicago dogs, pastrami reuben, and a variety of po'boys comprise the menu. Throw in twice-a-week live music, and it's no secret why this joint is jumpin'.

{ PERFECT PATIOS }

Each with its distinctive charms, united by one theme: these are spots to covet in temperate weather. Join the crowds at **McGurk's** (1200 Russell Blvd., 314-776-8309, mcgurks.com; enormous, and with a lovely fountain; ask bartenders for fish food for kids to toss, pictured below); **Joanie's** (2101 Menard St., 314-865-1994, joaniespizzeria.com; sunny spot for pizza); **Vin de Set** (2017 Chouteau Ave., 314-241-8989, vindeset.com; view of the Arch, downtown, bustling rooftop spot); **Venice Café** (1903 Pestalozzi St., 314-772-5994, thevenicecafe.com; psychedelic mosaic party paradise, but bring your cash); **Yemanja Brasil** (2900 Missouri Ave., 314-771-7457, yemanjabrasil.com; tropical oasis complete with hammocks); **Molly's** (816 Geyer Ave., 314-241-6200, mollysinsoulard. com; get shrimp and grits or fried green tomatoes, alfresco); **Hammerstone's** (2028 S. 9th St., 314-773-5565, hammerstones.net; great spot for a breakfast pizza!); and **Square One Brewery** (1727 Park Ave., 314-231-2537, squareonebrewery.com; tranquil water feature and fantastic house brews/spirits).

33 WINE SHOP & TASTING BAR
1913 Park Ave.
314-231-9463
33wine.com
Wine shop and tasting bar

1860 SALOON
1860 S. 9th St.
314-231-1860
1860saloon.com
Live music and dancing nightly, plus bar food

BASTILLE
1027 Russell Blvd.
314-664-4408
1920s-era tiger-oak bar, mostly gay clientele, Monday drag shows

BENTON PARK CAFÉ
1900 Arsenal St.
314-771-7200
bentonparkcafe.com
Boozy brunch cocktails and lip-smackin' spiked coffees

BIG DADDY'S
1000 Sidney St.
314-771-3066
bigdaddystl.com
Party bar with free sports shuttle

CARSON'S
1712 S. 9th St.
314-436-2707
Karaoke! Regulars make this a don't-miss.

CAT'S MEOW
2600 S. 11th St.
314-776-8617
catsmeowstl.com
Cheap and off the beaten path, opens early and takes washers seriously

CLEMENTINE'S
2001 Menard St.
314-664-7869
Favorite gay dive spot, with Oh My Darlin' café slinging steaks and more in back

DB'S SPORTS BAR
1615 S. Broadway
314-588-2141
Wings, sports, and women in their skivvies

ERNESTO'S WINE BAR
2730 McNair Ave.
314-664-4511
ernestoswinebar.com
Tucked-away spot for wine and great apps

GREAT GRIZZLY BEAR
1027 Geyer Ave.
314-231-0444
greatgrizzlybear.net
Bar apps, wraps, and a pretty patio

ITAP
1711 S. 9th St.
314-621-4333
internationaltaphouse.com
Beer paradise (and nary an A-B product in sight)

JOHNNY'S
1017 Russell Blvd.
314-865-0900
johnnysinsoulard.com
Raucous and scantily clad; with burgers

KEYPER'S
2280 S. Jefferson Ave.
314-664-6496
keypersstl.com
Piano bar, mostly gay clientele, giant drinks

NADINE'S GIN JOINT
1931 S. 12th St.
314-436-3045
nadinesginjoint.com
Darts, jukebox, kickin' chili

PLANTER'S HOUSE
1000 Mississippi Ave.
314-696-2603
plantershousestl.com
Adventurous forays in both drink and cuisine

SHAMELESS GROUNDS
1901 Withnell Ave.
314-449-1240
shamelessgrounds.com
Coffeehouse with wide-open arms for everyone, from polyamorous to plain-Jane

THE SHANTI
825 Allen Ave.
314-241-4772
soulardshanti.com
Live music/open mics, easy-going hippie vibe

SOCIAL HOUSE
1551 S. 7th St.
314-241-3023
socialhousesoulard.com
DJs and dance

TRUEMAN'S PLACE
1818 Sidney St.
314-865-5900
truemanssoulard.com
Big menu, shots, sports shuttle, sand volleyball, darts

WAY OUT CLUB
2525 S. Jefferson Ave.
314-664-7638
Bric-a-brac packed and home to some mighty loud rock-punk shows

{ DEATH BY CHOCOLATE }

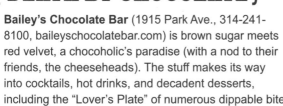

Bailey's Chocolate Bar (1915 Park Ave., 314-241-8100, baileyschocolatebar.com) is brown sugar meets red velvet, a chocoholic's paradise (with a nod to their friends, the cheeseheads). The stuff makes its way into cocktails, hot drinks, and decadent desserts, including the "Lover's Plate" of numerous dippable bites. Excellent beer selection and roses you can buy right from your table. Feel the love.

{ BUD PLUS }

The free tour is fine, but real brewing aficionados will be better served by **Anheuser-Busch's Beermaster Tour** (St. Louis Budweiser Tour Center, 12th and Lynch Sts., 314-577-2626, budweiser-tours.com/toursBeermaster.htm), an upgrade that for $25/person (or $10 for those 13–20) gets you behind the scenes to fermentation cellars, the historic Brew House, the Clydesdale Stable and Tack Room, a packaging/bottling line, and a private VIP tasting room. Some folks get super-excited, too, to sample Budweiser directly from a finishing tank. Reservations required, along with closed-toe shoes. The newest feature, an expansive, outdoor Biergarten, offers tasting flights, a small food menu, and the opportunity to participate in one of A-B's long-held traditions: a 3 P.M. tasting concurrent with that of A-B brewmasters around the country, to ensure the quality of the day's brews.

RECREATION

Plenty in the way of DIY-ethos diversions, plus a few heavy hitter annual events like **Mardi Gras** and **home tours** in Lafayette Square and Soulard. A smattering of galleries makes for an interesting arts scene, too.

FESTIVITIES

BENTON PARK
SUMMER CONCERT SERIES
Summer/fall
& CHALK ART FESTIVAL
Late fall
bpnastl.org
Monthly concerts bring a diverse musical range and crowd to the park, as does a pro and amateur chalk art exposition.

LAFAYETTE PARK
SUMMER CONCERT SERIES
June–Sept, every other Saturday, 6–9 P.M.
lafayettesqr.com

LAFAYETTE SQUARE
HOME & GARDEN TOUR
First weekend in June

HOLIDAY PARLOR TOUR
December
lafayettesqr.com/Events/Tour/default.aspx
See how the Victorians and their latter-day real-estate inheritors live

MARDI GRAS
February–March
mardigrasinc.com
From stuff-yourself-silly food events to parades to races, there's something for just about everyone over the weeks-long celebration.

SOULARD HOLIDAY PARLOR TOUR
December
soulard.org/HistoricSoulardHoliday ParlourTour.php
Inside scoop from homeowners and tour guides, with a variety of buildings included

EXERCISE

RAMP RIDERS
2324 Salena St.
314-776-4025
rampriders.net
Make all your BMX/skateboard/ rollerblade dreams of glory come true; the indoor skatepark facility offers open sessions daily, private instruction, equipment rental, demonstrations, contests, and overnight events.

BUMBERSHOOT AERIAL ARTS
2200 Gravois Ave.
314-898-3259
thebumbershoot.com
Wants you to "find your inner monkey" by learning skills most of us have only seen at the circus. Trapeze, silks, hoop, juggling, and more are the specialties at this studio, with classes for kids, teens, and adults. Want to try before you buy? Stop by most any Saturday from 4 to 5 P.M. for a free hour on the trapeze (ages 13+), no experience necessary.

The **Gateway Cup** (gatewaycup.com) brings professional criterium cycling to both Lafayette Square and Benton Park (in addition to the Hill and St. Louis Hills) in multiple events over Labor Day weekend. Neighbors often turn their front sidewalks into party patios, kids on bikes and in wagons abound, and when the peloton whizzes by you at a corner turn, it'll blow your skirt up.

ARTS, ENTERTAINMENT, & EDUCATION

CONCRETE OCEAN GALLERY
2257 S. Jefferson Ave.
314-497-0199
Local contemporary artists, rotating
monthly exhibits

KOKEN ART FACTORY
2500 Ohio Ave.
314-771-9000
kokenartfactory.com
Home of annual "Naughti Gras" erotica
show, plus other themed happenings

LEMP NEIGHBORHOOD ARTS CENTER
3301 Lemp Ave.
314-814-3633
lemp-arts.org
All-ages venue for underground shows
from folk to math-rock, along with arts
programs for community kids

MAD ART GALLERY
2727 S. 12th St.
314-771-8230
madart.com
Re-imagined former Art Deco police
station, site of events and art happenings
including traveling film fests, visual
exhibitions, and live music

OLD ROCK HOUSE
1200 South 7th St.
314-588-0505
oldrockhouse.com
Three-level live music venue for local
and touring shows

SOULARD ART MARKET
2028 S. 12th St.
314-258-4299
soulardartmarket.org
Artists' collective exhibits monthly,
in range of media

SOUTH BROADWAY ATHLETIC CLUB
2301 S. 7th St.
314-776-4833
Sheer oddball entertainment, in the
form of monthly local wrestling matches,
complete with grudges, girl fights, chair
breaking and can't-look-away people
watching; family-friendly, if you don't
mind your kid watching cartoonish vio-
lence and seeing drunk people

SHOPPORTUNITIES

COMESTIBLES

GRAND PETITE MARKET
2017 Chouteau Ave.
314-241-7799
grandpetitemarket.com
Specialty culinary goodies, from fancy oils and salts to copper cookware, picnic baskets, and table linens

KAKAO CHOCOLATE
2301 S. Jefferson Ave.
314-771-2310
kakaochocolate.com
Artisan chocolate including hand-dipped truffles, indulgent hot chocolate mix, and marshmallow pies

MILLER HAM
3345 Lemp Ave.
314-776-0190
millerham.com
Family-run and tucked-away, they sell to some local meat markets and do private-label product for Straub's, but you can still walk in the door (a phone call before Easter or other ham-loving holidays is advised) and walk out with a ham.

VINO VITAE
1637 S. 18th St.
314-771-8466
vinovitae.com
Cozy wine shop specializing in "educational retail," which means best experienced at one of the frequent tasting events and classes, where you'll get to sip (and nibble) your way to discover new favorites from the wine, beer, and spirits selection.

{ TO MARKET, TO MARKET }

Another unbeatable people-watching spot, **Soulard Market** (730 Carroll St., 314-622-4180, soulardmarket.com) on a Saturday morning provides both entertainment and provisions (and if you're not careful, maybe a pet). Market regulars have their own partisan picks, but most agree that the mini-donut stand, the Schmitz Spice Shop (averaging 600–800 pounds of spices sold per week!), and Scharf's produce are tops. But if you need a kitten, socks, or soap, you might just be in luck, too; as one happy shopper put it, Soulard is one of those rare locales that "continues to marinate in its own freaky juices."

{ KID ZONE }

You can buy 'em on many city corners, but it's worth a pilgrimage to the mothership of **Gus' Pretzels** (1820 Arsenal St., 314-664-4010, guspretzels.com), where, in addition to the regular stick variety, you'll find numbers, letters, baby carriages, hearts, sports logos, the Arch, and many seasonal shapes. Visit before noon and you'll likely see some twisted behavior in the bakery. Sandwiches, pretzel dips, and other snacks available. Cash only.

HOME/GARDEN/BODY

LA BELLE HISTOIRE
2501 S. 12th St.
314-556-0156
labellesoulard.com
French Quarter feel pervades this fanciful boutique full of jewelry, exquisite hand-made masquerade masks, candles, and incense.

MISSOURI CANDLE & WAX
707 Park Ave.
314-241-3544
mocandle.net
Supplies for the home candlemaker, including paraffin wax, soy wax, beeswax, wicking, hundreds of fragrances, and more. In business for more than a century and willing to show you the ropes.

GIFTS

LOOKING GLASS DESIGNS
1917 Park Ave.
314-621-3371
lookingglassemb.com
Handbags, scarves, baby gifts, and an emphasis on personalization and monogramming

THE PORCH
1700 S. 9th St.
314-436-0282
soulardporch.com
Combo wine shop and gift emporium is the perfect spot en route to a girlfriend's birthday party; grab a fun present and a bottle of vino and you're good to go!

ANTIQUES/COLLECTIBLES

R. EGE ANTIQUES

1304 Sydney St.
314-773-8500
regeantiques.com
It's antiquing minus the fussy, with an eye here towards outsider and funky art, including industrial artifacts, former church furnishings, and whole gobs of curiosities and thingamajigs. Need a baby-doll head mold or antique bird cage? This is your spot.

FABRICATION ARTS CENTER

1916 Park Ave.
314-776-4442
fabartscenter.com
A collection including art glass, wrought iron, lampwork beading, mosaic, and period lighting in one Lafayette Square storefront work space. Shop or take a class!

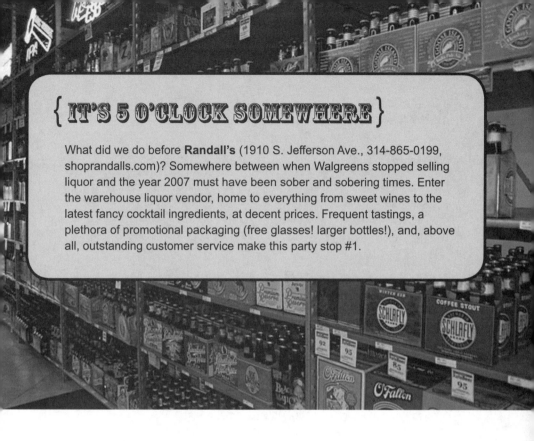

{ IT'S 5 O'CLOCK SOMEWHERE }

What did we do before **Randall's** (1910 S. Jefferson Ave., 314-865-0199, shoprandalls.com)? Somewhere between when Walgreens stopped selling liquor and the year 2007 must have been sober and sobering times. Enter the warehouse liquor vendor, home to everything from sweet wines to the latest fancy cocktail ingredients, at decent prices. Frequent tastings, a plethora of promotional packaging (free glasses! larger bottles!), and, above all, outstanding customer service make this party stop #1.

{ FOR THE DOGS }

Four Muddy Paws (1711 Park Ave., 314-773-7297, fourmuddypaws.com), located near a city park, is a holistic animal supply store/self-serve dog wash that serves as a de facto meeting place for the pets' people, too!

{ READY TO WEAR }

Easier than losing fifteen pounds, more attainable than an Oprah makeover: get some clothes that actually fit! **Daniel Morgan, Tailor** (2701 S. Jefferson Ave., 314-664-6366), runs a ship-shape shop where you can take your current threads for fitting, nip/tucking, repair, and even pretty solid wardrobe advice. (He'll gently talk you out of the dated silhouettes that aren't doing you any favors.) And you won't feel a thing but fabulously fashionable.

As far as you can get from the Wii, take the family to a St. Louis **Perfectos old-time baseball game** (perfectos.vintagenine.com) in Lafayette Park and show them the meaning of "old school." In vintage uniforms and playing by vintage rules, the team (taking on opponents like the St. Louis Brown Stockings, the University City Lions, and the St. Charles Capitals) is faithful to the game circa 1860. Among the differences? Ye olden men considered it unmanly to wear protective gear.

{ PILLARS OF FAITH }

Like so many city neighborhoods, this area has a wealth of religious institutions that have played pivotal historical roles. Two especially stand out: **St. John Nepomuk** (1625 S. 11th St., 314-231-0141, saintjohnnepomuk.org, at right), dating from the mid-1800s and originally serving a Bohemian congregation (when the surrounding streets were known as "Bohemian Hill" and a Czech newspaper was published on-site) and **St. Francis de Sales** (2653 Ohio Ave., 314-771-3100, institute-christ-king.org/stlouis), also called "the Cathedral of South St. Louis," an imposing Gothic edifice with a three-hundred-foot-plus spire, and also home to a daily, traditional Latin mass.

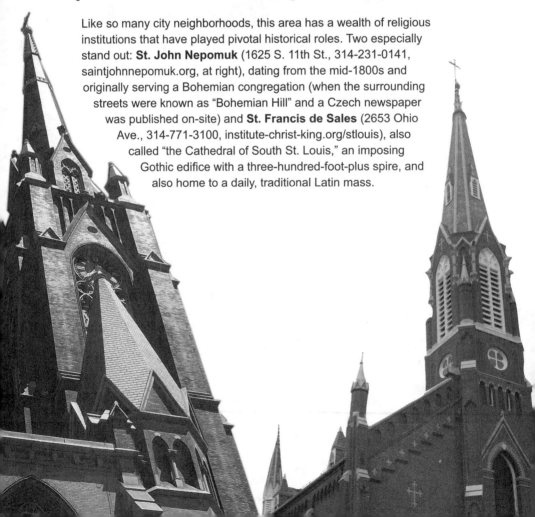

SOUTHWEST CITY

CLIFTON HEIGHTS ★ THE HILL ★ LINDENWOOD ★ NORTH HAMPTON ★ PRINCETON HEIGHTS ★ ST. LOUIS HILLS ★ SOUTHAMPTON

HISTORY

The southwest corner of St. Louis City teems with architectural charm, parks, and gourmet and family restaurants. Walkable, tree-lined neighborhoods, an abundant collection of city parks, annual block parties, and neighborhood festivals give these neighborhoods a small-town feel in a metropolitan city. It's no wonder this area is one of the top choices for the best of city living.

THE HILL

The Hill is a place where family businesses are owned for generations, where most folks know their neighbors, and where visitors will find some of the finest Italian food in the country. *The Italian Immigrants* monument in front of St. Ambrose Catholic Church pays homage to the immigrant heritage of the neighborhood. Fire hydrants on the Hill are red, green, and white in a nod to the colors of the flag of the mother country. Lines form on weekends and holidays at Volpi Salumeria and Viviano's Market for Italian delicacies. The Missouri Baking Co. is also a destination, known for its marvelous Italian-inspired baked goods. Hill restaurants are continually recognized for dining excellence.

Baseball fans know famed New York Yankee Yogi Berra and former St. Louis Cardinal and national baseball broadcaster Joe Garagiola are sons of the Hill. Both grew up on Elizabeth Avenue, now carrying the ceremonial name Hall of Fame Place. Beloved broadcaster Jack Buck bought his first home on Elizabeth. All three homes are marked with granite plaques.

ST. LOUIS HILLS

A ride or stroll through St. Louis Hills reveals Art Deco–influenced architecture and elegant stonework. Francis Park, the crown jewel and neighborhood centerpiece, has churches at all four corners and enjoys daily visits from walkers, joggers, and cyclists. Willmore Park is located in the neighborhood and has fishing lakes, bike trails, a playground, picnic areas, a dog park, tennis courts, a roller hockey rink, and ball fields.

SOUTHAMPTON

Southampton is architecturally similar to St. Louis Hills but with narrower lots, giving the neighborhood more of a gingerbread feel. Stunning art glass, faux fireplaces, Cuban mosaics, and hardwood floors, some with inlaid wood, are representative of a Southampton home. A walk through the neighborhood reveals few homes alike. Many of the homes built in the 1920s and 1930s took more than a year to build. Macklind Avenue is the heart of Southampton, with cafés, restaurants, and shops anchoring the neighborhood's renaissance.

CLIFTON HEIGHTS

Clifton Heights contains a magical little valley and lake, known as Clifton Park, in its neighborhood. Many homes surrounding the park have Victorian-inspired architecture. Other Clifton Heights home styles include Arts and Crafts bungalows and frame homes. The neighborhood's natural topography with hills and prominent valleys is unique when compared to other city neighborhoods, rendering it both hidden and convenient.

LINDENWOOD

Parks are the anchors of many Southwest St. Louis neighborhoods, and Lindenwood is no exception. Lindenwood Park's soccer and baseball fields and roller hockey rink have hosted tournaments both formal and informal. Ivanhoe is the neighborhood's "downtown" with shops and cafés. Like neighboring Southampton and St. Louis Hills, Lindenwood has a significant number of homes that were built in the Art Deco style of the 1920s and 1930s with art glass and hardwood floors. A walk through the neighborhood or around Lindenwood Park is a treat any time of year.

FOOD AND DRINK

Southwest City has its share of award-winning eateries. **Aya Sofia** (6671 Chippewa St., 314-645-9919, ayasofiacuisine.com) is an upscale Turkish restaurant with an intimate atmosphere. Weekend entertainment offers belly dancing, an unexpected novelty in this part of St. Louis. **Onesto Pizza and Trattoria** (5401 Finkman St., 314-802-8883, onestopizza.com) is making the world better one meal at a time, using only local or organically grown produce as well as hormone- and antibiotic-free meats and fish. If you're looking for pizza of the non-Provel persuasion, here you'll find some of the best in the city.

A BITE TO EAT

ADRIANA'S
5101 Shaw Ave.
314-773-3833
adrianasonthehill.com
Mouthwatering Italian sandwiches, pastas, salads for the lunch crowd

AMIGHETTI'S
5141 Wilson Ave.
314-776-2855
www.amighettis.com
Original location; Amighetti Special is a lunchtime favorite

ANTHONINO'S TAVERNA
2225 Macklind Ave.
314-773-4455
anthoninos.com
Pizza, Italian, and Greek for lunch or dinner; laid-back and kid friendly

ARI'S
3101 Hampton Ave.
314-644-4264
arisrestaurantstl.com
Greek-American, casual

BARTOLINO'S OSTERIA
2103 Sulphur Ave.
314-644-2266
bartolinosrestaurants.com
Italian fine dining

BIGGIE'S
3332 Watson Rd.
314-781-0060
biggiesrestaurant.com
Family friendly, made-from-scratch dressings and pasta sauces

BRAZIE'S
3073 Watson Rd.
314-481-5464
Classic Italian just south of the Hill

CHARLIE GITTO'S
5226 Shaw Ave.
314-772-8898
charliegittos.com
Italian; make a reservation, look spiffy

CUNETTO'S
5453 Magnolia Ave.
314-781-1135
www.cunetto.com
Traditional Italian, family owned, and worth the wait

DOMINIC'S
5101 Wilson Ave.
314-771-1632
dominicsrestaurant.com
Italian dining with romantic ambience; reservations recommended

EL PAISANO
3315 Watson Rd.
314-645-7455
Mexican cuisine and entertainment (often mariachi)

EL TAPATIO
3279 Hampton Ave.
314-645-7676
Family-friendly Mexican spot with a better-than-average chile relleno

EOVALDI'S DELI
2201 Edwards St.
314-771-5707
delionthehill.com
The Godfather or the
meatball sandwiches are
favorites

FARMHAUS
3257 Ivanhoe Ave.
314-647-3800
farmhausrestaurant.com
Contemporary American,
can be a tough seat to get

FAVAZZA'S
5201 Southwest Ave.
314-772-4454
favazzas.com
Laid-back Italian, outdoor
seating in season

FIVE BISTRO
5100 Daggett Ave.
314-773-5553
fivebistro.com
Fresh, locally sourced,
New American menu

GIAN-TONY'S
5356 Daggett Ave.
314-772-4893
gian-tonys.com
Southern Italian fare; fresh
herbs and vegetables
from garden

GIOIA'S DELI
1934 Macklind Ave.
314-776-9410
gioiasdeli.com
Italian deli; hot salami
sandwich is their signature
item

GIOVANNI'S ON THE HILL
5201 Shaw Ave.
314-772-5958
giovannisonthehill.com
Four-star Italian
establishment; jacket is
required

GUIDO'S PIZZERIA & TAPAS
5046 Shaw Ave.
314-771-4900
guidosstl.com
Casual Italian, tapas, and
Basque fare

JOE FASSI SAUSAGE AND SANDWICH FACTORY
2321 Sublette Ave.
314-647-5158
joefassisandwiches.com
Italian deli decorated with
local baseball memorabilia

JOEY B'S ON THE HILL
2524 Hampton Ave.
314-645-7300
joeybshill.com
Sports bar and Italian
restaurant

LILY'S
4601 S. Kingshighway
Blvd.
314-352-1894
lilysfreshmex.com
Home-style Mexican food;
family owned; casual

LORENZO'S TRATTORIA
1933 Edwards St.
314-773-2223
www.lorenzostrattoria.com
Contemporary northern
Italian; house-made
risotto and gnocchi and
patio dining

LORUSSO'S CUCINA
3121 Watson Rd.
314-647-6222
lorussos.com
Italian dining, business
casual

LOU BOCCARDI'S
5464 Magnolia Ave.
314-647-1151
louboccardis.com
Great version of St.
Louis–style pizza

MAMA CAMPISI'S
2132 Edwards St.
314-776-3100
mamasonthehill.com
Allegedly the birthplace
of the world-famous St.
Louis toasted ravioli

**MAMA TOSCANO'S
RAVIOLI**
2201 Macklind Ave.
314-776-2926
www.mamatoscano.com
Handmade ravioli, regular
or toasted to take home

MATHEW'S KITCHEN
5625 Hampton Ave.
314-351-1700
mathewskitchenstl.com
Meatloaf, crab cakes,
shepherd's pie; these
comfort faves, but gussied
up, rule the menu.

MODESTO TAPAS
5257 Shaw Ave.
314-772-8272
www.modestotapas.com
Bona fide taste of Spain

PLATO'S CAFÉ
5912 Hampton Ave.
314-477-9677
Coffeehouse, outdoor
seating, cash only

PIETRO'S
3801 Watson Rd.
314-645-9263
pietrosdining.com
Italian, pizza, home-style
comfort food

PIZZA-A-GO-GO
6703 Scanlan Ave.
314-781-1234
pizzaagogo.blogspot.com
Serving St. Louis–style
pizza since 1967; no
alcohol; cash only

PIZZERIA TIVOLI
5861 S. Kingshighway
Blvd.
314-832-3222
Brick-oven pizza

PUEBLO SOLIS
5127 Hampton Ave.
314-351-9000
pueblosolisstl.com
Award-winning Mexican
fare

RIGAZZI'S
4945 Daggett Ave.
314-772-4900
rigazzis.com
32-ounce frozen fishbowl
beer

RUSSELL'S CAFÉ
5400 Murdoch Ave.
314-553-9994
russellscafe.com/portfolio/
locations
Beloved neighborhood
café has changed
ownership and upgraded
its lovely patio: full menu
for breakfast, lunch, and
dinner, plus drool-worthy
baked goods.

SOUTHWEST MARKET
5224 Columbia Ave.
314-776-5220
Lunch sandwiches

STELLINA PASTA CAFÉ
3342 Watson Rd.
314-256-1600
stellinapasta.com
Italian, house-made
pastas and great salad

{(ALMOST) 24-HOUR EATS}

After a night of continuous happy hour excitement or when
you're craving breakfast after dinner, head on over to the 24/7
Courtesy Diner (1121 Hampton Ave., 314-644-2600) or **Chris'
Pancake and Dining** (5980 Southwest Ave., 314-645-2088,
chrispancakeanddining.com), which serves weekends until 1:30 A.M.

{ CLASSIC SOUTHWEST CITY }

For tweens and teens, the deli-markets of Southwest City are what the hamburger stand was to the *Happy Days* set. **Mom's Deli** (4412 Jamieson Ave., 314-644-1198), **LeGrand's Market** (4414 Donovan Ave., 314-353-4059, legrandsmarketcatering.com), and **Macklind Avenue Deli** (4721 Macklind Ave., 314-481-2435, macklindavenuedeli.biz) are where the after-school set in the know heads to cure hunger pangs on weekday afternoons, weekends, and school vacations.

SPIRO'S RESTAURANT
3122 Watson Rd.
314-645-8383
spirossouth.com
Greek family-owned
family restaurant

THREE FLAGS TAVERN
4940 Southwest Ave.
314-669-9222
threeflagstavern.com
The flags in question are Spanish, French, and American: the flags in succession that flew over the Louisiana Territory. They're also the primary cuisines represented on the menu here: lobster beignets to posole and Indian fry bread.

TRATTORIA MARCELLA
3600 Watson Rd.
314-352-7706
trattoriamarcella.com
Spiffy, "be seen," highly rated

ZIA'S
5256 Wilson Ave.
314-776-0020
www.zias.com
Classic Italian and St. Louis–style cuisine, with a wait most nights

{ KID ZONE }

Fill 'er up! But we're talking ice cream and (local G&W) brats, not 89 octane, at **The Filling Station**, a converted gas station now chock full of nostalgia like Betty Boop art, larger-than-life cartoon statues, and the like. A tasty treat for the kids, and a kitsch-trip down memory lane for the grown folks (5323 S. Kingshighway, 314-457-0238).

SOMETHING SWEET

You can still get your kicks on Route 66, but one can also satisfy even the most serious sweet tooth. **Gooey Louie** (6483 Chippewa St., 314-352-2253, gooeylouiecake.com) offers up a favorite treat, gooey butter cake. And if that's not enough sugar to make you comatose, **Donut Drive-In** (6525 Chippewa St., 314-645-7714) can seal the deal with their hand-cut donuts. Loyal customers come from miles around. **Gelato Di Riso** (5204 Wilson Ave., 314-664-8488, gelatodiriso.com) offers the authentic Italian confection in flavors such as lemon, pear, and pistachio, as well as espressos, lattes, teas, and smoothies.

{ LANDMARK }

On any given summer evening, traffic barriers slow the cars as the crowds make their way to **Ted Drewes Frozen Custard** (6726 Chippewa St., 314-481-2652, teddrewes.com), the frozen custard mecca on Route 66. Winters thin the crowds a bit but locals and tourists alike crowd around the sidewalk heaters while enjoying concrete treats like All Shook Up (Elvis-inspired banana and peanut butter cookie), Terramizzou (a pistachio treat inspired by the University of Missouri), and Dutchman Delight (in honor of the Scrubby Dutch of the South Side).

{ DRINKS FOR MARTINI MAVENS }

The Famous Bar (5213 Chippewa St., 314-832-2211, thefamousbar.com) pours some of the best around. Their seasonal selections alone are reason enough to stop in and toss back a martini. Lovers of the local music scene will not be disappointed. With plenty of parking in back for those with designated drivers, it's a destination for lovers of martinis and music alike.

SOMETHING TO DRINK

Classic South Side bars with games, pub food, and locals are in plentiful supply. However, aspiring sommeliers now too have a place to call their own at **3500 Winehaus** (3500 Watson Rd., 314-353-9463, 3500winehaus.com).

. . . .

BABE'S TAVERN
3215 Ivanhoe Ave.
314-647-3436
Classic South Side bar;
spring, summer, and fall
beer garden

DOUBLE-D'S DEN
5204 Hampton Ave.
314-481-4794
Not for serious non-
smokers; fun place to sing
karaoke on weekends

JOHNNY GITTO'S
6997 Chippewa St.
314-781-8111
eatjohnnygittos.com
3 A.M. karaoke bar

THE MACK
4615 Macklind Ave.
314-832-8199
Great burgers and pub
food

MILO'S BOCCE GARDEN
5201 Wilson Ave.
314-776-0468
www.milosboccegarden.com
As the natives say, "If you
want to play bocce, you
gotta come to the Hill."

POP'S BLUE MOON
5249 Pattison Ave.
314-776-4200
popsbluemoon.com
Tucked-away dive with
friendly patrons and fre-
quent live music, cash only

SHAW'S COFFEE, LTD.
5147 Shaw Ave.
314-771-6920
shawscoffee.com
Dark-roasted, European-
style espresso and non-
coffee drinks, pastries, and
confections

**SOUTHTOWN PUB &
SMOKE SHACK**
3707 S. Kingshighway Blvd.
314-832-9009
southtownpub.net
A great place to watch the
game or play games while
you have a beverage

Go back in time and experience old-world grocery shopping—no need for a trip across the pond. A sensory experience awaits: imported and domestic cheeses, olives and oils, meats, spices, pastas, and so much more. Everything a cook needs to prepare gourmet Italian dinners can be found at Di Gregorio's, Vivianos, or Urzi's markets. Volpi is nationally recognized as a premier salumeria; be sure to visit for scrumptious samples. A lemon ice from Urzi's hits the spot on hot St. Louis summer days. There are not many U.S. cities with as many family-owned (for decades) shopping treasures all in one neighborhood.

DI GREGORIO'S MARKET
5200 Daggett Ave.
314-776-1062
digregoriofoods.com
Italian corner market; authentic and tasty homemade specialties available for lunch; a wide variety of pastas, sauces, specialty oils, and herbs

MISSOURI BAKING COMPANY
2027 Edwards St.
314-773-6566
Vast assortment of traditional, fabulous, Italian baked breads, biscotti, cannoli, and more; cash only

SALUME BEDDU
3467 Hampton Ave.
314-353-3100
salumebeddu.com
Artisan-cured meats garnered national attention when *Forbes* called it "the best salami in the country"; try the soppressata Siciliano, with fennel and red wine; great spot for lunch, too.

URZI'S MARKET
5430 Southwest Ave.
314-645-3914
Family-owned, authentic Italian market with many specialty items; cash only

VITALE'S BAKERY
2130 Marconi Ave.
314-664-6665
vitalesbakerystl.com
Breads, cannolis, pizza shells, and Italian cookies (sesame and anise)

VIVIANO AND SONS MARKET
5139 Shaw Ave.
314-771-5476
shopviviano.com
Step into this old-world Italian grocery filled with enticing authentic specialties: pastas, spices, domestic and imported cheeses, wines; everything imaginable for an Italian kitchen

VOLPI
5258 Daggett Ave.
314-772-8550
volpifoods.com
Lovingly handcrafted Italian salami and cured meats; nationally known gourmet salumeria treasure

RECREATION

Residents of the city of St. Louis treasure their parks, and Southwest City is no exception. **Francis, Willmore, Lindenwood, Clifton, Tilles,** and **Christy Parks** provide a gathering place for joggers, dog walkers, picnics, concerts, and festivals. A variety of athletic practice fields provide exercise within walking distance for neighborhood kids or big kids still living in their glory days. Willmore Park is home to the **Southwest City Dog Park**, a fenced-in oasis where dog owners allow their canine companions to run and play off-leash.

....

FESTIVITIES

CHRISTMAS

Yearly lighting contests create a magical look during the holiday season. Candy Cane Lane and Snowflake Street, along with neighboring blocks, always do a bang-up job. Candy Cane Lane collects donations on weekends during the season to help the less fortunate. A home on the corner of the 6300 block of Devonshire and Childress, called by some "the Mary House," features a house-sized painting of the nativity, a gift to the original owners years ago.

CHRISTMAS ON THE HILL & CHILL ON THE HILL RUN

hill2000.org
First weekend in December
Visitors enjoy carolers, carriage rides, nativity scenes around the neighborhood, and a concert at St. Ambrose Church.

COLUMBUS DAY

hill2000.org
October
This annual celebration honors the gentleman from Genoa, Italy. Festivities include a parade, food (it is the Hill after all), music, and fun at Berra Park.

GATEWAY CUP

gatewaycup.com
Fall
Francis Park brings cyclists from across the country to St. Louis for the second leg of the Gateway Cup. The Hill hosts the longest-running bike race in St. Louis—the Giro Della Montagna, the third stop of the Gateway Cup.

HALLOWEEN

October 31
Halloween brings out hundreds of ghosts, ghouls, and goblins in the annual quest for treats. Be sure to have a joke ready if you're out and about in Southwest City.

SHOPPORTUNITIES

ARCHANGELS BOOKS
3461 Hampton Ave.
314-645-2256
archangelsbooks.com
An Orthodox store (Greek, Russian, Romanian, Bulgarian, etc.) with a unique and interesting gift selection

BERTARELLI CUTLERY
1927 Marconi Ave.
314-664-4005
bertarellicutlery.com
Top-notch cutlery and cooking accessories store; in-house sharpening

BIG RIVER RUNNING COMPANY
5352 Devonshire Ave.
314-832-2400
bigriverrunning.com
Shoes and gear for runners

CATHOLIC SUPPLY OF ST. LOUIS
6759 Chippewa St.
314-644-0643
catholicsupply.com
Gifts, books, and supplies for the faithful

THE FUTURE ANTIQUES (TFA)
6514 Chippewa St.
314-865-1552
tfa50s.com
1950s vintage furniture and furnishings store

GIRASOLE GIFTS & IMPORTS
2103 Marconi Ave.
314-773-7700
store.girasolegiftsandimports.com
Italian imported and themed merchandise

THE GREEN GOOSE
5611 Hampton Ave.
314-352-5000
greengooseresale.com
Well-edited consignment home goods, from big furniture pieces to frames, candles, pillows, artwork, and much more. Selection changes frequently.

HANNEKE HARDWARE
5390 Southwest Ave.
314-772-5120
hanneke.com
Expert home restoration advice

HERBARIA
2106 Marconi Ave.
866-OAT-SOAP
herbariasoap.com
Natural soaps and gifts made on-site; take a tour and learn how their soaps are made

THE HILL CIGAR CO.
5360 Southwest Ave.
314-776-4455
hillcigarco.com
Smoker-friendly retail shop and lounge, with knowledgeable folks to guide your purchase

KNITORIOUS
3268 Watson
314-646-8276
knitorious.com
Well stocked with yarns from basic to fancy, notions, designer patterns, lots of helpful advice, and comfy chairs

SKIF INTERNATIONAL
2008 Marconi Ave.
314-773-4401
skifo.com
Fashion designer Nina Ganci creates and sells one-of-a-kind, natural fiber, USA-made garments from her Hill studio.

{ THE HALLOWED HALL }

Soccer has a storied legacy in this town (see, for example, *The Game of Their Lives*), and this DIY **St. Louis Soccer Hall of Fame** (Inside Midwest Soccer Academy, 5247 Fyler Ave., stlsoccerhalloffame.com) tells the tale, from prominent players who called our town home to memorabilia from the 1950s–1970s heyday of the sport. Not open on a regular basis, it's still worth keeping an eye out for special events and the annual induction dinner.

{ YOU AND THE CHOCOLATE FACTORY }

No dipping your fingers in the stream of flowing chocolate, but a guided tour of the production floor at the **Chocolate Chocolate Chocolate Factory** might be the next best thing! You'll get to see the line rolling, hear more about what goes into crafting everything from molasses puffs to caramels, and—of course—sample the wares. Conveniently, the tour ends up right back in the gift shop. (5025 Pattison Ave., 314-338-3501, chocolatechocolate.com)

{ LOCAL FLAVOR }

Move over Frito-Lay. **The Billy Goat Chip Company** (3136 Watson Rd., 314-353-4628, billygoatstl.com) has become a homegrown success with hand-selected, sliced, seasoned, packaged potato chips.

{DON'T MISS}

Most of Southwest City's architecture—gingerbread bungalows, Arts and Crafts–styled abodes, stately homes with turrets (affectionately called Pencil Houses)—were built in the 1930s, and often took almost a year to build. Hardwood floors, leaded glass, rounded doorways and walls (some over one foot thick) are prevalent in this part of St. Louis City. Fireplaces are often decorative; homeowners didn't want the bugs from firewood and smoke but still desired the ambience of a fireplace. These homes with their distinctive and unique architectural features make this area a sought-after place to live in St. Louis.

{A WALK IN THE PARK}

Join the locals in a stroll around or through **Francis Park** (bounded by Tamm, Eichelberger, Donovan, and Nottingham), the crown jewel of the St. Louis Hills neighborhood. The park features *Francine the Mermaid* and other eclectic mosaic sculptures, a state-of-the-art playground, soccer and baseball fields, tennis courts, and a roller hockey court. On summer Sunday evenings, bring a lawn chair (and some bug spray) and enjoy the sounds of music courtesy of the Compton Heights Concert Band's summer series. Best of all, it's free.

NORTH CITY

BADEN ★ BELLEFONTAINE AND CALVARY CEMETERIES ★ FOUNTAIN PARK ★ O'FALLON PARK ★ PENROSE PARK ★ RIVERVIEW ★ THE VILLE

HISTORY

THE VILLE

Elleardsville, named for its location near the farm of horticulturist Charles Elleard, is today known by its nickname, the Ville. The Ville is renowned as the cradle of African American culture in St. Louis. Early twentieth-century restrictive covenants on property ownership banned African Americans from living in many areas of St. Louis. The Ville, an unrestricted area, became the self-contained neighborhood of choice for the upper and middle African American classes.

Annie Malone, the Ville's most prominent resident and a beloved philanthropist and civic leader, was one of the first African American woman millionaires in the United States. Solid cultural institutions, like Homer G. Phillips Hospital and Annie Malone's Poro College, provided neighborhood employment.

In 1948, restrictive covenants were finally ruled unconstitutional. As in many other neighborhoods, residents of the Ville began moving to the suburbs, and the neighborhood lost a significant chunk of its population between 1950 and 1970.

Sumner High School was the first high school in St. Louis, and the first west of the Mississippi, open to African Americans. It was named after U.S. Senator Charles Sumner, the first U.S. politician to call for full emancipation of African Americans. Noted Sumner High alumni include Chuck Berry, Tina Turner, and tennis great Arthur Ashe.

BADEN

Extensive German migration in the 1840s and 1850s helped Baden earn the nickname "Germantown." With the establishment of a post office in 1853, Germantown was formally named Baden to honor the German city Baden-Baden. True to St. Louis's eccentric habit of mispronouncing its ancestral namesakes, Baden is pronounced "BAY-den" versus its German namesake's pronunciation "BAH-den." Evidence of German heritage can be found in the neighborhood's architecture. Baden was another location of several Indian mounds, lost to development.

PENROSE PARK

Neat as a pin, the architecture of Penrose mirrors the Scrubby Dutch brick bungalow and hobbit-esque houses of its sister neighborhoods on St. Louis's South Side. Penrose Park was once the headquarters of Rexall Drugs until its closing in 1985. It still is home to the Mathews-Dickey Boys' & Girls' Club, which was founded in 1960 by two neighborhood baseball coaches and has served more than forty-thousand metro-area youth. Ashland School's ornamental details are the signature of famed architect William Ittner. St. Elizabeth's Church contains stained glass created by world-famous St. Louisan Emil Frei.

O'FALLON PARK

The country estate of John O'Fallon is today known as O'Fallon Park. O'Fallon, a nephew of William Clark (of Lewis and Clark), was one of St. Louis's most highly regarded benefactors, donating the land for St. Louis University.

O'Fallon Park anchors the neighborhood. Visitors may note the park's boathouse architecture is similar to that of Carondelet Park in St. Louis's South Side. Both parks were part of a compromise that established parks in both north and south St. Louis City as conditions for the approval of building Forest Park, and similar architectural plans were used.

The O'Fallon Park Jazz Concert Series, a new jogging path, renovated basketball courts, and a renovation of the boathouse are drawing residents back to the area. More information can be found at ofallonpark.org.

RIVERVIEW

This lightly populated neighborhood alongside the mighty Mississippi feels like you are in the country while within the St. Louis City limits. Riverview's northern boundary is Chain of Rocks Road, leading to the historic Chain of Rocks Bridge.

A vast network of partner organizations, from the Incarnate Word Foundation to the Saint Louis Chess Club, have joined forces with residents of the O'Fallon and Penrose neighborhoods to create a zone known as the **North Campus**, seeking to provide a pipeline of success from birth through college graduation for the children living and going to school within its boundaries. Related programming is undertaken at the **Sanctuary**, a former church that's now home to constructive, structured activities for kids from 11 to 18 years old (4449 Red Bud Ave., 314-769-9000).

FOOD AND DRINK

A BITE TO EAT

BISSELL MANSION RESTAURANT
4426 Randall Pl.
314-533-9830
bissellmansiontheatre.com
Historic home of Captain Lewis Bissell, built in the mid-1820s—St. Louis's oldest home—serves as a comedy/mystery dinner theatre.

COUNTRY GIRL'S PIE SHOP
3330 Union Blvd.
314-383-8509
Southern and soul food

C-W FRIED & GRILL
9009 Riverview Dr.
314-867-6899
St. Paul sandwich is a specialty

GOODY GOODY DINER
5900 Natural Bridge Ave.
314-383-3333
goodygoodydiner.com
Since 1948; try the chicken and waffles

GREGG'S BAR & GRILL
4400 N. Broadway
314-421-1152
Bar food done right, from crispy chicken sandwiches to burgers and daily specials worth exploring; outdoor seating for the temperate months

SOMETHING TO DRINK

Bars on the North Side tend to have a heavy pour when it comes to mixed drinks, so be aware and plan your intake accordingly. And don't be surprised to find establishments that proclaim themselves "30 and up" or even "35 and up" . . . these spots are only for the grown and sexy people. For the fun fact file: there is an active, and hotly contested, North Side tavern dart scene. Here are a few suggestions to get you started.

BEULAH'S RED VELVET LOUNGE
4769 Martin Luther King Dr.
314-652-6154
Pool and darts, music, pull tabs, and drinks

HARLEM TAP ROOM
4161 Martin Luther King Dr.
314-531-2965
Friendly corner bar, in business for decades

J'S HIDEOUT
4257 Martin Luther King Dr.
314-531-4050
Cozy spot for a nightcap or a birthday celebration

PREMIER LOUNGE
5969 Martin Luther King Dr.
314-717-1100
Upscale night out, with plenty of room for private parties

VALERIE'S SIT & SIP
3701 Sullivan Ave.
314-531-5085
Mature crowd and cozy booth seating mean you really can sit and sip

{ VANTAGE POINTS }

OUR LADY OF THE HOLY CROSS CHURCH
(8115 Church Rd., 314-381-0323, ourladyoftheholycross.com/index.htm). Built in 1909, spires from this Baden house of worship are visible for miles.

CHAIN OF ROCKS BRIDGE
(10950 Riverview Dr., 314-436-1324 ext. 107). An engineering marvel when it opened in 1929, the bridge's 22-degree bend let shipping pass through without hitting the castle-like water intake towers located nearby in the center of the river. Spanning the Mississippi River, the Chain of Rocks Bridge shortened travel time between St. Louis and Edwardsville and was part of the nostalgic Route 66 between 1936 and 1968.

The 5,353-foot-long bridge is on the National Register of Historic Places and is one of the world's longest bicycle and pedestrian bridges. It is a vital link in the bi-state trail system, connecting the St. Louis Riverfront Trail to the MCT Confluence Trail on the Illinois side of the river. Visitors will wax nostalgic at historic Route 66 displays.

LANDMARKS

ANNIE MALONE CHILDREN AND FAMILY SERVICE CENTER

2612 Annie Malone Dr.
314-531-0120
anniemalone.com

In 1922, at age fifty, Annie Malone donated $10,000 to help fund a permanent location for the St. Louis Colored Orphans Home. On the National Register of Historic Places, it continues its service to and is an anchor of the Ville neighborhood.

BELLEFONTAINE CEMETERY

4947 W. Florissant Ave.
314-381-0750
bellefontainecemetery.org

Take a journey into St. Louis's past with a trip through Bellefontaine Cemetery, where some of the finest memorial art in the United States can be found. Adolphus Busch (amazing mausoleum); Thomas Hart Benton, Missouri's first U.S. senator and experienced dueler; William Clark of Lewis and Clark; "Beat Generation" writer William Burroughs; and poet Sara Teasdale are laid to rest here. Visitors will also see many family names recognizable today as local place names, like Eads, Cupples, Hawken, Lemp, McDonnell, and Campbell.

BISSELL WATER TOWER

aka "New Red"

Built in 1885–1886, it was the second of three standpipe water towers in St. Louis. The 196-foot Bissell tower was designed to regulate water pressure rather than to store water. The water tower was used through 1912 and remains a favorite local landmark. Located at Bissell St. and Blair Ave.

CALVARY CEMETERY

5239 W. Florissant Ave.
314-792-7738

Following the 1849 cholera epidemic, city ordinance mandated all future cemeteries be built outside the city limits. In 1853, Catholic archbishop Peter Kenrick purchased the estate of James Clay, son of legendary Kentucky politician Henry Clay. The archbishop used half of the property as his summer residence. The remaining half became Calvary Cemetery. Calvary was once an ancient Native American burial

ground and also the final resting place of soldiers from nearby Fort Bellefontaine. The Native American and military remains were collected and buried in a mass grave under a large crucifix, located at one of the highest points of the cemetery. Wandering through Calvary, you will see familiar names from your history books, like Dred Scott, General William "War is Hell" Sherman, and playwright Tennessee Williams.

HALLS FERRY CIRCLE ROUNDABOUT

One of the few roundabouts in Missouri and one of just a handful in the U.S. when it opened in 1933, this area was still "in the country"; the intersections of Lewis and Clark Blvd., Riverview Blvd. (east), Halls Ferry Rd. (south), Riverview Blvd. (south), Goodfellow Blvd., and Halls Ferry Rd. (northwest) meet here.

HOMER G. PHILLIPS HOSPITAL

In segregated times, this hospital served the Ville neighborhood. A civic achievement for African Americans who long lobbied for a hospital of their own. Attorney Homer Phillips, who was killed before it opened, was instrumental in getting the project financed. When desegregation finally came about, the area suffered large population losses. The hospital closed in 1979. Lovingly restored, this North Side landmark on the National Register of Historic Places now provides 220 units of housing for the elderly.

KULAGE HOUSE

This home, at 1904 E. College Ave., was reconfigured in the early twentieth century, adding a pipe organ with 1,700 pipes housed in a stone tower. Still a private residence.

MARTIN LUTHER KING JR. STATUE

The Fountain Park neighborhood is home to a bronze statue honoring Dr. King. Inscribed with the message "His Dream, Our Dream," this is the only statue of Martin Luther King Jr. in St. Louis.

NORTH GRAND WATER TOWER

This landmark 154-foot Corinthian column served as a standpipe water tower from 1871 to 1912. Local legend wants to believe it was built by Jeff Whitman (brother of famed poet Walt); however, Walter Barnett was the actual builder. No slouch himself, Barnett also built Shaw House in the Botanical Garden, and his sons designed the New Cathedral on Lindell. This landmark, with lights added in the 1930s, served as a navigational beacon so pilots (including Charles Lindbergh) could find Lambert Field on foggy nights. Located at N. Grand Blvd. at 20th St.

ROBISON FIELD

Today the site of Beaumont High School. From the Browns came the Perfectos, which were to become St. Louis's beloved Cardinals. From 1893 to 1920, this was home to the Redbirds. From 1911 to 1917 the St. Louis Cardinals had the first female owner in Major League Baseball, Helen Hathaway Robison Britton. A commemorative marker can be found at Beaumont.

UNION AVENUE CHRISTIAN CHURCH

Built during the 1904 Romanesque Revival; the architect, Albert Groves, also designed City Hall and numerous Central West End manses. Located at 733 Union Blvd.

RECREATION

PARKS AND RECREATION

FAIRGROUND PARK
3715 Natural Bridge Ave.
314-289-5330
stlouis-mo.gov
Built in 1855 with land purchased from John O'Fallon, annual fairs were held in the park until 1902. Fairground Park housed St. Louis's first zoological garden, monkey house, bear pits (these gates still stand at Grand and Natural Bridge), carnivore house, and an aviary that once housed a twelve-thousand-seat amphitheater, the largest in the U.S. in its time, with standing room for ten-thousand more. In 1902, St. Louis's first auto race was held here. The winner's average speed was 33 mph. The 1904 World's Fair at Forest Park as well as the abolition of horse racing in 1905 led to the demise of the fairs. The fairgrounds were abandoned and sold to the city as a park, which opened in 1909. Today, visitors enjoy a nine-acre stocked fishing lake, a swimming and spray pool, as well as tennis, softball, baseball, soccer, and basketball fields.

O'FALLON PARK
1900 E. Adelaide Ave.
314-289-5300
stlouis-mo.gov
In the compromise that added the establishment of parks in North and South St. Louis as conditions for the approval of the Forest Park plan, O'Fallon Park was the North Side entrant. Amenities include the boathouse, picnic shelters, tennis and basketball courts, a softball field, and a spray pool.

O'FALLON PARK REC COMPLEX
4343 W. Florissant Rd.
314-932-1423
ymcastlouis.org/ofallon-park-rec-complex
A spiffy, long-promised new branch of the YMCA of Greater St. Louis operates this facility, which is home to all sorts of athletic offerings, community programming, and an outdoor swimming pool (pictured above).

PENROSE PARK VELODROME
The Penrose Park Velodrome brings cyclists from all over to St. Louis for the rare track cycling experience. One of only fourteen cycling tracks left in the nation, the velodrome is located at the intersection of Interstate 70 and N. Kingshighway Blvd. Built in 1962 for the national championships, this track replaced one located near Forest Park, which had been removed for the building of Highway 40 (I-64). The one-fifth-mile track has seen a rebirth in recent years as volunteers have secured corporate donations and have worked to restore the track and ensure its continuity. Local cycling shop Big Shark sponsors weekday track races during the summer months.

SPORTSMAN'S PARK

Stan the Man had his glory years playing at Sportsman's Park. Located at Grand and Dodier, today it's the site of the Herbert Hoover Boys and Girls Club. From 1881 until the opening of "old Busch Stadium" in 1966, this is where Cardinal Nation gathered to take in the national pastime. The 1940, 1948, and 1957 All-Star games were played here as well as ten World Series: 1926, 1928, 1930, 1931, 1934, 1942, 1943, 1944, 1946, and 1964.

{ HOLY GROUND }

Mount Grace Convent and the Pink Sisters (1438 E. Warne Ave., 314-381-5686, mountgraceconvent.org). "The Pink Sisters" get their name from the rose-colored habits they wear. Although this is a cloistered convent, the chapel and some of the gardens are open to the public. Pope John Paul II visited St. Louis in January 1999. The Pink Sisters prayed for good weather for months before the visit. Some of the best winter weather in St. Louis history occurred during the pope's visit. The local media had a field day with this legend when the weaher the day of the parade turned out to be nearly 70 degrees. Winter returned within hours of the pope's departure.

NEAR COUNTY

BRENTWOOD ★ CLAYTON ★ GLENDALE ★ KIRKWOOD ★ LADUE ★
MAPLEWOOD ★ OAKLAND ★ OLIVETTE ★ RICHMOND HEIGHTS ★ ROCK
HILL ★ UNIVERSITY CITY ★ WARSON WOODS ★ WEBSTER GROVES

HISTORY

St. Louis County is a separate entity from St. Louis City, which is also a county. Outside the state of Virginia—whose state constitution makes them a special case—Baltimore, Maryland, and Carson City, Nevada, are the only other major U.S. cities with this unusual governmental arrangement.

In 1876, the city of St. Louis chose to separate itself from its countrified cousins and split from St. Louis County. After much consideration, county officials chose **Clayton** as the county seat. The site was donated by two native Virginian farmers, Ralph Clayton and Martin Hanley. Hanley's 129-year-old farmhouse still stands on the edge of downtown Clayton, a testament to the city's unique combination of urban flair and quiet community.

Most municipalities in this area began as satellite communities based around transportation hubs. **Brentwood**, incorporated in 1910 to avoid annexation by the nearby city of Maplewood, was a stop on the Manchester trail. **Olivette** grew around the intersection of Olive Blvd. and Price Road. Other towns, like **Glendale** and **Oakland**, were developed from country estates for the wealthy.

Named for French pioneer Peter Ladue and established in the mid-1930s, **Ladue**'s median income is more than triple the national average. Ladue is notorious for its strict enforcement of codes that some might find strange or antiquated. A couple was forced to marry or move in 1985, political yard signs until recently were verboten, and city government sparred with the police chief about escorting drunk drivers home versus arresting them.

Maplewood was laid out by James C. Sutton on a tract of land purchased in 1835. It was permanently settled in 1848, when Sutton built a log cabin in this area. The city adopted its present name in the 1890s and was incorporated in May 1908.

Richmond Heights was incorporated in 1907. Local legend has it that Robert E. Lee surveyed in the area during his pre–Civil War stay in St. Louis. He named it Richmond Heights because the area reminded him of his native Richmond, Virginia.

KIRKWOOD

Kirkwood was platted in 1852 and named for James P. Kirkwood, the first chief engineer of the Missouri Pacific Railroad. After the cholera epidemic and the great fire of 1849, Kirkwood's higher elevation and spacious lots offered an appealing alternative for the middle and upper class.

Kirkwood's historic train station is a step into the past. Travelers daily leave by train for Chicago or Kansas City from the station. Kirkwood maintained strong ties to the city of St. Louis in part because of rail travel. Whether going to work or to a cultural event, St. Louis City was just a forty-minute train ride away. A drive through downtown or nearby neighborhoods is proof positive that Kirkwood's diligent efforts to preserve its past are a big success.

UNIVERSITY CITY

U. City was developed by E. G. Lewis, publisher of the popular *Woman's Magazine*. The octagonal City Hall was originally the magazine's headquarters. The Delmar Loop was the turnaround in U. City for the Delmar streetcar line. The Loop is a great example of a cultural alliance between business and the arts and a top choice for locals to eat, drink, listen to music, dance, or shop.

WEBSTER GROVES

Webster's location along the Pacific Railroad line led to its development as a suburb. Families could escape the noise of the city and live in a more bucolic environment. Businessmen could commute by train to work in the city.

The area took its name from Webster College, which was established by Artemas Bullard, a New Englander, in honor of fellow New Englander Daniel Webster. When establishing a post office, it turned out that there was already a Webster, Missouri. In light of this and because of the area's many trees, "Groves" was added to the name. Today, the natives have reverted to the original name, referring to their town as simply "Webster."

FOOD AND DRINK

A BITE TO EAT

BRENTWOOD

CARL'S DRIVE IN
9033 Manchester Rd.
314-961-9652
Known for delicious
homemade root beer and
outstanding burgers

TRAINWRECK SALOON
9243 Manchester Rd.
314-962-8148
trainwrecksaloon.com
Burgers are mouthwatering
at one of the oldest con-
tinuously operating taverns
in the area

CLAYTON

**ALMOND'S
RESTAURANT**
8127 Maryland Ave.
314-725-1019
almondsrestaurant.com
Southern, soul, and
Cajun-influenced menu

**BARCELONA TAPAS
RESTAURANT**
34 N. Central Ave.
314-863-9909
barcelonatapas.com
Small plates and home-
made sangria

CAFÉ MANHATTAN
511 South Hanley Rd.
314-863-5695
Known for their burgers
and soda fountain

CAFÉ NAPOLI
7754 Forsyth Blvd.
314-863-5731
cafenapoli.com
Romantic, highly
regarded Italian

**CARDWELL'S
IN CLAYTON**
8100 Maryland Ave.
314-726-5055
cardwellsinclayton.com
Classic restaurant,
reservations recom-
mended; dress nice and
be sure to try the ribs

**CARL'S DELICATESSEN
RESTAURANT**
6401 Clayton Rd.
314-721-2393
Home of the famous over-
stuffed sandwich; reubens
are a customer favorite.

{ AN INNOVATOR }

In 1980, Mai Lee left her native Vietnam with her husband and young son in
search of a better life. She worked as a waitress at St. Louis–area Chinese
restaurants in order to make ends meet for her family. In 1985, Mai Lee
opened a small, six-table Chinese restaurant on Delmar. Vietnamese dishes
were added over time to honor her homeland, to enthusiastic response from
her customers. **Mai Lee Restaurant** (8396 Musick Memorial Dr.; 314-645-
2835; maileerestaurant.com) has thrived for more than twenty years, known
for its enormous menu, delicious pho soup, spring rolls, and coffee. She
moved to a more spacious Brentwood location, but the tradition of offering
some of the finest Vietnamese and Chinese food to be found in St. Louis
continues.

CLAYTON DINER

6 S. Central Ave.
314-727-2828
Old-school diner serving
up buck burgers and
slingers

COMPANION

8143 Maryland Ave.
314-721-5454
companionstl.com
Left Coasters need look
no further for sourdough
that's as good or better
than San Francisco's

THE CROSSING

7823 Forsyth Blvd.
314-721-7375
fialafood.com
Serving American,
Italian, and French food;
seasonal menu ensures
locavores will be happy.

FIVE-STAR BURGERS

8125 Maryland Ave.
314-720-4350
5starburgersstl.com
Green-chile cheeseburger
leads the pack at this
gourmet burger joint.

HALF AND HALF

8133 Maryland Ave.
314-725-0719
halfandhalfstl.com
Half breakfast, half lunch:
fried chicken livers, veggie
hash, brioche French
toast, fresh donuts. And
the coffee . . . oh, the
coffee.

I FRATELLINI

7624 Wydown Blvd.
314-727-7901
ifrattelini.com
Moderately priced Italian,
serving lunch and dinner

JENNIFER'S PHARMACY & SODA SHOPPE

30 N. Central Ave.
314-862-7400
jenniferspharmacy.com
Jennifer's is the real deal;
try an egg salad sitting at
the counter, old-school on
a stool.

JOHN P. FIELDS PUB & RESTAURANT

26 North Central Ave.
314-862-1886
A hockey fan favorite
serving pub fare

THE LIBERTINE

7927 Forsyth Ave.
314-862-2999
libertinestl.com
Chef Josh Galliano's
home, serving fresh, local
fare for lunch and dinner.
Sunday Suppers are a
popular option, with the
crave-worthy fried chicken
served every second
Sunday.

NORTHWEST COFFEE ROASTING CO.

8401 Maryland Ave.
314-725-8055
northwestcoffee.com
Bring the kiddos; fun,
dynamic atmosphere

OCEANO BISTRO

44 N. Brentwood Blvd.
314-721-9400
oceanobistro.com
Delicious seafood,
booth ambience

POMME RESTAURANT

40 N. Central Ave.
314-727-4141
pommerestaurants.com
Lovely high-end café

POSH NOSH

8115 Maryland Ave.
314-862-1890
poshnoshdeli.com
A don't-miss; ask for the
free pickles (not on the
menu) kept behind the
counter

PROTZEL'S DELICATESSEN

7608 Wydown Blvd.
314-721-4445
protzelsdeli.com
Kosher Jewish deli
in the spirit of NYC's
Carnegie Deli

REMY'S KITCHEN & WINE BAR

222 S. Bemiston Ave.
314-726-5757
remyskitchen.net
Greek and Mediterranean
fare; browse-worthy wine
list

ROXANE ON MERAMEC

12 N. Meramec Ave.
314-721-7700
roxaneonmeramec.com
This eclectic bistro is a hot
spot for happy hour.

TANI SUSHI BISTRO

16 S. Bemiston Ave.
314-727-8264
tanisushi.com
The OMG roll is a favorite, but check out the Hot Rock Beef cooked in front of you on a 400-degree hot rock

FRONTENAC

KREIS' RESTAURANT

535 S. Lindbergh Blvd.
314-993-0735
kreisrestaurant.com
Classic steakhouse cuisine renowned especially for prime rib

KIRKWOOD

AMIGOS CANTINA

120 W. Jefferson Ave.
314-821-0877
amigoskirkwood.com
Traditional Mexican fare in the heart of Kirkwood

CITIZEN KANE'S STEAKHOUSE

133 West Clinton Pl.
314-965-9005
citizenkanes.com
A top choice if you're looking for beef

DEWEY'S PIZZA

124 N. Kirkwood Rd.
314-821-7474
deweyspizza.com
Real pizza, good salads; kitchen windows allow the kiddos to watch the pizza skins fly

FIVE-STAR BURGERS

312 S. Kirkwood Rd.
314-394-2250
5starburgersstl.com
Green-chile cheeseburger leads the pack at this gourmet burger joint.

FILOMENA'S ITALIAN KITCHEN

9900 Manchester Rd.
314-961-9909
filomenasitalian
kitchen.com
Authentic red sauce and Italian wedding soup at a reasonable price; BYOB, no corkage fee

KING DOH CHINESE RESTAURANT

10045 Manchester Rd.
314-821-6988
kingdoh.com
Local favorite of residents and food critics for many years

KIRKWOOD STATION RESTAURANT & BREWING CO.

105 E. Jefferson Ave.
314-966-2739
kirkwoodstationbrewing.com
If beer is your bailiwick, then give this hometown brewer a try; plenty of food options.

{ THE EMPIRE OF CRAFT }

There were, of course, great chefs in this town before Gerard Craft arrived. He'll be the first to acknowledge the collegial restaurant community that thrives here. A strong case can be made, however, that he did much to put St. Louis on the national foodie map, with the opening of Niche several years back. Now Craft has consolidated two of his endeavors—**Niche** (perhaps the most coveted reservation in town) and **Pastaria** (the family-friendly, come-as-you-are joint next door)—in one Clayton location (7734 Forsyth Blvd., 314-773-7755 and 314-862-6603, nichestlouis.com and pastariastl.com). Two other Craft spots (Brasserie and Taste) snuggle up next to each other in the Central West End. Nothing, it seems, attracts a crowd like a crowd.

MIKE DUFFY'S PUB & GRILL

124 W. Jefferson Ave.
314-821-2025
mikeduffys.com
Old-school burgers
with all the fixings,
served until 1 A.M.

ONE 19 NORTH TAPAS & WINEBAR

119 N. Kirkwood Rd.
314-821-4119
one19north.com
Unique selections,
sangria, live but not
too loud music

PEPPE'S APT. 2

800 S. Geyer Rd.
314-909-1375
peppesapt2.com
Authentic Italian food,
generous portions

RICHARD'S RIBS

10727 Big Bend Rd.
314-966-1015
richardsribs.com
The place for ribs in
Kirkwood; kid-friendly

SPENCER'S GRILL

(aka Kirkwood Grill)
223 S. Kirkwood Rd.
314-821-2601
Hometown old-school
grill filled with the locals

STEAK & RICE

951 S. Kirkwood Rd.
314-965-2082
steakandrice.com
Basic but consistent
Chinese

LADUE

FLACO'S COCINA

8400 Delmar Blvd.
314-395-4343
flacoscocina.com
Try the fish tacos or
freshly made guacamole

HOUSE OF INDIA RESTAURANT

8501 Delmar Blvd.
314-567-6850
hoistl.com
Authentic Indian,
vegetarians have a lot
to choose from; great
lunch buffet

LESTER'S SPORTS BAR AND GRILL

9906 Clayton Rd.
888-651-5843
lestersrestaurant.com
Deli sandwiches have
meat stacks measured
in inches; peruse all the
local sports memorabilia
after lunch or dinner.

SPORTSMAN'S PARK RESTAURANT

9901 Clayton Rd.
314-991-3381
sportsmansparkladue.com
Get the wings, baby; a
Ladue institution

MAPLEWOOD

ACERO

7266 Manchester Rd.
314-644-1790
fialafood.com
An intimate northern
Italian dining spot; try the
daily ragu special

BOOGALOO

7344 Manchester Rd.
314-645-4803
boogalooswings.com
Enjoy Cuban food or
happy hour from a swing;
seriously, the bar seats
are swings instead of
stools.

HOME WINE KITCHEN

7322 Manchester Rd.
314-802-7676
homewinekitchen.com
Risk No-Menu Monday for
a chef's-choice meal

MAYA CAFÉ

2726 Sutton Ave.
314-781-4774
mayacafestl.com
Distinctive pan-Latin food
and margaritas

SCHLAFLY BOTTLEWORKS

7260 Southwest Ave.
314-241-2337
schlafly.com
Burgers, real brews, and
a menu featuring locally
grown produce; brewery
tour; farmers' market on
summer Wednesdays

WATER STREET CAFÉ

7268 Manchester Rd.
314-646-8355
waterstreetstl.com
Vintage vibe, with classic
cocktails and salads,
escargots, flatbreads,
pastas, and more

OLIVETTE

DURANGO TAQUERIA AND GROCERY
10238 Page Ave.
314-429-1113
Fried pig esophagus for the adventurous, tacos for the conservative

HAVELI INDIAN RESTAURANT
9720 Page Ave.
314-423-7300
havelistl.com
Authentic, vegetarian (and non-vegetarian) Indian cuisine with varying degrees of spice

I LOVE MR. SUSHI
9443 Olive Blvd.
314-432-8898
mrsushistl.com
Good sushi in a small space; sushi chef has nice singing voice

KATIE'S PIZZERIA CAFÉ
6611 Clayton Rd.
314-727-8585
katiespizzacafe.com
Be it provel or mozzarella on your pizza, both are done well here

LU LU SEAFOOD RESTAURANT
8224 Olive Blvd.
314-997-3108
luluseafood.com
Dim sum available weekends; fresh, fast

MEI HUA CHINESE RESTAURANT
9626 Olive Blvd.
314-569-0925
meihuastl.com
Skip the buffet and instead order hot braised pork or scallops in hot chili sauce

MS. PIGGIES SMOKEHOUSE
10612 Page Ave.
314-428-7776
mspiggiessmokehouse.com
Ribs, pork steaks, catfish, and chicken; pass the homemade BBQ sauce!

NOBU'S JAPANESE RESTAURANT
8643 Olive Blvd.
314-997-2303
nobusushistl.com
Sushi is the menu mainstay; sake and other beverages of the Asian persuasion available; one of the first sushi places in the region.

OLIVETTE DINER
9638 Olive Blvd.
314-995-9945
Traditional diner fare, bring cash and coin

PHO LONG
8629 Olive Blvd.
314-997-1218
Vietnamese; good for pho and spring rolls

POINTERS PIZZA
1023 S. Big Bend Blvd.
314-644-2000
pointersdelivery.com
A longtime local favorite

STARRS
1135 S. Big Bend Blvd.
314-781-2345
starrs1.com
Restaurant and wine shop with wines available from just about anywhere in the world

SUGARFIRE SMOKEHOUSE

9200 Olive Blvd.
314-997-2301
sugarfiresmokehouse.com
The next generation of St. Louis BBQ, with menu items like the Big Muddy (brisket "debris" and smoked sausage), PBLT (the P is for "pimiento cheese"), and a slap-yo-momma chicken biscuit. Plus, boozy shakes!

RICHMOND HEIGHTS

FRANK PAPA'S RISTORANTE

2241 S. Brentwood Blvd.
314-961-3344
frankpapas.com
Local favorite on the Richmond Heights–Clayton corridor; a taste of Italy served in a cozy, intimate atmosphere

HARVEST SEASONAL MARKET CUISINE

1059 S. Big Bend Blvd.
314-645-3522
harveststlouis.com
Seasonal menu using locally sourced and organic produce whenever possible; always looking for sustainable methods and delicious practices

YEN CHING

1012 S. Brentwood Blvd.
314-721-7507
Exactly what everyone expects Chinese food to be

ROCK HILL

A'MIS

9824 Manchester Rd.
314-963-1822
amispizza.com
Italian food and pizza à la New York, Chicago, or St. Louis style

CHARCOAL HOUSE

9855 Manchester Rd.
314-968-4842
charcoalhouse.us
Think of this as your parents' steakhouse; a special occasion, old-school, dressy kind of place

FAROTTO'S ITALIAN RESTAURANT & PIZZERIA

9525 Manchester Rd.
314-962-0048
farottos.com
St. Louis–style pizza institution if you're into provel on your pies, and popular happy hour spot

HACIENDA MEXICAN RESTAURANT

9748 Manchester Rd.
314-962-7100
haciendastl.com
Enjoy 'ritas and the party on the patio at this happy hour spot

KATIE'S PIZZERIA & PASTA OSTERIA

9568 Manchester Rd.
314-942-6555
katiespizzaandpasta.com
Wood-fired pizzas, house-made pastas (which you'll see draped and drying about the kitchen), fresh salads, and a full bar

NACHOMAMA'S

9643 Manchester Rd.
314-961-9110
nachomamas-stl.com
Fresh and fast Tex-Mex, from burritos to tamales, plus frequent daily specials

---

{ FULLY CAFFEINATED }

City Coffeehouse and Creperie (36 N. Brentwood Blvd., 314-862-2489, citycoffeeandcreperie.com); **Foundation Grounds** (7298 Manchester Rd., 314-601-3588, foundationgrounds.com); **Meshuggah Café** (6269 Delmar Blvd., 314-726-5662, meshuggahcafe.com) offer your morning fix in an independent environment.

{ (ALMOST) ANYTIME EATS }

Tiffany's Original Diner (7402 Manchester Rd., 314-644-0929) is a real diner with counter seating, good food, and fun. Open 24 hours.

UNIVERSITY CITY

AL-TARBOUSH DELI
602 Westgate Ave.
314-725-1944
Falafel is freshly made; you can purchase hummus, tabbouleh, dolmahs, and tahinis to go along with a hookah.

BLUEBERRY HILL
6504 Delmar Blvd.
314-727-4444
blueberryhill.com
Restaurant/music club filled with pop-culture memorabilia; burgers, soups, and Chuck Berry in the Duck Room

CHEESE-OLOGY MACARONI & CHEESE
6602 Delmar Blvd.
314-863-6365
cheese-ology.com
Comfort food mavens and vegetarians will be happy and leave full.

CICERO'S
6691 Delmar Blvd.
314-862-0009
ciceros-stl.com
Huge beer selection, Italian eats; people watch from your sidewalk café table spot on a St. Louis summer evening

ECLIPSE
6177 Delmar Blvd.
314-726-2222
eclipsestlouis.com
Interplanetary culinary adventure in the Moonrise Hotel; also check out the rooftop bar

FITZ'S AMERICAN GRILL & BOTTLING WORKS
6605 Delmar Blvd.
314-726-9555

fitzsrootbeer.com
See how root beer, orange soda, and cream soda are made, right from your table; plenty of healthy food options so you won't feel guilty about the root beer float

FORK & STIX
549 Rosedale Ave.
314-863-5572
forknstix.com
Intimate dining room serving the best dishes of northern Thailand: deep-fried dumplings, green and red curry, tempura udon soup

FRANK & HELEN'S PIZZERIA
8111 Olive Blvd.
314-997-0666
frankandhelens.com
Pizza with mozzarella cheese! The fried chicken is very good; the only other place in St. Louis where you can get Crown Candy ice cream besides Crown Candy.

{ KID ZONE }

Old school reigns at **Fizzy's Soda Fountain & Grill** (29 N. Gore Ave., in Webster Groves, 314-395-4550, fizzyssodafountain.com), where the kids can oversee the creation of their own soda concoction, or go ape with the Colossal, Gargantuan, Enormous Sundae ($25 for ten scoops of ice cream and a gazillion toppings). Fresh burgers, fries, pizza, and salads are available, but only if you finish all your dessert.

LA PIZZA
8137 Delmar Blvd.
314-725-1230
lapizzamenu.com
Hand-tossed New York–
style pizza

MI RANCHITO
887 Kingsland Ave.
314-863-1880
mi-ranchitostl.com
Mi Ranchito offers good,
inexpensive, authentic
Tex-Mex.

MISSION TACO
6235 Delmar Blvd.
314-932-5430
missiontacostl.com
Street-taco style at the
eastern end of the Loop;
casual and bustly

MOMOS
630 North and South Rd.
314-863-3511
saucemagazine.com/
momos
Authentic Greek with a
tapas-style menu and
belly dancers

QUEEN OF SHEBA
6665 Olive Blvd.
314-727-7057
Ethiopian food; try the
goat curry

RANOUSH
6501 Delmar Blvd.
314-726-6874
ranoush.com
Syrian food with a
multitude of options for
vegetarians; baklava is
made fresh daily

SEOUL TACO
571 Melville Ave.
314-863-1148
seoultaco.com
From the road to the
Loop: got its start as a
food truck sensation, and
now offers a small-but-
mighty Korean/Mexican
mash-up menu.

U-CITY GRILL
6696 Enright Ave.
314-721-3073
Korean specialties just off
Delmar in the Loop; the
bulgogi beef is a favorite,
cash only

**WEI HONG SEAFOOD
RESTAURANT & BAKERY**
7740 Olive Blvd.
314-726-0363
weihongseafood.com
Local favorite for dim sum

WINSLOW'S HOME
7213 Delmar Blvd.
314-725-7559
winslowshome.com
A cool place for breakfast
or lunch; try the scrump-
tious blueberry pancakes

WONTON KING
8116 Olive Blvd.
314-567-9997
On many folks' "best
Chinese" list, both for its
standard menu and week-
end dim sum carts

WEBSTER

BIG SKY CAFÉ
47 S. Old Orchard Ave.
314-962-5757
allgreatrestaurants.com
Great place to begin or
finish an evening at the
Rep

THE BLOCK
146 W. Lockwood
314-918-7900
theblockrestaurant.com
Casual room; meaty menu
includes roasted chicken
meat pies, house-made
bacon jam, chops, trout,
braised pork

C.J. MUGG'S
101 West Lockwood Ave.
314-963-1976
cjmuggs.com
Come for martinis before
the Rep or sip while
people watching from the
sidewalk in the summer;
local music venue for
the over-30 crowd

CYRANO'S
603 E. Lockwood Ave.
314-963-3232
cyranos.com
Scrumptious desserts
before or after the Rep
or a play at Nerinx Hall
High School

CHINA INN
9737 Manchester Rd.
314-968-8823
Serves a mean "Happy
Family"

HWY 61 ROADHOUSE
& KITCHEN
34 S. Old Orchard Ave.
314-968-0061
hwy61roadhouse.com
Cajun, Creole, and BBQ;
local brews and music

MILAGRO
MODERN MEXICAN
20 Allen Ave., Suite 130
314-962-4300
milagromodernmexican.com
An upscale taste of Mexico;
enjoy freshly made margaritas
at happy hour; house-made
chorizo and grilled fish tacos

RACANELLI'S
8161 Big Bend Blvd.
314-963-1111
racanellis.com
Local-based New York–style
pizza chain

STRATTON'S CAFÉ
8103 Big Bend Blvd.
314-961-2900
strattonscafe.com
A good bet for breakfast; also
try the house-made gelato

{ REMINDERS OF OUR PAST }

Hanley House (at right, 7600 Westmoreland Ave., 314-290-8553, hanleyhouse.
blogspot.com) is a reminder of how Clayton was
in the early days. Hawken House (1155 South
Rock Hill Rd., 314-968-1857, hawkenhouse.
org) is the 1857 home of the rifle manufacturing
Hawken family. Quinette Cemetery (12120 Old
Big Bend Blvd.) is a historic African American
burial ground that was established in 1866 and is
one of the oldest west of the Mississippi. Mudd's
Grove, the massive, red-brick Greek Revival
home in Kirkwood, dates from 1859, and also
serves as the home of the Kirkwood Historical
Society (302 W. Argonne Dr., 314-965-5151,
kirkwoodhistoricalsociety.com).

SOMETHING SWEET

**CHOCOLATE
CHOCOLATE
CHOCOLATE**
112 N. Kirkwood Rd.
314-965-6615
chocolatechocolate.com
Enjoy handcrafted
chocolate on the day it
was made

HANK'S CHEESECAKES
1063 S. Big Bend Blvd.
314-781-0300
hankscheesecakes.com
Scrumptious; a favorite
is the white chocolate
raspberry cheesecake

JILLY'S CUPCAKE BAR
8509 Delmar Blvd.
314-993-5455
jillyscupcakebar.com
Enjoy the six-cheese mac
and cheese; stay for the
delectable cupcakes,
oversized and filled

**LAKE FOREST
CONFECTIONS**
7801 Clayton Rd.
314-721-9997
www.lakeforest
chocolates.com
If it's Hanukkah gold coins
you need, don't go any-
where else; staff has more
than one-hundred years
of combined confectionery
experience

**LUBELEY'S
BAKERY & DELI**
7815 Watson Rd.
314-961-7160

lubeleysbakery.com
Stollens (the German
pastry treat), hot cross
buns, and a cool retro
highway sign

PICCIONE PASTRY
6197 Delmar Blvd.
314-932-1355
piccionepastry.com
Authentic Italian temp-
tations, served late on
weekends for that post-
concert or Loop stroll
craving. Cannoli, biscotti,
gelato, plus coffee drinks
and Italian sodas

ST. LOUIS CUPCAKE
39 S. Old Orchard
314-961-1111
stlcupcake.com
Perfect spot for that after-
school cupcake craving:
cookie dough, key lime,
PB&J, and other homey
flavors

**SERENDIPITY HOME-
MADE ICE CREAM**
8130 Big Bend Blvd.
314-962-2700
serendipity-icecream.com
Sold by the ounce, Seren-
dipity is currently served
in one hundred local
restaurants

STRANGE DONUTS
2709 Sutton Ave.
314-932-5851
strangedonuts.tumblr.com
These fellows broke the
mold of St. Louis donut

shops (and possibly the
record for "longest time
between announced
concept and actual shop
opening"), and are now
the place if you're jone-
sing for a Fat Elvis (ba-
nana and peanut butter),
Butterfinger, or Campfire
(s'mores-inspired) donut.

SUGAR SHACK
151 W. Argonne Dr.
314-966-0065
kirkwoodsugarshack.com
Old-time sweets, sodas,
phosphates, floats, and
cake balls; parties with
theme names like Candy
Carnival, Candy Land,
and Pirate Party

**SWITZER
CANDY COMPANY**
27 N. Gore Ave.
314-961-1101
switzercandy.com
This is authentic,
traditional candy; known
nationally for licorice but
also try the many fruit twist
flavors as well as Butter-
mels, a favorite of Switzer
Candy's founder, Grandfa-
ther Frederick Switzer.

YO MY GOODNESS
237 W. Lockwood Ave.
314-963-3590
yomystl.com
Sold by the ounce; nonfat
and low-calorie frozen
delights in a variety of
flavors

BLUEPRINT COFFEE

6255 Delmar Blvd.
888-863-8053
blueprintcoffee.com
Serious coffee from folks
serious about coffee;
roasted and served on-
site, and shipped all over

FALLON'S PUB

9200 Olive Blvd.
314-991-9800
fallonspub.com
Irish-themed sports bar
with sixteen TV screens;
happy hour features
live music, weekly trivia
contests, patio dining, live
music on the weekends

POST SPORTS
BAR & GRILL

7372 Manchester Rd.
314-645-1109
thepostsportsbar.com
Learn the art of "Posting";
game-day specials

ST. LOUIS BUBBLE TEA

6677 Delmar Blvd.
314-862-2890
Refreshing on a hot,
humid St. Louis summer
evening, plus warming
winter selections

WINE A LITTLE

BRANICA'S WINE BAR

449 S. Kirkwood Rd.
314-984-9595
Kirkwood hot spot for
happy hour; limited late-
night dining menu

GRAPEVINE WINES AND
CHEESE

309 S. Kirkwood Rd.
314-909-7044
grapevinewinesand-
cheese.com
Over one thousand wines
to choose from plus sixty
malt scotches, gourmet
cheeses, foods, and ac-
cessories

ROBUST WINE BAR,
SHOPPE & CAFÉ

227 W. Lockwood Ave.
314-963-0033
robustwinebar.com
An elegant spot for wine
flights and thoughtful food
pairings

SASHA'S
WINE BAR & MARKET

706 DeMun Ave.
314-863-7274
sashawinebar.com
Very nice wine bar;
seasonal outdoor
atmosphere is delightful

WINE AND CHEESE
PLACE

7435 Forsyth Blvd.
314-727-8788
wineandcheeseplace.com
Wine, as the name says,
gourmet foods, classes,
and events

THE WINE MERCHANT

20 S. Hanley Rd.
314-863-6282
winemerchantltd.com
Considered a top stop
for wine, this also was
one of the first wine stores
in St. Louis.

CLAYTON

Public art abounds; a trip through town reveals works by Renoir as well as Milles.

Folke Filbyter, *by Carl Milles*
Located in front of City Hall, 10 N. Bemiston. Milles studied with Renoir and also created the *Meeting of the Waters* at St. Louis's Union Station. On loan from the St. Louis Art Museum.

Venus Victorious, *by Pierre-Auguste Renoir* located in Shaw Park's Centennial Garden. On loan from the St. Louis Art Museum.

The Uncertainty of Ground State Fluctuations, *by Alice Aycock*
Located in front of the Center of Clayton at 50 Gay Avenue.

FM/6' Walking Jackman, *by Ernest Trova*
Located at the intersection of Maryland Ave. and Brentwood Blvd.

Clayton Caryatid, *by Howard Ben Tre*
Located at 150 Carondelet Pl.

Still Point, *by Ruth Keller Schweiss*
Located in front of the Ritz Carlton at 100 Carondelet Pl.

KIRKWOOD

The Kirkwood Chairs
The work of Marianist Brother Mel Meyer
A whimsical stack of colorful chairs located at the entry to the Kirkwood Farmers' Market on Argonne Ave.

UNIVERSITY CITY

The *Gates of Opportunity* are the gateway to the Loop and are a beloved landmark of all St. Louisans.

Rain Man, *by Gregory Cullen*
Rain Man, at Delmar and Kingsland, Epstein Plaza, was intended to be a temporary seven-month display. Its removal created an uproar. A group formed to raise funds for a more permanent bronze statue and the rest, as they say, is history.

Lion in the Grass, *by Robin Murez*
Sits playfully in the center of a rotary surrounded by native Missouri tall grass at Skinker and Olive. Murez also has art on display at St. Louis's Francis Park.

Musical Lion Benches, *by Robert Cassilly*
In front of University City's city hall at Delmar and Trinity, a saxophone-playing lion and a lute-playing lion invite you to sit and enjoy the view.

St. Louis Walk of Fame
This walking lesson in local history was the brainchild of Joe Edwards in 1988. Honorees must have been born in St. Louis or spent their formative or creative years here. Their accomplishment must have had a national impact on our cultural heritage. Currently there are more than 130 honorees, each represented by a brass-starred sidewalk plaque.

Chuck Berry Statue, *by Harry Weber*
Unveiled in 2011 in honor of one of St. Louis's favorite sons, the legendary rock 'n' roller Chuck Berry. The eight-foot-tall bronze stands near beloved music venue and eatery Blueberry Hill, site of many Chuck Berry performances in that venue's Duck Room.

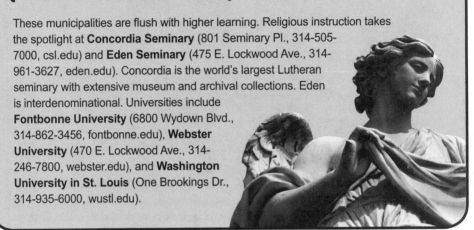

These municipalities are flush with higher learning. Religious instruction takes the spotlight at **Concordia Seminary** (801 Seminary Pl., 314-505-7000, csl.edu) and **Eden Seminary** (475 E. Lockwood Ave., 314-961-3627, eden.edu). Concordia is the world's largest Lutheran seminary with extensive museum and archival collections. Eden is interdenominational. Universities include **Fontbonne University** (6800 Wydown Blvd., 314-862-3456, fontbonne.edu), **Webster University** (470 E. Lockwood Ave., 314-246-7800, webster.edu), and **Washington University in St. Louis** (One Brookings Dr., 314-935-6000, wustl.edu).

RECREATION

FESTIVITIES

ART AND AIR
wcaf.org
June
Webster Groves
Art and Air features more than one hundred artists in twelve categories on the grounds of beautiful Eden Seminary. Purchase the best of fine food and enjoy the sights and sounds of great music. Now that you're feeling artsy, head to the Art and Air Studios and create your own masterpiece. Free parking.

ART OUTSIDE
7260 Southwest Ave.
314-241-BEER
Art Outside is a three-day, juried alternative art fair featuring affordable works from St. Louis–based artists. With Bottleworks as the host, the opportunity to multitask, supporting both local art and beer, is just too good to pass up.

GREEN TREE FESTIVAL
September
Geyer and Adams, Kirkwood
September drought and Dutch elm disease were taking a serious toll on Kirkwood's trees. In 1961, the city offered several varieties of trees for sale for just a dollar. This gradually grew into a festival that draws crowds from across the metro area. There's also a folklife festival. Artisans dress in period costumes from the 1700s and 1800s and bring history to life with crafts, food, and fiddle music. There's a kids' dog show, a canine Frisbee competition, crafters, and entertainment. Admission and parking are free.

LET THEM EAT ART
July
Maplewood
An inner-ring burb Bastille bash, featuring whimsical costume contest, public art,

unique performances (music in all styles, belly dance, hooping), face painting, film screenings, and more, throughout downtown Maplewood.

LOOP ICE CARNIVAL
January
University City
Ice, Ice, Baby. Dozen of ice sculptors and their creations; there's a Snow Ball (as in dance) and for the brave, a Frozen Buns Run. Free for all.

POTPOURRI SALE
April
Ladue
755 S. Price Rd.
314-993-4040
Sponsored by John Burroughs School, this is an annual five hundred–family yard sale. Bring cash, a backpack, and get there early for best parking. There's no yard sale quite like this one. Food available for purchase.

ST. LOUIS ART FAIR
September
Clayton
Clayton Business District
314-863-0278
Billed as the top art fair in the nation, it takes over the heart of downtown Clayton.

ST. LOUIS INTERNATIONAL FILM FESTIVAL
November
University City
Hosted at the beautiful Tivoli Theatre in University City, which dates back to 1924, this is local film lovers' best bet to catch new international films, documentaries, features, and short features.

TURKEY BOWL
Thanksgiving
For the past one hundred years or so, Kirkwood and Webster Groves High Schools have met up for a classic football rivalry, one of a handful still in existence. To the winner goes the coveted Frisco Bell Trophy and to the loser, the Little Brown Jug—kept at school until the following year's Turkey Bowl. There are many other events leading up to the big game, including bonfires, chili cook-offs, alumni gatherings, and a Friendship Dance held at the school not hosting that year's Turkey Bowl.

WEBSTER COMMUNITY DAYS
Fourth of July
This is an all-American, family-friendly, Fourth of July celebration that includes a parade, carnival, BBQ, and fireworks after dark.

{ TOE-TAPPING }

The **Old Webster Jazz and Blues Festival** (*September*, Webster Groves, 314-961-4656, oldwebsterjazzfestival.com) offers nonstop jazz and blues from two stages. Street entertainers, jugglers, face painters, and balloon artists make the festival a family-friendly affair. Local restaurants sell food and drink to go with the music. Strollers and lawn chairs are welcome at this award-winning festival, which showcases some of the best musical talent St. Louis has to offer. Best of all, admission is free. A portion of the festival food and drink sales proceeds are donated to music programs in the Webster Groves School District.

PARKS AND RECREATION

St. Louis's immigrant population left behind a European world where parks were primarily for the wealthy and noble classes. Their legacy to future generations is a long list of green spaces accessible to the masses. Although these communities have a number of excellent parks, take special note of Oak Knoll and Shaw Parks, both in Clayton.

Oak Knoll Park is home to one of the last large native stands of 150-year-old post oak trees, along with walking paths, a native plant area, rain, sunken and flowering island gardens, and popular Musical Nights, a summer concert series on the fourth Sunday, June–September. The St. Louis Artists' Guild, a fabulous art space and gallery, also calls Oak Knoll Park home.

The forty-seven-acre Shaw Park is an urban oasis and Clayton's oldest and largest park, named in honor of former Clayton mayor Charles Shaw. Centennial Gardens hosts sculpture by a Renoir (on loan from the St. Louis Art Museum) in its bicentennial garden. There is also an aquatic center with a fifty-meter competition pool, and an outdoor ice rink.

Step back in time at the retro (and historic) **Saratoga Lanes** (2725 Sutton Blvd., #A, 314-645-5308, saratogalanes.com). They've been rolling here since 1916, but improvements, like a second-story patio, keep the crowds coming back. **Pin-Up Bowl** (6191 Delmar Blvd., 314-727-5555, pinupbowl.com) takes a different approach with posh surroundings and fancy cocktails.

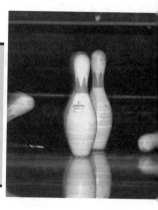

ARTS, ENTERTAINMENT, & EDUCATION

CONCORDIA HISTORICAL INSTITUTE MUSEUM
1333 S. Kirkwood Rd.
314-505-7900
lutheranhistory.org
Also known as "the Lutheran museum," preserves and shares the history of Lutheranism in America, at the Lutheran Church–Missouri Synod's International Center

THE FOCAL POINT
2720 Sutton Blvd.
314-560-2778
thefocalpoint.org
An eclectic mix of local art and culture. Hear a concert, listen to a poetry reading, watch dancing, or sit in on a jam session. While no beverages are served you can bring a margarita or two in from the Maya Café, located in the same building.

FRANK LLOYD WRIGHT HOUSE IN EBSWORTH PARK
120 N. Ballas Rd.
314-822-8359
ebsworthpark.org
Dubbed FLWHEP, this pristine example of Wright's architectural and design aesthetic (including original Wright-designed furniture and fabrics) is one of just five in the state. Tours by appointment only, W–Su.

THE GREEN CENTER
8025 Blackberry Ave.
314-725-8314
thegreencenter.org
Acres of prairie, wetlands, and woods, along with demonstration gardens, make this nonprofit environmental education center worth a visit; grounds open daily, visitor headquarters open Wednesday only.

Imagine a mommy (and maybe daddy) dreamland: tasty and nutritious food for you and bebe; yoga for you (and bebe!), with on-site babysitting; a place for the kids to play while you and the hubby have dinner and a glass of wine. All this and more is available when you perch at **The Nest**, a hybrid of a private club (members get free classes, babysitting, and other perks) and a public restaurant/play space in Frontenac (10440 German Blvd., 314-942-3521, theneststl.com).

THE REPERTORY THEATRE (THE REP)
130 Edgar Rd.
314-968-4925
repstl.org
St. Louis's premier live theatre at the Loretto-Hilton Center for the Performing Arts located on the grounds of Webster University. This architectural gem was the first of its kind in the U.S., designed to house both a professional acting company and an undergraduate arts department. Conrad Hilton, in appreciation for the education given to him by the Sisters of Loretto, donated the building funds. Backstage tours are offered free to school or community groups, around production schedules, September through March.

{ INTERESTING, BUT DON'T TRY IT }

If you stood in the middle of Price Road where Delmar ends, you'd be in three cities (Olivette, University City, and Ladue) at one time!

{ LANDMARK }

Driving by on 40/64 you'd really have to not be paying attention to miss this outlandishly large **Amoco sign** anchoring the Clayton Road exit. Although Amoco has been swallowed into another conglomerate, the sign remains, because after all, there is still a gas station there and St. Louisans are known for their love of tradition, however quirky. If the sign were ever removed though, it is highly doubtful that any planning commission would allow another as big and obnoxious, which is possibly the key to the survival of this unusual landmark.

SHOPPORTUNITIES

Fans of local, independent business will jump for joy. Many towns are unique shopping destinations unto themselves. This list is only the tip of the retail iceberg.

....

SEASONAL PROVISIONS

CLAYTON FARMERS' MARKET
North Central Ave.
314-913-6632
claytonfarmersmarket.com
Wednesdays, May through October

KERRY COTTAGE
2119 S. Big Bend Blvd.
314-647-0166
kerrycottage.com
Clothing, jewelry, Waterford, and other fine crystal and china straight from the Emerald Isle

KIRKWOOD FARMERS' MARKET
150 East Argonne Dr.
314-822-0084
downtownkirkwood.com/kirkwood-farmers-market.asp
April through September,
Monday–Saturday

MAPLEWOOD FARMERS' MARKET
7260 Southwest Ave.
314-241-2337
Wednesdays, May through October,
at Schlafly Bottleworks

WEBSTER GROVES FARMERS' MARKET
4 East Lockwood Ave. Gazebo Park
314-963-5696 ext. 888
webstergrovesfarmersmarket.com
Thursdays, May through October

{ ALL ABOARD! }

Kirkwood Train Station (at S. Kirkwood Rd. and Argonne Dr.) was an endangered species saved from closure by a unique Amtrak and Kirkwood partnership. In 2003, the city of Kirkwood purchased the historic train station from Amtrak. Since then, the station has been staffed by a legion of volunteers who give out schedule information, help passengers embark, issue parking passes (which must be obtained in advance of your trip), and keep the station open from approximately an hour prior to the first passenger train of the day until about an hour after the last one. Tickets can be purchased at the station via an automated machine or direct from Amtrak. Next time you're pining for a ride on the rails, do it old-school style and leave from Kirkwood.

{ THE LANDMARK LIONS }

Gates of Opportunity
The feline gatekeepers of University City sit forty-nine feet above the entry. Commissioned by E.G. Lewis (U. City founder), artist George Zolnay was a prominent designer and sculptor for the 1904 World's Fair. This art treasure symbolizes all things University City.

BRENTWOOD

Manchester Road's shopping opportunities weave through multiple municipalities, including Brentwood.

THE GIFTED GARDENER
8935 Manchester Rd.
314-961-1985
thegiftedgardener.com
Great home touches and gifts for those who love their little backyard slices of heaven: fancy hand tools, gloves and clogs, plus urns, welcome mats, birdbaths, fountains, pots, and gardening books

K. HALL DESIGNS
8416 Manchester Rd.
314-961-1990
khalldesigns.com
Serene apothecary ambience is retail home for St. Louis–made (and nationally sold) fragrances, candles, diffuser oils in natural scents like sugared magnolia and Siberian fir; small selection of ceramics and fine linen gifts, too.

T. HARGROVE FLY FISHING
9024 Manchester Rd.
314-968-4223
thargrove.com
Learn what you need to from passionate practitioners, buy what you need to tie flies, and then go out and practice your cast in the front lot! Drive by any temperate weekend morning and see for yourself.

CLAYTON

As the signs say, "This is Clayton, Missouri." Trendy, upscale, must-have, and luxe describe the shopping options here.

BARUCCI GALLERY
8101 Maryland Ave.
314-727-2020
baruccigallery.com
Original paintings and contemporary art, glass, framing, and jewelry. Nationally recognized as a Top 100 Gallery in the U.S.

CITY SPROUTS
8807 Ladue Rd.
314-726-9611
citysprouts.com
A fun place to grab gear for the kids; wide and unique selection; gift registry for expectant parents

LOLA & PENELOPE'S
7742 Forsyth Blvd.
314-863-5652
lolaandpenelopes.com
Fashions, food, and grooming services for the pampered pet

LUSSO
165 Carondelet Pl.
314-725-7205
lussohome.com
Find all the best names in home decor, candles, clothing, and accessories

SCHOLARSHOP
8211 Clayton Rd.
314-725-3456
scholarshopstl.org
Quality men's, women's, and children's clothing and accessories. For more than forty years, Scholarshop has raised money for the Scholarship Foundation of St. Louis, assisting thousands of now-successful St. Louisans with their education by providing interest-free loans. Check out their Webster Groves location.

WORLD NEWS, LTD.
4 S. Central Ave.
314-726-6010
Extraordinary newsstand with over two thousand periodicals, newspapers, and local books and a general store

KIRKWOOD

Grab the girls and shop til you drop. Start at Down by the Station, go buggy at the Bug Store, re-decorate the home at Christopher's, or get your gourmet kitchen on at Cornucopia. These are just a few of more than one hundred unique shopportunites that await in downtown Kirkwood.

BLUSH BOUTIQUE
110 N. Clay Ave.
314-965-4411
shopblushboutique.com
Fashion-forward designer boutique, appears on local "best of" lists

THE BUG STORE
113 W. Argonne Dr.
314-966-2287
Unique gifts and decor

CHECKERED COTTAGE
135 W. Jefferson Ave.
314-909-7233
checkeredcottage.com
Arts and craft supplies, home products, plus seasonal gift items

CHRISTOPHER'S
127 E. Argonne Dr.
314-909-0202
christophersgifts.com
Cool stuff for your casa; gifts and kid stuff you won't find elsewhere

CLAY & COTTON
159 W. Argonne Dr.
314-394-1400
clayandcottonkirkwood.com
Home goods in cheerful colors, unique fashion, hostess gifts

CORNUCOPIA
107 N. Kirkwood Rd.
314-822-2440
cornucopiakitchen.com
Fifteen thousand gourmet items in stock; coffees, teas, candy, food, cookware, and cutlery

DOWN BY THE STATION
150 W. Argonne Dr.
314-965-7833
downbythestation.com
Unique gifts, scented wax bowls, and collectibles

LASS AND LADDIE, A CHILDREN'S BOUTIQUE
161 W. Jefferson Ave.
314-822-1886
lassandladdiekirkwood.com
Modern, vintage, and handmade items for kids

O.K. HATCHERY FEED AND GARDEN STORE, INC.
115 E. Argonne Dr.
314-822-0083
Since 1927, has supplied feed, pet supplies, outdoor decor, and garden accessories; shoppers appreciate the old-school style; it's worth a visit to check out even if you don't need anything

PAPERDOLLS
110 E. Jefferson Ave.
314-965-3655
paperdollsboutique.webs.com
Women's clothing and accessories

PUZZLE WAREHOUSE
655 Leffingwell
314-856-4030
puzzlewarehouse.com
Stop in, if for no other reason, to see the twenty-four-thousand-piece puzzle; Ravensburger, MasterPieces, and all the top brands, with fun stuff for every age

VELLUM
120 W. Monroe Ave.
314-909-1640
velluminc.com
Hip and haute from the world of stationery and invitations

LADUE

Creativity and fashion abound on Clayton Road.

GIDDYUP JANE
9670 Clayton Rd.
314-993-9944
giddyupjane.com
Handmade belt buckles, gorgeous boots, and Western wear for Midwestern ladies

IMAGINATION TOYS
9737 Clayton Rd.
314-993-6288
imagination-toys.com
Awesome toys, games, and diversions for kids of all ages and interests, with great advice (and free gift wrap) if you're en route to a birthday party and don't know much more than the kid's age.

IVY HILL BOUTIQUE
8835 Ladue Rd.
314-721-7004
ivyhillboutique.com
Second location of the popular women's shop carries denim, dresses, designer goods of all types. There's a build-your-own jewelry bar, too

SALLIE HOME
9821 Clayton Rd.
314-567-7883
salliehome.com
Enter a dream world of bed/bath/home, with vignettes of linens, frames, china, candles, serving ware, and much more

THE SERVICE BUREAU
9773 Clayton Rd.
314-991-1104
stlservicebureau.com
Charitable shopping, you can call it: fine stationery and paper goods, monogrammed gifts, and home decor, with all profits donated to local charities

MAPLEWOOD

Maplewood turned their downtown upside down with stellar results. Boutiques like Femme and Maven are regular stops on professionally guided shopping tours. Its eclectic, walkable shopping has topped off a textbook revitalization effort.

THE BOOK HOUSE
7352 Manchester Rd.
314-968-4491
bookhousestl.com
New location for longtime bookseller means avid readers and browsers will continue to have access to a wide array of new and used books in every genre.

FEMME
7270 Manchester Rd.
314-781-6868
Step inside and you'll see unique high-end fashion and accessories; there's a yoga class one evening a week

MAVEN
7290 Manchester Rd.
314-645-1155
mavenstl.com
Bath and beauty boutique featuring Maven's own line of soaps, candles, and skin care; they also offer apparel, jewelry, and lighting

ST. LOUIS SALT ROOM
2739 Sutton Blvd.
314-647-2410
mysaltspa.com
Take the cure of halotherapy, a European import involving spending time in a full-salt-surround environment, from walls to floor; it's a practice its beneficiaries swear by to alleviate symptoms of everything from asthma to pneumonia

TIGERLILY
7328 Manchester Rd.
314-646-0061
tigerlilystore.com
Mom and her two girls have a cute boutique and their tagline says it all: "For Baby, For You, For Home, For Fun"; women's accessories, tabletop, baby apparel, and monogramming

WEBSTER GROVES
Webster has two local shopping areas, Old Webster and Old Orchard. Each is home to independent bookstores, restaurants, boutiques, and more.

APPLE OF YOUR EYE
20 N. Gore Ave.
314-968-9698
appleofyoureyegifts.com
Fun to funky personalized gifts for over thirty years

THE CLOVER
8150 Big Bend Blvd.
314-467-0436
the-clover.com
"Core," "Lab," "Refine[d]," and "Capsule": yeah, there's some high concept branding going on here, but at its (ahem) core, this women's boutique offers a well-edited selection of everything from basics to bling.

INITIAL DESIGN
25 N. Gore Ave.
314-968-8300
theinitialdesignstl.com
Monogramming of just about anything you can imagine

KIND SOAP CO.
20 Allen Ave., Suite 105
314-942-2024
kindsoap.com
Super, natural (but not supernatural!) soaps, cosmetics, scrubs, lotions, and more that will make you soft, supple, and yummy-smelling; manufactured on site.

KRUEGER POTTERY SUPPLY

8153 Big Bend Blvd.
314-963-0180
kruegerpottery.com
Come out and play; classes for all skill
levels, supplies for all things clay

RED LEAD

27 N. Gore Ave.
314-962-0433
redleadpaperworks.com
Paper, art, and stamp store for the
creative type

ROLLING RIDGE NURSERY

60 N. Gore Ave.
314-962-3311
rollingridgenursery.com
Keeping Webster's landscape well planted
with plants of merit; holiday decoration
and Christmas tree destination for more
than fifty years

RUNG & SPRUNG BOUTIQUES

9739 and 9741 Manchester Rd.
314-918-0575
shoprung.org
Dot.org? Yep, two side-by-side consignment boutiques – one for children, one for
women – donating 100 percent of their
profits to local charities helping the same
audiences. High-quality goods and display
talents that rival any department store's,
plus frequent sales and events

VERDE KIDS

27 S. Old Orchard Ave.
314-962-5437
verdestl.com
The cutest/softest/funnest stuff for babies
and kids, all with a focus on environmental
sustainability and eco-friendliness.
Apparel, toys, cooperative games, and a
great book corner

WEBSTER GROVES BOOKSHOP

100 W. Lockwood Ave.
314-968-1185
Independent store with a cozy,
comfortable literary ambience; wide
selection of local books

YUCANDU ART STUDIO

20 Allen Ave., Suite 110
314-963-4400
yucandu.com
No appointment needed; drop in to paint,
collage, or do mosaics; classes for all
ages and skill level and parties too

THE LOOP IN UNIVERSITY CITY

It's hip, it's fun, and there are many options. Vintage clothing and Vintage Vinyl, fair trade shopping, artist guilds and galleries, even cool duds for the small fry. Shop, dance, or drink until you drop. It's so cool, in fact, it's one of America's "Ten Great Streets," according to the American Planning Association. The Loop shopping district is loaded with public art and friendly to those on foot, bikes, or blades.

CRAFT ALLIANCE
6640 Delmar Blvd.
314-725-1177
craftalliance.org
Nonprofit arts education, gallery, and shop; great place for one-of-a-kind gift shopping and jewelry

GOOD WORKS
6323 Delmar Blvd.
314-726-2233
goodworksfurniture4u.com
A different kind of furniture store; contemporary or traditional designs; you'll want one of everything

LORI COULTER
6138 Delmar Blvd.
314-727-9870
loricoulter.com
Made-to-order swimwear

MACROSUN INTERNATIONAL
6273 Delmar Blvd.
314-726-0222
macrosun.com
Fair trade items from places like Thailand, Nepal, India, Tibet, and Sri Lanka; global jewelry and international fashions, exotic decor

MISS M'S CANDY
6193 Delmar Blvd.
314-721-7000
missmscandy.com
Classic candy store— every kid's, and many adults', dream

PLOWSHARING CRAFTS
6271 Delmar Blvd.
314-863-3723
plowsharing.org
Staffed primarily by volunteers, this store offers fair trade handicrafts from forty countries and three continents.

SILVER LADY
6364 Delmar Blvd.
314-727-0704
thesilver-lady.com
A jewelry store that specializes in silver and artist-made pieces.

SOLE AND BLUES
6317 Delmar Blvd.
314-863-3600
soulandblues.com
Cutting-edge shoes for men and women; jewelry and accessories; shoe mavens should definitely have a look

SUBTERRANEAN BOOKS
6275 Delmar Blvd.
314-862-6100
store.subbooks.com
Independent urban bookstore

SUNSHINE DAYDREAM
6608 Delmar Blvd.
314-727-9043
sunshinedaydream.com
A 1970s flashback that fits well in the new millennium

{ **HOT WAX** }

Vintage Vinyl (6610 Delmar Blvd., 314-721-4096, vintagevinyl. com) is a destination with a national reputation. It has an extensive collection of rare CDs and vinyl, both new and used, plus concert DVDs, T-shirts, and merch from your favorite bands. You can often catch free in-store performances from national acts coming through town. Allow plenty of time, and enjoy the soundtrack from the live DJ while you shop.

WARSON WOODS

The Manchester Road shopping continues through Warson Woods.

AMERICAN VISIONS
9999 Manchester Rd.
314-965-0060
american-visions.com
Exquisite and functional craft pieces from the U.S. and Canada, from measuring spoons to handbags

JANIE LOU QUILTS
10041 Manchester Rd.
636-579-0120
janielouquilts.com
Fabric, notions, and inspiration for the modern quilter

KANGAROO KIDS
10030 Manchester Rd.
314-835-9200
kangarookidsonline.com
Mecca for new parents, especially those into breastfeeding and attachment parenting; free support and educational groups are popular; buy a sling, learn to use it, and buy/sell quality consignment kids' clothes and gear

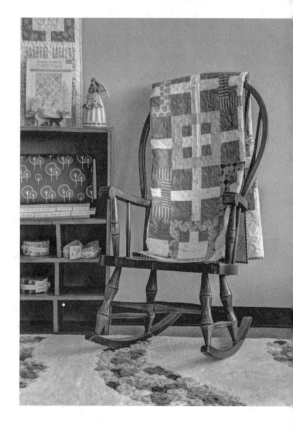

"For over 125 years this **Woman's Exchange** (8811-A Ladue Rd., 314-997-4411, woexstl.org) helps those in need lead productive lives through their own industry." It is known as one of *the* top places in the metro area for unique, handmade children's clothing and locally known for the cherry dress. The Tea Room at the Woman's Exchange is where the girls gather for the Woman's Exchange salad bowl with Mayfair dressing or a piece of lemon meringue pie. Dinner is served and there is a takeout menu as well. It's a St. Louis tradition, which helps those in need. Win-win.

FOODSTUFF

BAUMANN'S FINE MEATS
8829 Manchester Rd.
314-968-3080
baumannsfinemeats.com
Experienced full-service meat shop

EXTRA VIRGIN, AN OLIVE OVATION
8829 Ladue Rd.
314-727-6464
extravirginoo.com
A celebration of cooking and all things olive

FREDDIE'S MARKET
9052 Big Bend Blvd.
314-968-1914
freddiesmarket.com
Third-generation, family-owned neighborhood market with organic items, hand-cut meats, farm-fresh produce

GLOBAL FOOD MARKET
421 N. Kirkwood Ave.
314-835-1112
globalfoodsmarket.com
Globetrot while you shop; local produce and household products from England to Pakistan

KAKAO CHOCOLATE
7272 Manchester Rd.
314-645-4446
kakaochocolate.com
For the serious chocolate lover, mind-blowing treats

PENZEY'S SPICES
7338 Manchester Rd.
314-781-7177
penzeys.com
More than 250 herbs and spices, plus advice on what to do with them

SEAFOOD CITY GROCERY STORE
8020 Olive Blvd.
314-993-2800
seafoodcitysupermarket.com
Top retail location for seafood

STRAUB'S IN CLAYTON
8282 Forsyth Blvd.
314-725-2121
straubs.com
Local gourmet supermarket

VOM FASS
7314 Manchester Rd.
314-932-5262
vomfassusa.com
Vinegars, oils, wines, liqueurs straight from the cask

SOUTH COUNTY

AFFTON ★ CONCORD ★ CRESTWOOD ★ JEFFERSON
BARRACKS ★ LEMAY ★ MEHLVILLE ★ OAKVILLE ★
SHREWSBURY ★ SAPPINGTON ★ SUNSET HILLS

HISTORY

While the affluent built Victorian homes and European-style avenues, hardy
pioneers moved to the fertile land of the Meramec River floodplain to farm
and raise families. The winding river reminded the many German immigrants
of their homeland's Rhine, and their love of the land is shown in city planning
for these communities, as many towns were planned around the natural
sweeping curves and dips instead of typical city grids. In most cases, they
made special efforts to preserve trees or other nature-made beauties.

These farmlands stretched from the Mississippi River to the Meramec.
After World War I and World War II, the surrounding areas—including
Crestwood, Shrewsbury, Sunset Hills, Mehlville, and Oakville—began to see
an influx of residents seeking an escape from the city, and the population
expanded in just a few short years. Today, these communities still have that
mid-century suburban feeling.

AFFTON

Affton was originally a plantation owned by a Scotsman, but it became
known as "Aff's Town" for the man who opened a general store and became
the postmaster. Back in the days of buggies and carriages, the only road
markers were buildings; Aff's general store became known as the "Ten Mile
House," as it was ten miles away from the courthouse. This neighborhood
was briefly a stand-alone village and enjoyed its own police force. However,
the Affton residents voted to disincorporate in 1935 due to lack of revenue. It
is now a part of St. Louis County but still has much of its charm, as many of
its homes were built before World War II.

JEFFERSON BARRACKS

As the oldest operating military base in the country, Jefferson Barracks has seen much of America's history. Founded on the day of President Thomas Jefferson's death in 1826, it played host to Civil War generals Robert E. Lee and Ulysses S. Grant, as both men were stationed here. Strategically important in multiple wars and westward expansion, it was home to the nation's first permanent cavalry unit, the dragoons. Its military hospital treated more than eighteen thousand soldiers during the Civil War, and the base served as the main training grounds for the Spanish-American War. During World War I, it became the first base to train soldiers in aviation parachuting and during World War II it was one of the first Army Air Corps bases. Today, much of its land has been sold to the county for parks and residential developments, and the nearby national cemetery is one of the nation's oldest military cemeteries. More than twenty thousand soldiers are buried here, including one thousand Civil War casualties interred according to their home state.

LEMAY

Crossing the Mississippi has always featured prominently in St. Louis's economic and cultural history. Fragments of the mom-and-pop contributions of ferry river crossing remain. Such is the case with Lemay. Francois LeMais and his son operated a ferry across the Meramec River, and a road was laid out in 1834 from their ferry to Carondelet. As Lemay became a bustling epicenter of river traffic, it was briefly considered as a candidate for our nation's capital, due to its strategic importance and central location in the rapidly expanding country.

FOOD AND DRINK

A BITE TO EAT

BARTOLINO'S SOUTH
5914 S. Lindbergh Blvd.
Affton
314-487-4545
bartolinosrestaurants.com
Fine Italian, seafood, and
steaks since 1982

BERIX
2201 Lemay Ferry Rd.
Mehlville
314-845-3711
berixcoffee.com
Eastern European special-
ties and Turkish coffee
produced in-house

BREAKFAST & BURGER
10024 Gravois Rd.
Affton
314-669-9555
thebreakfastandburger.com
It's hard to improve upon the
description! French toast,
omelettes, pancakes, and
their ilk, along with more
than twenty specialty burgers from the grill

CAFÉ AFFTON
8713 Gravois Rd.
Affton
314-457-8000
cafeaffton.com
Classic South County sports
bar with better food than
you'd expect

CAFÉ TELEGRAPH
2650 Telegraph Rd.
Lemay
314-200-9952
cafetelegraph.com
Cozy neighborhood spot

a block from Jefferson
Barracks, serving wings,
meatloaf, burgers, and
other comfort foods, plus
their signature dessert:
hand grenades (aka home-
made donuts) cooked
to order. Military and St.
Louis–memorabilia provide
the décor, and lots of area
Catholic and other schools
get their own menu items.

COURTESY DINER
8000 S. Laclede Station Rd.
Affton
314-553-9900
www.courtesydiner.com
The newest member of
the locally owned Cour-
tesy family, and faithfully
serving up the St. Louis
slinger and other cus-
tomer favorites 24/7

**CRUSOE'S
RESTAURANT & BAR**
5591 Oakville Shopping Ctr.
Oakville
314-892-0620
crusoerestaurant.com
American; "Feed the
Crew" family special for
takeout orders

**DRUNKEN NOODLES
TASTE OF THAI**
5496 Baumgartner Rd.
Oakville
314-845-8808
A taste of pad thai deep in
South County

FORTEL'S PIZZA DEN
7932 Mackenzie Rd.
Affton
314-353-2360
fortelspizzaden.com
Where little leaguers and big
leaguers go after a game to
chow down

**FRAILEY'S
SOUTHTOWN GRILL**
4329 Butler Hill Rd.
Concord
314-892-1866
fraileysrestaurant.com
Traditional American;
try the wings

GARVEY'S GRILL
5647 Telegraph Rd.
Oakville
314-846-8881
garveysgrillonline.com
Traditional pub fare, with a
solid following among the
Oakville crowd

HELEN FITZGERALD'S
3650 S. Lindbergh Blvd.
Sunset Hills
314-984-0026
helenfitzgeralds.com
Pub, Italian, and American
fare; a happening party spot,
especially on St. Paddy's Day

**KING EDWARD'S
CHICKEN AND FISH**
8958 Watson Rd.
Crestwood
314-843-3474
kingedwardschicken.com
Family-owned Southern-
style (Louisiana, to be exact)
chicken

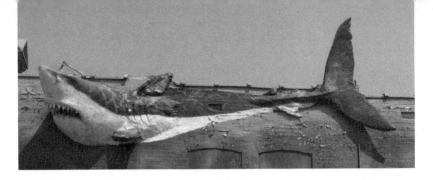

LEMAY WOK
4530 Lemay Ferry Rd.
Mehlville
314-487-8834
A hole-in-the-wall-esque
Chinese eatery that's
worth the wait

PHIL'S BBQ
9205 Gravois Rd.
Affton
314-638-1313
Home of the St. Louis
pork steak; an old-
school original

P'SGHETTI'S PASTA &
SANDWICHES
5540 S. Lindbergh Blvd.
Concord
314-849-5332
psghettis.com
Feed the masses for a
song

RICH & CHARLIE'S
SOUTH COUNTY
4487 Lemay Ferry Rd.
Mehlville
314-894-1600
richandcharlies.com
Longtime eatery that
changed the way St. Louis
ate salad and pasta. (Its
next generation of restaurants became the Pasta
House Company.)

ROBERTO'S TRATTORIA
145 Concord Plaza
Shopping Ctr.
Concord
314-842-9998
robertosstl.com
A favorite off-the-Hill
Italian spot

RUMA'S DELI
1395 Covington Manor Ln.
Mehlville
314-892-9990
rumasdeli.com
Hometown Italian deli,
hot sandwiches, and
mostaccioli

SPANKY'S
FROZEN CUSTARD
11616 Concord Village Ave.
Concord
314-843-9529
Traditional custard stand
in the heart of South
County

SAM'S STEAKHOUSE
10205 Gravois Rd.
Affton
314-849-3033
samssteakhouse.com
Romantic neighborhood
gem, aged steaks

SMUGALA'S PIZZA PUB
10150 Watson Rd.
Crestwood
314-842-5900
6346 Telegraph Rd.
Oakville
314-846-9500
smugalas.com
Mozzarella-provel pizza
with game room

SOCO'S GYROS
5530 S. Lindbergh Blvd.
Concord
314-843-7600
Gem of a Greek deli

SYBERG'S
7802 Gravois Rd.
Affton
314-832-3560
sybergs.com
A local favorite known for
their wings; the building's
resident shark appears
about to dive onto Gravois

TRATTORIA TOSCANA
11686 Gravois Rd.
Affton
314-849-1499
trattoriatoscanastl.com
Italian fine dining in an
unassuming strip mall
location: veal Milanese,
eggplant Parmigiana,
penne alla Bolognese,
and more

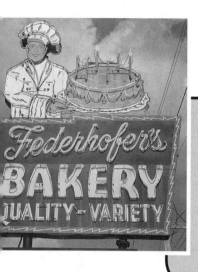

SOMETHING TO DRINK

THE BEERHOUSE
777 River City Casino Blvd.
Lemay
888-578-7289
Massive bar (inside the casino complex) specializes in—guess what?—beer and German-inspired, beer-complementary foods

FRANKIE G'S BAR AND GRILL
4565 Chestnut Park Pl.
Oakville
314-894-9292
frankiegs.com
Enjoy a burger or trashed wings with your adult beverage

HESSLER'S PUB
11804 Tesson Ferry Rd.
Concord
314-842-4050
hesslerspubandgrill.com
Traditional pub fare, karaoke, and keno

O'LEARY'S
3828 S. Lindbergh Blvd.
Sunset Hills
314-842-7678
Actor and Affton native John Goodman was formerly an owner of this bar and grill.

THE PINK GALLEON
410 Butler Hill Rd.
Mehlville
314-845-2386
pinkgalleon.com
Neon pool tables, darts, arcade games, and shot specials in enormous club

SOMETHING SWEET

THE DONUT STOP
1101 Lemay Ferry Rd.
Lemay
314-631-3333
thedonutstopinc.net
Listed in *Bon Appetit*'s 2010 "Top 10 Best Places for Donuts" in the U.S.; closes at 12:30 P.M. daily

MCARTHUR'S BAKERY
3055 Lemay Ferry Rd.
Mehlville
314-894-0900
mcarthurs.com
Main location; also in Kirkwood and Chesterfield; paczki available for a limited time right before Lent

{ LANDMARK }

Jefferson Barracks County Park (345 North Rd., stlouisco.com/parks/j-b. html) was a military post that opened in 1805, following the Lewis and Clark Expedition, and became a fort in 1826 with the closing of Fort Bellefontaine. Names from history like Robert E. Lee, William Sherman, Zachary Taylor, and Dwight Eisenhower were stationed here. It served as a gathering point for troops and supplies for wars beginning with the Mexican-American War through World War II. It's now a county park with biking/hiking trails, corkball, soccer, softball, and baseball fields, and picnic shelters. World War II Weekend is held the last weekend in April and draws fifteen-thousand spectators for the three reenacted battles and numerous encampments. Kids get to pick up the spent shell casings after each battle for souvenirs.

SHOPPORTUNITIES

BAKED GOODS POTTERY
11557 Gravois Rd.
Sappington
314-842-0110
www.bakedgoodspottery.com
Ceramic and art glass studio; parties for kids of all ages

KENRICK'S MEAT MARKET
4324 Weber Rd.
Affton
314-631-2440
kenricks.com
High-quality meats and ready-to-cook meals

SCHAEFER'S HOBBY ARTS AND CRAFTS
11659 Gravois Rd.
Sappington
314-729-7077
schaeferhobby.com
The second generation continues a family tradition; wide selection for the consummate hobbyist

SHARPSHOOTERS ST. LOUIS
8135 Gravois Rd.
Affton
314-353-BANG
sharpshooterstl.com
Were you thinking of acquiring a new fire-arm, testing it out at the shooting range, and then maybe tucking into a plate of ribs? All your American dreams can come true here, from the retail store to the Pit and Grill restaurant on-site.

THE TEACHERS' LOUNGE
21 Ronnies Plaza
Concord
314-894-2227
the-teachers-lounge.com
Stuffed with educational products/toys, instruments, classroom decorations, and tools, plus free weekly story time and activities popular with pre- and home-schoolers

{ ANIMAL FARM }

Suson County Park (6073 Wells Rd., 314-615-8822, stlouisco.com/parks/suson), located not far from the Meramec River, offers picnics and playgrounds, a stocked fishing pond, and an animal farm with petting opportunities. The farm is open daily at 10:30 A.M. year-round and closes at either 3 P.M. or 5 P.M., depending on the season. The farm is home to pigs, sheep, goats, horses, ponies, cows, ducks, and chickens and offers information about different breeds and their histories.

Grant's Farm (10501 Gravois Rd., 314-843-1700, grantsfarm.com) is the location of Ulysses S. Grant's cabin and farm, which was purchased by the Busch family in 1907. August Busch Sr. had the cabin moved and reassembled approximately one mile from its original location. Attractions include exotic animals in the wild, animal shows, a hospitality center (read here: free beer for adults), and a tram ride of the eighty-acre grounds. Days/hours vary depending on the time of year; closed Nov. 1–April 15.

UNCLE SAM'S MILITARY SURPLUS AND SAFARI OUTFITTERS
8380 Watson Rd.
Affton
314-499-8338
unclesams.com
Not planning a safari? No worries—Uncle Sam's has gear for the outdoorsman, law enforcement, and paint ballers

THE WOMEN'S CLOSET EXCHANGE
11575 Gravois Rd.
Sappington
314-842-8405
womensclosetexchange.net
Nationally recognized extreme upscale resale; guaranteed authentic designer labels from Dolce and Gabbana, Christian Louboutin, Prada, Chanel, Dior, and many more

{ LANDMARK }

Jefferson Barracks National Cemetery (2900 Sheridan Rd., 314-845-8320, cem.va.gov/cems/nchp/jeffersonbarracks.asp) opened in 1866 after the Civil War. The 331-acre cemetery at Jefferson Barracks hosts hundreds of thousands of visitors each year. Memorial Day is quite a sight with an endless sea of white markers and American flags.

There are more than 4,400 burials each year and more than 180,000 veterans buried here from every U.S. war, including Confederate soldiers and German and Italian prisoners of war. Johnnie Johnson, Robert McFerrin Sr., and Jack Buck are a few household names who are buried at Jefferson Barracks National Cemetery.

RECREATION

ARTS & EDUCATION

CONCORD LANES AND FAMILY FUN CENTER
11801 Tesson Ferry Rd.
Concord Village
314-843-9200
concordlanes.com
Bowling, mini-golf, batting cages, and more

LAUMEIER SCULPTURE PARK & MUSEUM
12580 Rott Rd.
Sunset Hills
314-615-5278
laumeiersculpturepark.org
Stroll and play in a park while surrounded by world-class sculptures; the Mother's Day art fair is a big draw

THE NEUTRAL ZONE ARCADE
4239 Reavis Barracks Rd.
Mehlville
314-301-8697
Classic arcade games (about seventy-five of them) from Tekken and Centipede to massive multiplayer games line the room; a flat fee of about $15/adults, $10/kids under twelve gets you into open hours on the weekends, the games are set to free play, and you can school the kids and grandkids in the fine art of wasted youth.

POLE POSITION RACEWAY INDOOR KARTING
8800 Watson Rd.
Crestwood
314-925-7545
polepositionraceway.com/st-louis/
Feed the need for speed at this indoor race kart track, featuring vehicles for kids (48 inches or taller) and adults, and races that reach 45 mph

RIVER CITY CASINO EVENT CENTER
777 River City Casino Blvd.
Lemay
888-578-7289
Bet you can guess the scene inside the casino: slots, tables, lights, buffets. Step

{ HINT OF HISTORY }

Quite unbelievably, our city didn't really have an institution devoted to its significant role in the Civil War until the indefatigable Mark Trout undertook the restoration of a sixteen-thousand-square-foot Federal-style building on the campus of Jefferson Barracks, known as the Post Exchange. Now it's home to the excellent **Missouri Civil War Museum**, displaying a wide-ranging collection of artifacts, weaponry, medical instruments, uniforms, medals, photography, and much more (222 Worth Rd., Jefferson Barracks, 314-845-1861, mcwm.org).

into the thousand-or-so capacity Event Center, though, for a pretty sweet concert experience. Booking acts from the Charlie Daniels Band to Chippendales dancers, it's a diverse draw.

RONNIE'S 20 CINE
5320 S. Lindbergh Blvd.
Sappington
314-843-4336
So, in one sense, it's a movie theater. But it's the extras here, like the faux drive-in setup in the lobby, that put Ronnie's over the top as a movie-going experience.

WHITEHAVEN
7400 Grant Rd.,
Affton
314-842-1867
nps.gov/ulsg
The National Park Service runs this ten-acre plot that was the childhood home of Gen. Grant's wife, Julia, and the spot where the Grants planned to return after the war

FESTIVITIES

AFFTON DAYS AND FESTIVAL
Third Saturday in September
Annual parade and festival that, despite the name, is a one-day event

{ THEY'RE CRAFTY }

Something about South County brings out the crafty in folks: the area is host to a clutch of long-running arts/crafts shows each fall. The largest in the area is the **Rotary Fall Arts and Crafts Fair**, held the weekend before Thanksgiving. Held at **Lindbergh High School**, this event features over 450 booths and draws more than ten thousand shoppers (rotaryfair.com). Other fall shows are held at the **South County YMCA** (October), **Affton High School** (November), **Oakville High School** (December), and **Lutheran South High School** (December).

NORTH COUNTY

BELLEFONTAINE NEIGHBORS ★ BELLERIVE ★ BEL-NOR ★ BEL-RIDGE ★ BERKELEY ★ BEVERLY HILLS ★ BLACK JACK ★ BRIDGETON ★ CHARLACK ★ DELLWOOD ★ FERGUSON ★ FLORISSANT ★ HAZELWOOD ★ JENNINGS ★ MOLINE ACRES ★ NORMANDY ★ NORTHWOODS ★ OVERLAND ★ PAGEDALE ★ PASADENA HILLS ★ PINE LAWN ★ ST. ANN ★ ST. JOHN ★ SPANISH LAKE ★ UM–ST. LOUIS

....

HISTORY

St. Louis County is known for its inordinate amount of small municipalities. North County is filled with these mini-municipalities. They are quaint in some respects, but they present governmental challenges in many others. Bel-Nor, Bel-Ridge, Dellwood, and Charlack (well-known for their I-170 ticket-writing ability), Pagedale, Jennings, and Black Jack are representative of dozens of these mini-municipalities, which add to the character and uniqueness of North County. The end of World War II created a housing shortage. Old communities like Bridgeton and newly incorporated Bellefontaine Neighbors experienced an unprecedented building boom lasting into the early 1950s.

....

FLORISSANT

Florissant is one of Missouri's first settlements. As part of the Louisiana Territory, it saw several governmental changes between 1762 and 1803 when Spain and France passed the land back and forth, first from France to Spain and back again to France. The Louisiana Purchase in 1803 was the final transfer of governmental authority.

The French gave Florissant its name. *Fleurissant* means blossoming or prosperous. French remained the primary language well into the nineteenth century. Old Town is an ever-present reminder of Florissant's French heritage.

FERGUSON

William Ferguson deeded part of his farm to the railroads in return for a regular rail stop in Ferguson. The promised "regular stop" led to the town's expansion during the streetcar era. Ferguson became a popular place for the upper middle class looking for more pastoral digs outside the city. Today, the town offers plenty of charm, along with the Ferguson Farmers' Market and annual Ferguson Streetfest.

NORMANDY

Charles Lucas named the area after the French coastal region where his father had been born. Lucas was involved in two duels with Thomas Hart Benton (later a U.S. senator); the second one was fatal. Lucas's land later became the first location of Bellerive Country Club, and today it includes Incarnate Word Catholic High School and the campus of the University of Missouri–St. Louis. Ironically, UMSL's first building was named for Lucas's nemesis, Thomas Hart Benton.

{ PROTOSUBURBIA }

Take a spin (and in your car is the way to do it) through **Pasadena Hills** (Lucas and Hunt Rd., off I-70, pasadenahills.com/historic-district) for a look at the emergence of the auto-centric suburb, as it developed in St. Louis in the 1920s and 1930s. Among the first local communities of the automobile age, this collection of stunning private homes (and the meandering streets, driveways, and massive entrance tower) is on the National Register of Historic Places, in its entirety.

FOOD AND DRINK

Here's what you need to know regarding North County's food scene: there are serious, well-staked-out camps around "best pizza." Like, to a more intense degree than anywhere else in St. Louis. So, tread lightly or better yet, try them all and choose your own favorite. (Plenty of non-pizza options abound, too.)

A BITE TO EAT

ADAMO'S
3264 Rider Trail S.
Earth City
314-291-3555
adamositalian.com
Pizza, pasta, subs

ANGELO'S PIZZERIA
4814 Parker Rd.
Florissant
314-355-3242
Family-owned pizza joint

BREAKAWAY CAFÉ
8418 Natural Bridge Rd.
Bel-Nor
314-381-3554
Pastas, pizzas, salads, and more in casual atmosphere

CATHY'S KITCHEN
250 S. Florissant Rd.
Ferguson
314-524-9200
cjenkinscompany.com/category_s/59.htm
From New Mexico to Florida, stops along her travels inspired owner Cathy Jenkins in creating the menu at this casual neighborhood diner.

CHUCK-A-BURGER DRIVE IN
9025 Saint Charles Rock Rd.
St. John
314-427-9524
chuckaburger.com
Hearkens back to the heyday of automobile culture and carhop service, with monthly car cruise events (classic cars plus live entertainment); chili mac, catfish sandwiches, burgers, and floats on the menu, and nostalgia in the air

CORK
423 S. Florissant Rd.
Ferguson
314-521-9463
corkwinebarstl.com
Wine bar and tasty small plates (Match Meat crab cakes recommended)

{ **WHAT'S BREWING?** }

At **Ferguson Brewing Company** (418 S. Florissant Rd., 314-521-2220, fergusonbrewing.com), it might be vanilla bourbon porter, or a distinctive pecan brown ale: whatever it is, it'll be innovative and fresh . . . and served in a glass for you to enjoy on-site with a bite, or now in party-proper kegs, too.

{ COLD WAR }

If you're not careful, you can start a fight by publicly naming a favorite ice cream/frozen custard stand in these parts. Among the contenders? **Fritz's** (1055 Saint Catherine St., 314-839-4100, fritzsfrozencustard.com), **Doozle's** (717 S. New Florissant Rd., 314-921-3452, doozlesfrozencustard.com), **Velvet Freeze** (7355 West Florissant Ave., 314-381-2384; the last of a once-dominant chain), and the **Whistle Stop** (1 Carson Rd., 314-521-1600, whistlestopdepot.com, inside the historic Ferguson train depot).

COSI DOLCE
425 S. Florissant Rd.
Ferguson
314-799-2157
cose-dolci.com
Charming bakery with cakes, cookies, biscotti, and to-die-for rugelach

CUGINO'S
1595 N. U.S. 67
Florissant
314-831-3222
dinecuginos.com
Pizza, steak, chicken, and Italian specialties

DELISH CHEESECAKE BAKERY & CAFÉ
1060 Rue Saint Catherine St.
Florissant
314-831-7400
delishcheesecakes.com
Quiche, sandwiches, and breakfast called "The Gladiator" that involves a pound of applewood-smoked bacon as its base, and goes on from there. And of course, there's cheesecake!

FARACI PIZZA
520 S. Florissant Rd.
Ferguson
314-524-2675
The thinnest of St. Louis–style crusts and provel

HELFER'S PASTRIES & DELI
380 Saint Ferdinand St.
Florissant
314-837-6050
helferspastries.com
Old-fashioned bakery with generations of birthday-cake fans (and known for seasonal/ethnic delights, too, like kringles, paczki, king cakes, etc.)

INDIA PALACE
4534 N. Lindbergh Blvd.
Bridgeton
314-731-3333
indiapalaceairport.com
Buffet lunch, menu dinner, airport runway view, surrounded by tiki-bar decor

KNODEL'S BAKERY
6621 W. Florissant Ave.
Jennings
314-385-2000
knodelsbakery.com
One hundred ten years of custom cakes and confections; if you need a retirement-party cake that looks like a bottle of Crown Royal, don't mess around with anyone else

NICK & ELENA'S
3007 Woodson Rd.
Overland
314-427-6566
Rave-worthy pizzas, salads, Italian specialties

OMAR'S
10111 St. Charles Rock Rd.
St. Ann
314-429-6881
omarstann.com
Pizza joint meets Mediterranean (shawarma, kabobs, hummus)

PIRRONE'S
1775 Washington St.
Florissant
314-839-3633
pirronespizza.com
St. Louis–style pizza and Italian lunch buffet; perennial "best pizza" mention

PEARL CAFÉ
8416 N. Lindbergh
Florissant
314-831-3701
Authentic dishes well executed, from curries and spring rolls to tender pork belly

PUEBLO NUEVO
7401 N. Lindbergh Blvd.
Florissant
314-831-6885
pueblonuevostl.com
Muy autentico. To wit, beef tongue tacos

REYNOLD'S BBQ
6409 Natural Bridge Rd.
Pine Lawn
314-385-3100
Carolina-style vinegar-based sauce for ribs, pork steaks, and more

ROBERTO'S
16 Mullanphy Garden Shopping Ctr.
Florissant
314-837-7674
Thin-crust pizza, fried chicken, Italian specialties

SWEETIE PIE'S
9841 West Florissant Ave.
Dellwood
314-521-9915
Lip-smackin' soul food

{ MODERN FOOD, HISTORIC SETTING }

At **Hendel's Market Café** (599 St. Denis St., 314-837-2304, hendelsrestaurant.com) in Florissant you'll find a lovely, casually elegant American restaurant housed in a historic brick building that began its life as a grocery in the 1870s. Dine inside and you'll enjoy a side of nostalgia (along with well-regarded seafood, steak, and pasta dishes) in the form of historic photos of the building and area; choose outside and while away the hours on one of the more pleasant, breezy patios in town.

TAM TAM AFRICAN RESTAURANT
35 Florissant Oaks Shopping Center
Florissant
314-921-3805
tamtamstl.com
Culinary melting pot for Senegalese, Moroccan, Ivorian cuisines, plus weekend music/dance events

VINCENZO'S
242 S. Florissant Rd.
Ferguson
314-524-7888
vincenzosstl.com
Italian dishes from pasta melanzani to a meaty, cheesy lasagna; all local beer on tap

WHITE BARN
2457 Chambers Rd.
Moline Acres
Burger shack also slings meatloaf, catfish, and Polish sausage.

{ RISE TO THE CHALLENGE }

The *Challenger* space shuttle disaster of 1986 provided impetus for the creation of a national network of educational and inspirational interactive space science centers. The St. Louis **Challenger Learning Center**, one of forty-five in the country, opened in the Ferguson-Florissant School District in 2003 (205 Brotherton Ln., Ferguson, 314-521-6205, clcstlouis.org). It provides space education programs for school classes, scout groups, community organizations, and the general public. Simulated, hands-on space missions and experiments run about $15/person for public programs, and a full schedule is available at theie website. Space continues to be the place!

{ GOURMAND GO-TOS }

When dinner calls for something special, a couple of shops will jazz up your menu: Hit **John's Butcher Shoppee** (2608 Walton Rd., 314-423-8066, johnsbutchershoppee.com) for just the cut of meat you want (or a smoked hambone), and **Goeke Produce** (449 Saint Ferdinand St., 314-831-1931, goekesmarket.com) for, well, everything else (veggies, eggs, local honey, and jams).

SOMETHING TO DRINK

ALASKA KLONDIKE COFFEE COMPANY
3200 N. U.S. 67
Florissant
314-830-3488
rrochat.com/akcc
Micro-roaster of top-notch (and many organic/rainforest-friendly) beans from around the world

BJ'S
184 Washington St.
Florissant
314-837-7783
Yep, it's open, and a dive fave for cheap drinks, tasty pizza, and pull-tabs; rotating selection of produce for sale behind the bar

DEAVER'S SPORTS BAR
2109 Charbonier Rd.
Florissant
314-838-0002
deaversrestaurant.com
Lots of screens, friendly service, and your kids are welcome, too

K.D. GRAY'S
6130 Madison Ave.
Berkeley
314-521-5309
Electronic darts, cozy tables, and surprisingly fancy drink options

MATTINGLY'S
8108 N. Lindbergh Blvd.
Florissant
314-831-9181
mattinglysportsbar.com
Casual hangout for after the Little League game or what have you

REDBIRDS SPORTS CAFÉ
9085 Dunn Rd.
Hazelwood
314-731-1234
redbirdscafe.com
Pool tables, darts, washers, and Wii, plus big screens to keep tabs on other athletes in the world

As the largest university in the area, the **University of Missouri–St. Louis** brings together a plethora of resources, people, and attractions that benefit far more than just its students. Among the spots worth setting foot on campus: the **Touhill Performing Arts Center** (1 University Blvd., 314-516-4949, touhill.org; though the "Tou-PAC" nickname never took off, you'll still find plenty of world-class entertainment options here, especially dance and musical performances); the **Schwartz Observatory** (new location on North campus near the Fine Arts Building, 314-516-5706, umsl.edu/~physics/astro; free and open to the public, monthly stargazing sessions, where an astronomy student can school you on constellations); **Gallery 210** (44 East Dr., 314-516-5976, gallery210.umsl. edu; a handsome, nationally renowned facility hosting a regular schedule of visual arts exhibitions, free and open to the public); and the **Mercantile Library** (314-516-7240, umsl.edu/mercantile; oldest library west of the Mississippi, rich in documents/artifacts/fine art/ephemera related to westward expansion, St. Louis history, river/rail transit systems, and more, plus regular exhibits from its collections, free and open to the public).

RECREATION

EXERCISE

AMF DICK WEBER LANES
4575 Washington St.
Florissant
314-838-4822
amf.com/dickweberlanes
Named for local legend Dick Weber, a pro bowler and ambassador for the sport

COACHLITE SKATE CENTER
3754 Pennridge Dr.
Bridgeton
314-739-2057
coachlitestl.com
Open skate sessions at various times on Saturday–Sunday, Tuesday, Friday, including weekly gospel music slots; cheap skate rental

CREST BOWL
650 New Florissant Rd. North
Florissant
314-837-0494
crestbowlmo.com
Plenty to do here, from thirty-two lanes of bowling to a hoppin' sports bar, darts, video games, and karaoke nights

ICE ZONE
5555 St. Louis Mills Blvd., Suite 345
Hazelwood
314-227-5288
stlicezone.com
Daily public sessions on the same ice used by the St. Louis Blues for practice

{ BACK TO THE LAND }

Two farms with deep roots in this neck of the woods offer food . . . and food for thought. At **Thies Farm** (4215 N. Hanley Rd., 314-428-9878, thiesfarm.com), a 125-year-old operation, a dedication to quality produce, flowers, and plants, and edible items like local honey and jams/jellies is the core business, and fun annual activities like the popular Pumpkinland, a hay bale/produce/petting zoo fall extravaganza. **EarthDance** (233 S. Dale Ave., 314-521-1006, earthdancefarms.org) took up the cause a little more recently, farming fourteen acres on a century-plus-old plot, and dedicated to preserving heirloom varieties, growing new farmers through its active apprenticeship programs, and engaging the community (e.g., summer camp for kids, film/music programs, and discussions).

{ KID ZONE }

Aviation buffs will find plenty of planes (both civilian and military, plus missiles and spacecraft) alongside a detailed mock-up of the International Space Station and informative video clips on the history of air/space travel and technology at the source of much of it: the Boeing company's **Prologue Room** (in Building 100 at the corner of McDonnell Blvd. and Airport Rd., 314-232-6896, boeing.com/companyoffices/aboutus/tours/prologueroom/index.html). It's free and open to the public, 9–4 on weekdays, June–August.

JAMES J. EAGAN CENTER
1 James J. Eagan Dr.
Florissant
314-921-4470
florissantmo.com
Florissant's modern civic center includes an indoor pool and ice-skating rink; open to the public.

NORTH COUNTY
GOLF & SPORTS CENTER
3555 N. U.S. 67
Florissant
314-837-7543
ncgasc.com
Covered driving lanes, large putting green

PLAN NINE SKATEPARK
5555 St. Louis Mills Blvd., Suite 373
Hazelwood
314-227-5294
plan-nine.net
Wheel demons, shred to your heart's content at this spiffy indoor skatepark for boards, scooters, blades, and BMX bikes

TED JONES BIKE TRAIL
Ferguson
traillink.com/trail/ted-jones-trail.aspx
2.2-mile paved path that links up with more extensive trail network and UM–St. Louis

WHITE BIRCH BAY
AQUATIC CENTER
1186 Teson Rd.
Hazelwood
314-731-0980
hazelwoodmo.org
Newish, fancy outdoor municipal water park in Hazelwood, with features like a bubble slide, lazy river, dumping water bucket, and more

It might be the most surprising feature of North County: how unbelievably wild and natural wide swaths of the area are. With rivers wrapping around much of the area (to the west, north, and east), you're never far from some remarkable topography and flora/fauna spotting. Among the best vantage points: **Columbia Bottom Conservation Area** (Take the Riverview Drive exit from I-270, then go north on Riverview about 2.5 miles, 314-877-6014, mdc4. mdc.mo.gov/applications/moatlas/AreaSummaryPage.aspx?txtAreaID=9736; a spectacular and informative visitor center; stop here to find out exactly where you'll find today's best birding, biking, and so on); **Sioux Passage Park** (17930 Old Jamestown Rd., 314-615-4386, bookit.stlouisco.com/cgi-bin/prp_fbk.exe?act=facInfo&facCode=SIOUX; a sprawling piece of land abutting the Mississippi, with horse trails and a lively disc golf scene); **Fort Belle Fontaine Park** (13002 Bellefontaine Rd., 314-615-5270, stlouisco.com/parks/ftbellefontaine.html; you gain access via a somewhat off-putting guard gate, thanks to the shared land with a state-run youth facility; it's worth the trouble to get to the massive, WPA-built stone staircase); and **Little Creek Nature Area** (2295 Dunn Rd., 314-831-7386, fergflor.schoolwires.com/115810130131529260/site/default.asp; a Ferguson-Florissant School District–owned collection of easy trails and a nature center, perfect for introducing young hikers to the great outdoors; open weekdays).

FRANZ GITTEMEIER HOUSE
1067 Dunn Rd.
Florissant
314-921-7055
historicflorissant.com
150-year-old home houses
Florissant's historical society,
local genealogical records.

GENERAL DANIEL BISSELL HOUSE
10255 Bellefontaine Rd.
Bellefontaine Neighbors
314-615-4386
stlouisco.com/parks/bissell.html
Outstanding Federal-style home from the
early 1800s, includes many original Bissell family furnishings and possessions;
open by reservation only

HAWTHORNE PLAYERS
1 James J. Eagan Dr.
Florissant
314-368-9909
hawthorneplayers.com
One of the area's oldest theatre
companies performs a repertoire
of drama, musical revivals, and
holiday favorites at the Florissant
Civic Center Theatre.

PAYNE-GENTRY HOUSE
4211 Fee Fee Rd.
Bridgeton
314-739-5599
bridgetonmo.com
Restored nineteenth-century home/doc-
tor's office with many original furnishings;
also perpetually reported to be haunted

ST. STANISLAUS
HISTORICAL MUSEUM
3030 Charbonier Rd.
Florissant
314-837-3525
Rural farmhouse provides a setting
for artifacts of the early frontier life
and interactions between Jesuit priests
(including Pierre De Smet) and Native
American tribes who lived and traded
in the area

{ KID ZONE }

Race fans! BE THERE! Make the wacky world of monster truck motorsports
a little more, uh, tame with a visit to the birthplace and world headquarters
of **Bigfoot 4x4** (6311 N. Lindbergh Blvd., 314-731-2822, bigfoot4x4.com) in
Hazelwood. Since the late 1970s, a small team of innovators (and engineers
and repairmen, natch) has built up a fleet of about seventeen Bigfoot monster
trucks, which are now dispatched nearly every weekend to events around the
country and world, including the ever-popular car crush. Your little fans can
crawl under and around some of the vehicles, learn what goes into making a
monster truck, and take home tons of related merch and souvenirs.

FESTIVITIES

EAGLE DAYS
January
Old Chain of Rocks Bridge
mdc.mo.gov/discover-nature/programs/
eagle-daysconfluencegreenway.org/
eagledays
Cold temps bring soaring eagles back
to the corridor along the Mississippi
River, and this two-day event provides
help spotting them and learning about
their habits.

FIESTA IN FLORISSANT
June
Knights of Columbus Park
(near the corner of Lindbergh and
Washington St.)
314-837-6100
Mexican heritage festival includes folk
dancers, music, puppets, and plenty of
delicioso food and drink.

ST. LOUIS STORYTELLING FESTIVAL
May
314-516-5961
stlstorytellingfestival.org
Chew the fat with locally treasured and
internationally renowned tellers of tales
for all ages, at locations throughout the
region, but based at UM–St. Louis

STREETFEST
September
fergusonstreetfest.com
Thousands flock to the live music festival
in Ferguson, but only a few are chosen
for the Manly Man High Heel Race.

VALLEY OF FLOWERS FESTIVAL
May
314-837-0033
florissantvalleyofflowers.com
Marking fifty years, the community
celebration in Florissant includes flower/
plant sales, a carnival midway, tons of
music, craft sales, kids' activities, and
a parade, plus the crowning of a queen
and court.

SHOPPORTUNITIES

ANDREA'S BOUTIQUE
1145 N. Lafayette St.
Florissant
314-831-7500
Great jewelry, handbags, and
vintage apparel

ARCADES-N-MORE
6 Patterson Plaza
Florissant
314-838-1210
arcadesandmore.com
Been wanting a full-size Centipede
game or pinball machine?

CR FRANK POPCORN & SUPPLY
5757 N. Lindbergh Blvd.
Hazelwood
314-731-4500
crfrankpopcorn.com
Popcorn machine and supply rental/
sales plus fresh-popped big bags,
ready to party

EL-MEL
6185 N. U.S. 67
Florissant
314-741-2117
Old-time lawn-garden-feed store,
with tons of pet supplies, bird feeders,
garden gear, and such

THE FANTASY SHOP
8232 N. Lindbergh Blvd.
Florissant
314-831-5211
fantasyshoponline.com
Graphic novels, comics, collectibles

FRISON FLEA MARKET
7025 St. Charles Rock Rd.
Pagedale
314-727-0460
All manner of stuff ranging from bizarre
to kinda useful, conveniently located
adjacent to the Rock Road MetroLink
station

GENERATIONS ANTIQUE MALL
250 Saint Catherine St.
Florissant
314-831-6070
150-year-old home, itself an antique of
sorts, houses more than thirty-five vendor
booths under one roof.

NAGLE'S
19 Patterson Plaza
Florissant
314-838-4444
Five-and-dime hanging on to a nostalgic
past of penny candy, toys, tchotchkes,
little gifty stuff, and craft and party
supplies

ST. LOUIS OUTLET MALL
5555 St. Louis Mills Blvd.
Hazelwood
314-227-5900
stlouisoutletmall.com
Massive space filled mostly with discount
retailers (outlets for Marshall's, Sears,
Gymboree, and Levi's), plus an IMAX-
equipped cinema, ice rink, and indoor
play spaces.

{ GET FRESH IN FERG }

The **Ferguson Farmers'
Market** (20 S. Florissant
Rd., 314-324-4298,
fergusonfarmersmarket.com)
is the place to be on Saturday
mornings during the growing
season: farm-fresh produce,
local handicrafts, and tempting
treats abound, along with an
engaging schedule of music,
kids' activities, and fun special
events (pie contests, bike
relays, etc.).

{ AFROCENTRIC }

All your African American heritage merchandise needs can be met
at **AfroWorld** (7276 Natural Bridge Rd., 314-389-5194, afroworld.
com). Think prints of famed ancestors, Obama campaign
memorabilia, African American devotional books, handmade
cards and jewelry, special occasion clothing, and hair and beauty
products. Super-friendly and community-minded staff. And as a
bonus, if you're looking to put a little color in your Christmas,
your brood can get a photo snapped with Soulful Santa around
the holidays.

ALL GOD'S CREATURES
WELCOME HERE

{ PETS RIP }

Put aside any lingering Stephen King fears and instead marvel at the soul connections betwixt man and beast at the **Imperial Crown Pet Cemetery** (115 N. U.S. 67, 314-921-1558, imperialcrownpc.com), the oldest in St. Louis. Founded by a local veterinarian in the 1920s, it's still in use today and provides a rather unlikely, but definitely tranquil, spot to remember your furry (or feathered, or finned) friend.

{ SAINTS AMONG US }

Old St. Ferdinand Shrine (1 Rue St. Francois, 314-837-2110, oldstferdinandshrine. com), the oldest Catholic church west of the Mississippi, forms the centerpiece of this well-preserved complex, also including a convent, church, and rectory. A fascinating glimpse into the French and Spanish forebears of the area's early development. Tours for any size/age group, by appointment. The convent was home to St. Philippine Rose Duchesne.

WEST & SOUTHWEST COUNTY

BALLWIN ★ CHESTERFIELD ★ CREVE COEUR ★ DES PERES ★ ELLISVILLE ★ EUREKA ★ FENTON ★ FRONTENAC ★ MANCHESTER ★ MARYLAND HEIGHTS ★ TOWN AND COUNTRY ★ VALLEY PARK ★ WILDWOOD

HISTORY

West and Southwest County sit on the edges of the Ozark foothills. The tree-lined country roads, limestone bluffs along the Meramec River, and richness in preserved history make this region distinct. Pro athletes, local celebrities, and other affluent residents call the area home. Olive Boulevard follows an old Indian trail, which once ran between the Missouri and Mississippi Rivers. The trail became a widely used road by farmers, stagecoaches, and travelers heading into or out of St. Louis. Manchester Road, a road to market and a link between St. Louis and Jefferson City, was designated a part of Route 66 in the 1930s. Businesses sprang up along the route, which today are part of Ballwin, Manchester, and Ellisville.

Bellefontaine, Hilltown, Gumbo, Hog Hollow, Monarch, Eatherton, and Bonhomme were former towns with post offices, which today are part of **Chesterfield**. Gumbo Flats—now called Chesterfield Valley—was submerged in the flood of 1993. Levees were built, and today one of the country's longest strip malls can be found here. Thornhill Estate, built by Missouri's second governor, Frederick Bates, was later purchased by the Faust family. Wanting to preserve Thornhill's historical significance, the Fausts donated the estate and ninety-eight acres to St. Louis County, creating Faust Park, a Chesterfield treasure. Nearby, **Wildwood** is geographically comparable to St. Louis City but maintains its country-living ambience with a population of fewer than forty-thousand.

Creve Coeur is French for "broken heart." Legend has it that an Indian princess was distraught over the unrequited love of a French fur trapper and jumped off the ledge overlooking Creve Coeur Lake. It was then that the lake formed into the shape of a broken heart. Creve Coeur Lake hosted the rowing competition during the 1904 Olympics and remains a popular place for sailing. Originally a resort, Creve Coeur Lake Memorial Park in **Maryland Heights**

officially became a county park in 1945. Maryland Heights also is where the Verizon Wireless Amphitheatre and Harrah's Casino are located. The Holocaust Museum and Learning Center in Creve Coeur houses an extensive historical collection, including personal accounts of Holocaust survivors who came to St. Louis.

Town and Country residents have one of the highest median incomes in the state. Maintaining the pastoral heritage led to a soaring deer population with collisions between cars and deer becoming a regular occurrence. A deer management program, which harvests a select number of deer annually, has led to the donation of venison to local food banks via the Missouri Department of Conservation's Share the Harvest Program. **Frontenac**'s Benjamin Wood and his wife were frequent visitors to Quebec. Enamored with the history of Quebec's Chateau Frontenac, they named their Missouri property Frontenac. Today the Woods property is the central part of the town.

French Jesuit missionaries settled near the confluence River des Peres and were responsible for giving the river and area the name **Des Peres,** or in English "of the fathers." The name has stood the test of time as churches, post offices, schools, and societies adopted the Des Peres name as well.

Eureka's location near wonderful state parks like Lone Elk and Route 66 brings new residents looking for country living. **Fenton**, once a small village on the Meramec River, has blossomed into a full-fledged southwestern suburb of St. Louis. Seasonal flooding near its downtown has made relocation of some residents and businesses necessary. However, the Navajo Hotel, built in 1929, offers a glimpse of the kinds of resorts that were once popular getaways in places like Valley Park, Castlewood Park, and Fenton.

{ KID ZONE }

Ride the gold glass elevator to the 12th floor for an authentic Teppanyaki cooking experience at **Kobe Steakhouse** (111 Westport Plaza, Gold Tower, 12th Floor, 314-469-3900, kobesteakhouse.us): the antics of your table chef will keep the kiddos engaged. Gotta love a kids' menu with pint-sized portions of okosama chicken shrimp or steak. There's nary a nugget nor grilled cheese in sight.

FOOD AND DRINK

Take the time to explore strip malls and hidden commercial developments. Even if you can't see them from the street, some independent gems lurk there for your dining and drinking pleasure.

A BITE TO EAT

ADDIE'S THAI HOUSE
13441 Olive Blvd.
Chesterfield
314-469-1660
addiesthaihouse.com
White-tablecloth Thai, with fresh rolls and waterfall beef recommended

ANNA MARIE'S ICE CREAM
16497 Clayton Rd.
Wildwood
636-273-1900
annamariesicecream.com
Homemade ice cream and gourmet treats, including ice cream cakes

ANNIE GUNN'S
16806 Chesterfield Airport Rd.
Chesterfield
636-532-7684
anniegunns.com
Wood-paneled and homey while still feeling "special night out"; American cuisine and superlative wine list

BABBO'S SPAGHETTERIA
17402 Chesterfield Airport Rd.
Chesterfield
636-536-0000
babbosspaghetteria.com
Spaghetti, yes, and meatballs, chicken spiedini, risotto, and more

BARNEY'S BBQ
16011 Manchester Rd.
Ellisville
636-227-2300
barneysbbq.com
Vinegar-based sauce on ribs, chicken, pork, and beef; seasonal operation, May–Sept

IL BEL LAGO
11631 Olive Blvd.
Creve Coeur
314-994-1080
bellagostl.com
Fine dining Italian, fountain-side in strip center

BISTRO 1130
1130 Town and Country Crossing Dr.
Town and Country
636-394-1130
bistro1130.com
French haute cuisine (sauteed sweetbreads, vol-au-vent, escargot)

LA BONNE BOUCHEE
12344 Olive Blvd.
Creve Coeur
314-576-6606
labonnebouchee.com
Cafe and patisserie features croissants, quiche, and more, to say nothing of the tempting bakery cases

BRICKHOUSE TAVERN & TAP
2 McBride and Son Center Dr.
Chesterfield
636-536-6291
brickhousetavernandtap.com
Embrace your inner dude in this self-proclaimed man cave: beer, deviled eggs, meatloaf, and beer

CHARLOTTE'S RIB BBQ
15467 Clayton Rd.
Ballwin
636-394-3332
charlottesribbbq.com
Sweet, saucy ribs, pork steak, and standout sides

{ BAGELS BY THE BOOK }

Mass popularity has ruined many a noble foodstuff, and such is arguably the case with bagels. Forget the toothless variety you might be accustomed to pulling from your grocer's freezer section: go straight to the **Bagel Factory** (11256 Olive Blvd., Creve Coeur, 314-432-3583; well, hit the ATM first, 'cause they don't take plastic) and stock up on the real deal. Water-boiled before baking, these are the bagels lesser bagels dream of being when they grow up. Poppyseed, onion, strawberry, egg, and a handful of other varieties; strictly grab-and-go atmosphere.

CIRCLE 7 RANCH
14412 Clayton Rd.
Ballwin
636-220-9707
circle7ranch.com
Fancified bar/grill food (smoked brisket nachos, mahi mahi lollipops, po'boys), but the real draw is table-side, serve-yourself beer taps at select booths

CLASSIC RED HOTS
41 Forum Shopping Center
Chesterfield
314-878-4687
classicredhots.com
Vienna beef dogs in many varieties, sandwiches, and hot tamales

CUISINE D'ART
701 North New Ballas Rd.
Creve Coeur
314-995-3003
cuisine-dart.com
French-inspired offshoot of catering service, with small chalkboard menu, Sunday brunch

DAVE & TONY'S PREMIUM BURGERS
12766 Olive Blvd.
Creve Coeur
314-439-5100
daveandtonys.com
BYOB: build your own burger, from four choices of bun (and six proteins!) on up

DREAM HOUSE & TEA ROOM
15425 Clayton Rd.
Ballwin
636-227-7640
dreamhouseandtearoom.com
Ladies, your lunch: soups, salads, quiche

EAST COAST PIZZA
17304 Chesterfield Airport Rd.
Chesterfield
636-536-7888
eastcoastpizza.net
Slices and pies (New York– and Chicago–style), stromboli, calzones

GERARD'S
12240 Manchester Rd.
Des Peres
314-821-7977
stlgerards.com
Old-school continental dining room, with plenty of seafood, beef, and serious wine

GIANFABIO
127 Hilltown Village Ctr.
Chesterfield
636-532-6686
gianfabio.com
Flash-fried spinach,
brick-oven pizzas, pastas

HAPPY CHINA
12921 Olive Blvd.
Creve Coeur
314-878-6660
Stomach-pleasing
buffet of pot stickers,
hot and sour soup,
sushi, crawfish, fried
squid, and plenty more

ICHIBAN
12388 Olive Blvd.
Creve Coeur
314-579-6002
Japanese specialties
and sushi

JOO JOO
12937 Olive Blvd.
Creve Coeur
314-469-1999
letseat.at/joojoo
Bibimbap! Fun to say,
fun to eat; Korean food
and karaoke rooms

KABOB PALACE
14424 Manchester Rd.
Manchester
636-230-8800
kabob-palace.com
Afghan/Persian, including
burani, sambosas, and
various kabobs

LAL QILA
15222 Manchester Rd.
Ballwin
636-527-4717
lalqilastl.com
Pakistani/Indian, with
weeknight dinner buffet

LAZY RIVER GRILL
631 Big Bend Rd.
Manchester
636-207-1689
lazyyellow.com
Steaks, fish, burgers
in "LL Bean–rustic"
atmosphere

MAGGIE'S LUNCHBOX
867 Horan Dr.
Fenton
636-326-4411
maggieslunchbox.com
Great soup/sandwich/
salad cafe, plus evening
menu; many off-the-menu
faves among regulars, so
don't be afraid to ask!

MATADOR
17304-115 Chesterfield
Airport Rd.
Chesterfield
636-536-6500
Casual Mexican spot
serving fajitas, enchila-
das, tacos, and more

MILLER'S CROSSING
14156 Olive Blvd.
Chesterfield
314-439-0400
Nary a hint of gangster
noir at this burgers and
beer sports bar

MONSOON
14248 Manchester Rd.
Ballwin
636-256-8838
monsoon-stl.com
Dumplings, pho, and
extensive entree menu,
upscale

NIPPON TEI
14025 Manchester Rd.
Ballwin
636-386-8999
nippontei-stl.com
Bento boxes, sukiyaki,
and other Japanese dish-
es, but sushi is the star

PM BBQ
161 Long Rd., #103
Chesterfield
636-536-1966
pmbbq.com
Memphis-style BBQ, from
ribs to pulled pork plus
wings and chicken 'n'
dumplings

PAUL MANNO'S
75 Forum Shopping Ctr.
Chesterfield
314-878-1274
Sicilian-Italian spot
that's generally packed

PUMPERNICKLES DELI
11036 Olive Blvd.
Creve Coeur
314-567-4496
pumpernickles.com
Deli/diner classics with
added Jewish flavor, from
mishagos, homemade lox,
and bialys

RAY'S DONUTS (FORMERLY LAMAR'S)
12414 Olive Blvd.
Creve Coeur
314-485-1686
raysdonutsandcoffee.com
Donuts and holes that will more than satisfy any sugar addiction

ROYAL CHINESE BBQ
8406 Olive Blvd.
314-991-1888
Chinese BBQ, congee (rice porridge), and shark fin soup are menu mainstays.

SHU FENG
8435 Olive Blvd.
314-983-0099
shufengstlouis.com
Chinese and Korean menu for lunch and dinner; one of the few Asian restaurants serving sizzling rice soup

SISTERS TEA HOUSE
505 W. Main St.
Fenton
636-305-1319
sistersteahouse.com
Luncheon is served: tuna salad, soups, croissants, or more traditional high tea service

ST. LOUIS KOREAN BAKERY
13357 Olive Blvd.
Chesterfield
314-523-1332
Korean baked goods and other treats like pat bing soo (shaved ice)

SURF & SIRLOIN
13090 Manchester Rd.
Des Peres
314-822-3637
surfandsirloin.com
Extensive seafood menu (red snapper, grouper, trout, sole), steaks, and Greek flourishes

SURF DOGS
137 Chesterfield Towne Ctr.
Chesterfield
636-537-8799
surfdogsgrill.com
Tons o' hot dogs, plus burgers, Polish sausage, fish baskets, and key lime pie

TABLE THREE
16765 Main St.
Wildwood
636-458-4333
table-three.com
Smart-casual contemporary American spot, from flat-screen-facing bar seats to lush patio

THE TAVERN
2961 Dougherty Ferry Rd.
Valley Park
636-825-0600
oghospitalitygroup.com
It's comfort food, with a punch: lobster ravioli, trout amadine, caramelized brussels sprouts, and more, in a convivial atmosphere

THAI NIVAS
11054 Olive Blvd.
Creve Coeur
314-567-8989
thainivassushibar.com
Sleek room for sushi
and Thai specialties
like tom yum soup,
massaman curry

VILLA FAROTTO
17417 Chesterfield
Airport Rd.
Chesterfield
636-519-0048
villafarotto.com
Multiconcept Italian fine-
dining restaurant/takeout/
patio/shop

WILD HORSE GRILL
101 Chesterfield Towne
Ctr.
Chesterfield
636-532-8750
wildhorsegrill.com
Spiffy place for
ambitious dishes like
duck Wellington, smoked
tenderloin lasagna

**THE WOLF PUBLIC
HOUSE**
15480 Clayton Rd.
Ballwin
636-527-7027
thewolfstl.com
Popular gathering spot,
early morning til late
evening, for coffee,
breakfast, sandwiches,
live music. Plus, grilled
cheese du jour. Yeah.

YOUNG'S ICE CREAM
206 Meramec Station Rd.
Valley Park
636-225-6677
youngs1954.com
Generations of family
(the Youngs, natch) have
owned this restaurant/
creamery, boasting lip-
smacking fried chicken,
BLTs, cones, sundaes,
shakes, and more.

ZOYA'S CAFE
725 N. New Ballas Rd.
Creve Coeur
314-432-5050
zoyascafe.net
Gyros, Greek salad,
and other quick lunch/
dinner bites

{ EAST MEETS WEST (COUNTY) }

Sample the wide variety of the Indian subcontinent without ever going
east of 270: recommended are **Gokul** (10633 Page Ave., 314-428-8888,
gokulrestaurant.com; 100% vegetarian), **Flavor of India** (11939 Olive Blvd.,
314-997-4224, flavorofindiastl.com; strong on northern Indian), **Mayuri**
(12513 Olive Blvd., 314-576-7272, mayuri.com; north and south Indian
dishes represented, plus a healthy dose of Indian-Chinese), **Saffron** (2137
Barrett Station Rd., 314-965-3822, saffronstl.net; lamb dishes are tasty), and
Taj Palace (92 THF Blvd., 636-728-1000; plenty of tandoori-cooked dishes).

SOMETHING TO DRINK

**BONE'S FRENCH
QUARTER**
14766 Manchester Rd.
Ballwin
636-391-8293
fqstl.com
Nonstop Mardi Gras
atmosphere, plus bar
food (and breakfast, from
7 A.M. daily)

EUREKA WINE HOUSE
107 S. Central Ave.
Eureka
636-938-5411
eurekawinehouse.com
120 wines, pet-friendly
patio, and live music

HARPO'S
136 Hilltown Village Ctr.
Chesterfield
636-537-1970
harposstl.com
Like you never left Miz-
zou, right down to the
Shakespeare's pizza

**THE HAUS PIZZERIA &
BAR**
14815 Clayton Rd.
Chesterfield
636-386-5919
Drink specials, karaoke,
occasional live music

THE HIVE
609 North New Ballas Rd.
Creve Coeur
314-569-1769
Post-office-work
hangout with nice,
smallish patio

{ MIND THE SCRUM }

The country's longest-running rugby tournament
(since 1949: imagine the urgent care visits in
that time!), the **St. Louis Gateway Ruggerfest**
hosts women's, men's, and high-school matches
between top clubs across the Midwest. The
two-day April event also features gear vendors,
entertainment, and food for participants and
spectators. Held at the Scott Gallagher Soccer
Complex (2350 Creve Coeur Mill Rd., Maryland
Heights, stlouisruggerfest.com).

INTERNATIONAL TAP HOUSE (ITAP)
161 Long Rd.
Chesterfield
636-537-8787
internationaltaphouse.com
Beer bonanza, with brews from around the globe. BYO food from neighboring establishments

POOR RICHARD'S
960 Brookwood Ctr.
Fenton
636-349-3438
poorrichardsstl.com
Burgers, wings, and beer for game day with the fam

THE SPORTS PAGE
13431 Olive Blvd.
Chesterfield
314-434-4115
thesportspage-barandgrill.com
A renowned burger, high-end TVs, and friendly atmosphere

VERITAS
15860 Fountain Plaza
Chesterfield
636-227-6800
veritasgateway.com
Weekend three-taste wine flights, plus stellar selection in retail tasting shop atmosphere

{ BASTA IN THE BASEMENT }

"Nondescript" isn't the half of it: **Balducci's Winefest** (12527 Bennington Pl., 314-576-5024, balducciswineryandrestaurant.com) shares a strip with, among other tenants, a hair stylist and a 7-Eleven. Descend the steps into the basement-level Italian restaurant, though, and you'll find a cheery, family-run joint that's been keeping its patrons happy for decades, with good food (pizza and t-ravs are tops) and homey decor (giant wire-spool tables, stained glass).

At **Lone Elk Park** (1 Lone Elk Park Rd., Valley Park, 314-615-7275, stlouisco.com/ParksandRecreation/Parkpages/LoneElk), yep, there are elk—and bison, wild turkeys, turtles, deer, and all manner of wildlife—roaming free and quite happy to meander up near you, your car, or your pic-a-nic. Take only pictures, leave only footprints (and perhaps a donation), then fly over to the neighboring **World Bird Sanctuary** (125 Bald Eagle Ridge Rd., Valley Park, 636-225-4390, worldbirdsanctuary.org) to see owls, hawks, bald eagles, falcons, parrots, and more, in habitat displays and in live animal encounters. And in the grandest St. Louis tradition, it's all free to visitors.

RECREATION

Perhaps it's the availability of big tracts of cheap, exurban real estate, but a cluster of indoor amusement facilities dots the West County landscape.

EXERCISE

AQUAPORT
2344 McKelvey Rd.
Maryland Heights
314-738-2599
marylandheights.com
Outdoor water park with slides, lazy river, splash playground, and more

THE CAGES
14918 Manchester Rd. Rear
Ballwin
636-391-0616
thecagesinballwin.net

Indoor batting cages and pitching mounds, with instructors for baseball and softball

CASTLEWOOD STATE PARK
1401 Kiefer Creek Rd.
Ballwin
636-227-4433
mostateparks.com/park/castlewood-state-park
Mountain-biking nirvana in these parts, plus Meramec hikes, horse trails, and playground

{ HIT THE TRACKS }

Romance the rails at several unique whistle-stops in West County. First (and free!), you can ride a large-scale model train in Eureka's Kircher Park on select dates under the auspices of the **St. Louis Live Steamers** (Kircher Park, on Williams Rd., stlouislivesteamers.org)—something like sitting atop a steam-operated footstool. Or take it up a notch and hop aboard the **Wabash Frisco and Pacific Railroad**'s (109 Grand Ave., Glencoe, 636-587-3538, wfprr.com) 12-inch gauge steam locomotive, which winds along the Meramec River near Glencoe for a two-mile, thirty-minute loop. (You'll be sitting single file on bench seats; $4/ages four and up). Budding engineers will be in choo-choo heaven at the **Frisco Train Store** (24 Front St., Valley Park, 636-529-1660, friscotrainstore.com), a store/play space selling American-made, lead-paint-free wooden trains and accessories. It's not all pushy retail, though; tons of tracks make up a free play area, there's coffee for the tall people, and upstairs in the historic building are rooms for parties and special Family Fun nights, held monthly.

CHESTERFIELD SPORTS FUSION
140 Long Rd.
Chesterfield
636-536-6720
chesterfieldsportsfusion.com
Indoor funplex of laser tag, mini-golf, climbing wall, dodgeball court

HIDDEN VALLEY SKI AREA
17409 Hidden Valley Dr.
Wildwood
636-938-5373
hiddenvalleyski.com
Manufactured snow covers thirty acres of terrain, from absolute beginner level to expert jumps and bowls. Plus, how fun is it to say "Ski Missouri"? Night skiing offered.

MILLENNIUM PARK SPRAYGROUND
2 Barnes West Dr.
Creve Coeur
creve-coeur.org
Must be accessed from Barnes West Dr. just south of Olive Blvd. A hidden treasure near Barnes West, featuring two playgrounds with modern equipment and a fun sprayground.

THE POINTE AT BALLWIN COMMONS
#1 Ballwin Commons Circle
Ballwin
636-227-8950
ballwin.mo.us
Indoor aquatic center features slide and water playground.

ROCKWOODS RESERVATION
2751 Glencoe Rd.
Wildwood
636-458-2236
mdc.mo.gov/regions/st-louis/rockwoods-reservation
Forested area with hiking trails, a stream through the Ozark hills, and a conservation education center with exhibits about the flora and fauna of the area. The February Maple Sugar Festival is highly recommended: educational, fun, and tasty for all ages.

SKYZONE SPORTS
17379 Edison Ave.
Chesterfield
636-530-4550
skyzone.com
Indoor trampoline park for all ages

SWING AROUND FUN TOWN
335 Skinker Ln.
Fenton
636-349-7077
swing-a-round.com
Go karts, bumper boats, mini-golf, batting cages

{ RELAXATION HARVEST }

Breathe deep at Eureka's **Winding Brook Estate** (3 Winding Brook Estate Dr., Eureka, 636-575-5572, windingbrookestate.com). You're surrounded by the state's only commercial lavender farm (don't breathe too deep: they also raise and sell lambs.) Pick your own tussie-mussie when the harvest comes in, or buy their organic bath, body, and culinary products.

On a hot day, or a rainy day, or a day not quite merry enough, hightail it to the **St. Louis Carousel** in Faust Park (15185 Olive Blvd., Chesterfield). A buck a spin on this circa-1920 merry-go-round—relocated from Forest Park Highlands Amusement Park with rousing musical accompaniment by the Stinson Band Organ; might be the best deal in town.

ARTS, ENTERTAINMENT, & EDUCATION

AKC MUSEUM OF THE DOG
1721 South Mason Rd.
Manchester
314-821-3647
museumofthedog.org
If your exposure to dog art begins and ends with them playing poker, visiting the seven-hundred-item collection of fine art here will be a treat. Handsome facility, and you can bring Fido along for the trip.

BACKSTREET JAZZ & BLUES
610 Westport Plaza Dr.
Maryland Heights
314-878-5800
Small jazz club in Westport Plaza draws tops from local blues scene.

BUTTERFLY HOUSE
15193 Olive Blvd.
Chesterfield
636-530-0076
butterflyhouse.org
Science and beauty on the wing (plus added attractions like hissing cockroaches, spiders, and scorpions), fun annual events like "Hot! Hot! Hot!" in the dead of winter (with steel drum music, tropical theme, and beachy activities)

THE ENDANGERED WOLF CENTER

6750 Tyson Valley Rd.

Eureka

636-938-5900

endangeredwolfcenter.org

Founded by Carol and Marlin Perkins (of *Wild Kingdom* fame), offers education programs, tours of wolf enclosures (featuring African wild dogs, red wolves, swift foxes, and more)

FUNNY BONE COMEDY CLUB

614 Westport Plaza Dr.

Maryland Heights

314-469-6692

stlouisfunnybone.com

Stand-up comedy and open mic for 18+ crowd

HOLOCAUST MUSEUM

12 Millstone Campus Dr.

Maryland Heights

314-432-0020

hmlc.org

Eye-opening detail and firsthand accounts of the Holocaust in artifacts, photos, letters, and exhibits dedicated to a future free of hatred and indifference

{ **AHOY** }

If you've ever thought longingly about living somewhere on the water, and perhaps getting a little boat and chucking it all for the coast, head out to **Creve Coeur Lake** (2143 Creve Coeur Mill Rd., stlouisco.com) on alternate Sundays for most of the year and cast your lot with the friendly folks from the Creve Coeur Sailing Association. They race small sailboats in the afternoon, but the preparation and rigging time is when even novice sailers can get in on the action, volunteering to crew for a few hours. It's great fun to participate or even watch, and you'll need that small craft experience if you ever trade up to the high seas, anyway.

{ TO OUTLET, TO OUTLET }

The area's long drought with no significant outlet-style shopping officially ended when not one, but two, outlet malls opened, almost within spitting distance of each other, in the Chesterfield Valley. **St. Louis Premium Outlets** (18521 Outlet Blvd., 314-399-8163, premiumoutlets.com) offers Armani, Coach, Kate Spade New York, and Saks Fifth Avenue Off 5th, while **Taubman Prestige Outlets** (17017 North Outer 40 Rd., 636-536-3014, taubmanprestigeoutlets. com) counters with Abercrombie & Fitch, Juicy Couture, Brooks Brothers, and J. Crew Factory. Check out the listings to make a plan, and you could easily spend a whole day in retail bliss.

KEMP AUTO MUSEUM
16955 Chesterfield Airport Rd.
Chesterfield
636-537-1718
kempautomuseum.org
Forty stunning cars showcase the art and history of European automobiles, including Mercedes, Porsche, and Rolls Royce models.

LONGVIEW FARM PARK
13525 Clayton Rd.
Town and Country
314-434-1215
town-and-country.org/LongviewPark.aspx
Thirty acres of bucolic parkland includes a spiffy playground, walking trail, and stables for equine-assisted therapy horses, which you're welcome to visit when the barn is open.

MYSEUM

283 Lamp and Lantern Village
Town and Country
636-220-7930
stlmyseum.com

Hands-on, interactive, and wildly fun kids' museum: a bit like a more down-home version of the popular Magic House. Kids love the slides and inflatables, the "seaweed swamp" (you've never seen such a use of pool noodles!), vet and animal medicine area, musical instruments, shadow wall, and more. They might even pick up a bit of scientific knowledge while they roam!

STAGES ST. LOUIS

1023 Chesterfield Pkwy. E.
Chesterfield
636-530-5959
stagesstlouis.org

One of the fastest-growing musical theatres around, in its twenty-eighth season of classic American musicals

{ DECLARATION OF INDEPENDENTS }

Right there in the mall, stereotypical purveyor to the mass market, is a haven of uniquity: **Artropolis**, in the Sears wing of Chesterfield Mall (636-536-0409, chesterfield-mall.com). It brings together seven local arts endeavors, from a black-box theatre (Dramatic License Productions, dramaticlicenseproductions. org) to a locally focused gallery (Mind Works). And if that's not enough indie cred for you, pop into **The Foundrie** (265 Chesterfield Mall, Chesterfield, 636-730-4130, thefoundrie.com), an all-local boutique for art, apparel, jewelry, gifts, tote bags, stationery, and more from area crafters and artists.

{ THE GREAT PUMPKIN }

Each year, when he finds the patch that's most sincere . . . well, you know the rest. Start a fall family tradition with an October visit (weekends offer the most activity) to **Rombachs Farm** (18639 Olive Street Rd., 636-532-7265, rombachsfarm. com; in Chesterfield, with pumpkins for sale, a pumpkin pyramid for pix and hayrides, plus a small country store) or **Stuckmeyer's** (249 Schneider Dr., 636-349-1225, stuckmeyers.com; in Fenton, offering pre- or you-pick pumpkins, hay and pony rides, corn maze, live music, and produce sales). Make sure you're prepared for a cute-photo-opp overload: think babies plunked in pumpkin patches, kids eating apples as big as their heads, and so on.

FESTIVITIES

ART FAIR AT QUEENY PARK
Labor Day weekend
Greensfelder Recreation Center,
Queeny Park
gslaa.org
Juried fine art and craft festival features more than one hundred artists in all media.

CREVE COEUR DAYS
June
Grounds of DeSmet Jesuit High School
crevecoeurdays.com
Large community-planned festival that has taken place since 1967, features carnival rides, games, food, and fun, including live music and a parade

FAUST HERITAGE & FINE ARTS FESTIVAL
September
Faust Park
Get your fine arts and folk arts fixes in one convenient location: everything from modern jewelry and paintings to rug-making demos and corn husk dolls

MISSOURI WINEFEST
February
Westport Plaza
westportstl.com
Charity wine-tasting event from the state's top vintners

SAINT LOUIS BLUES WEEK
This Memorial Day weekend event features concerts, workshops, parties, awards; also inaugurating a Blues Hall of Fame and Blues Trail markers throughout the city.

SPIRIT OF ST. LOUIS AIRSHOW
Spirit of St. Louis Airport
spirit-airshow.com
For those who love the high-flying, adrenaline-fueled exploits of flying machines, this spring airshow features craft both historic and new, along with guest flyers from around the country. Rides in everything from helicopters to B-25s are available, too . . . for a price.

SHOPPORTUNITIES

COTTON BABIES
1200 Town and Country Crossing Dr.
Town and Country
636-220-7720
cottonbabies.com
Cloth diaper and natural parenting HQ: get all your questions answered, supplies bought, toy and gear wish lists made

DREAM PLAY RECREATION
17373 Edison Ave.
Chesterfield
636-530-0055
dreamplayrec.com
Where the coolest outdoor swingsets and jungle gyms (and rock walls and playhouses) come from; you can buy here, sure, but savvy parents also take advantage of the pay-to-play sessions and birthday parties.

FAZIO'S FRETS & FRIENDS
15440 Manchester Rd.
Ellisville
636-227-3573
faziosmusic.com
Huge music store with instruments, accessories, rentals, performances, and instruction; after-school Rock Academy program

GABI'S WINE
14433 Manchester Rd.
Ballwin
636-527-2997
Vast selection including beer, plus good staff advice

GO!SPA
11735 Manchester Rd.
Des Peres
314-822-0772
gospagirl.com
Full menu of spa services in a fun, upbeat, drop-in-and-get-pampered-in-a-flash venue; great gift selection, too

LUKAS LIQUOR
15921 Manchester Rd.
Ellisville
636-227-4543
lukasliquorstl.com
The big daddy of West County booze superstores, with rave-worthy selection and service

THE NAKED VINE

1624 Clarkson Rd.
Chesterfield
636-536-0711
nakedvine.net
Avoid the Mondavis and Kendall Jacksons of the world here, and instead hone in on small-production wineries, craft beers, and handmade salumi

NEW DAY GLUTEN FREE

15622 Manchester Rd.
Ellisville
636-527-5000
newdayglutenfree.com
One meal in the café is great, but it's the grocery side where you'll find the dishes and ingredients to make every day in your home easier for a gluten-free lifestyle.

OLD HOUSE IN HOG HOLLOW

14319 Olive Blvd.
Chesterfield
314-469-1019
oldhouseinhoghollow.com
Folk art, linens, collectible figurines, pewter, holiday decor, and plenty more

ONE LUCKY MUTT

2414 Taylor Rd.
Grover
636-458-8838
oneluckymutt.com
Natural foods/treats, fancy pet fancies, and a DIY dogwash

RJ CHOCOLATIER

14882 Clayton Rd.
Chesterfield
636-230-9300
rjchocolatier.com
Small-batch, artisan chocolate confections almost too beautiful to eat. For true connoisseurs, ask about their eco-chocolate tours in Costa Rica!

{ THANKS FOR YOUR SUPPORT }

Laugh if you will at the "Got Bra Problems?" billboards, but we'll bet your wife (or your mom) nods in sympathy. **Ann's Bra Shop** (13483 Olive Blvd., Chesterfield, 314-878-4144, brashop. com) is nationally known for fitting, selection, and especially care and products for post-mastectomy patients. Even we giggle, though, at the drive-through window.

**ST. LOUIS WINE MARKET AND
TASTING ROOM**
164 Chesterfield Commons East
Chesterfield
636-536-6363
stlwinemarket.com
Retail space and tasting area means
you can find a new favorite and take
it home tonight

TOBAKKO'S
112 Chesterfield Commons E. Dr.
Chesterfield
636-536-0606
tabakkoscigars.com
Cigars and other manly accoutrements

TOY TYME
Chesterfield Mall (lower level near Sears)
Chesterfield
636-733-0088

TREASURE ROOMS
17373 Chesterfield Airport Rd.
Chesterfield
636-728-1899
treasurerooms.com
Trick out your nursery or big-kid room
with fancy furniture and all the extras

VJ COFFEE & TEA
12595 Olive Blvd.
Creve Coeur
314-542-9292
Independent coffee and tea retailer
glommed onto the front of Dierbergs

{ HANDIWORK }

For the county crafter, plenty of specialty shops can provide the
supplies, instruction, and inspiration for projects in a variety of
media. Beaders/jewelry makers: **Bizzy Beads** (135 Chesterfield
Towne Ctr., Chesterfield, 636-728-1515, bizzybeads.com) and
B&J Rock Shop (14744 Manchester Rd., Ballwin, 636-394-4567,
bjrockshop.com). Glass/metal fabrication: **Glasshopper Studio**
(13011 Olive Blvd., St. Louis, 314-205-0220, glasshopperstudio.
com). The edible arts: **Sallie's Cake and Candy Supplies** (14340
Manchester Rd., Manchester, 636-394-3030, salliesonline.com).
Textiles: **Susie Q Quilting** (131 S. Central Ave. #B, Eureka, 636-
587-2772, susieqquilting.com).

ST. CHARLES COUNTY

COTTLEVILLE ★ DARDENNE PRAIRIE ★ O'FALLON ★ LAKE ST. LOUIS ★ ST. CHARLES ★ ST. PETERS ★ WELDON SPRING ★ WENTZVILLE

HISTORY

The French were the first European settlers in St. Charles County, arriving late in the eighteenth century. Daniel Boone, a Spanish land grant recipient, came soon after. German immigrant Gottfried Duden, a neighbor of Boone's, spent a lot of time with the famous frontiersman exploring this area. Duden later returned to Germany and published a glowing report of life here, and his writings inspired Germans to immigrate to Missouri.

Until the arrival of the automobile, St. Charles County was largely rural. The building of the interstate highway system and the Blanchette Bridge linked St. Louis City and County with St. Charles. The population soon followed. By 1980, St. Charles County grew from a population of 14,000 to 50,000. The trend as one of the nation's fastest growing counties continues today, especially in St. Peters, O'Fallon, and Wentzville.

St. Charles is the county seat and the oldest city on the Missouri River. French founder Louis Blanchette, named it *Les Petites Côtes* (the little hills), which was changed by the Spanish to *San Carlos del Misuri*, or "St. Charles of the Missouri." After the Louisiana Purchase, the name became St. Charles. The city served as Missouri's first state capital from 1821 to 1826. Lindenwood University, established in 1827, has evolved into a highly respected educational institution. Main Street St. Charles is renowned for hosting some of the Midwest's best festivals and craft fairs.

St. Peters provides a prime example of St. Charles County's population boom over the last four decades. The 1970 census revealed a population of 486. The 1980 census listed the population as 15,700. By 2010, the population was over 52,500.

O'Fallon is another one of Missouri's fastest growing cities. In 1812, Zumwalt's Fort was built to protect settlers from Native Americans who'd been armed by the British. The *Spirit of Freedom 9/11 Memorial* is thirteen tons of twisted steel brought to Missouri from the Twin Towers in New York. Dedicated in 2003, it serves as a poignant reminder of one of the saddest days in U.S. history.

Lake St. Louis began as a private recreational lake and original planned community built in the spirit of Reston, Virginia, and Columbia, Maryland. Facing annexation to Wentzville or O'Fallon, after the developer declared bankruptcy, the residents came together and formed what today is Lake St. Louis. According to the 2010 census, **Wentzville** is Missouri's fastest growing city. Living history aficionados can relive life in sixteenth-century France at the Greater St. Louis Renaissance Faire. Get in the spirit of it all and wear period costume! There'll be jousting, sword fighting, strolling minstrels, period craftsmen, artisans, and food.

Over the years St. Charles County has undergone a transformation from a collection of small villages to a thriving part of the metro area. From the historical to the most modern conveniences, St. Charles has it all.

{ HINT OF HISTORY }

St. Charles, the final embarkation point of the Lewis and Clark Expedition, could not be more closely intertwined with that historic journey, and the **Lewis and Clark Boat House and Nature Center** (1050 Riverside Dr., St. Charles, 636-947-3199, lewisandclarkcenter.org) is a kind of one-stop interpretive shop for all things L&C. Dioramas illustrating the expedition's highlights, encounters with native peoples, animals, and habitats along the way, and more. The highlight, for many, is the Boat House, where full-scale replicas of the Corps of Discovery's vessels are displayed. A wetland marsh around the site makes for good birding, too.

FOOD AND DRINK

As in many suburban and exurban locales, chain eateries are ascendant, but independent options exist, too, even if you have to drive the strip mall to find them.

....

A BITE TO EAT

BC'S KITCHEN
11 Meadows Circle Dr.
Lake St. Louis
636-542-9090
billcardwell.com
Latest outing from chef-owner Bill Cardwell; upscale American food

CONCETTA'S ITALIAN RESTAURANT
600 S. 5th St.
St. Charles
636-946-2468
concettas-stcharles.com
Family-owned Italian for more than twenty-five years

HEAVEN SCENT BAKERY
1133 Bryan Rd.
O'Fallon
636-240-8311
heavenscentbakery.net
Donuts, gourmet desserts, frozen custard, 24-hour drive-thru

HENDRICK'S BBQ
1200 S. Main St.
St. Charles
636-724-8600
hendricksbbq.com
Ribs, brisket, and more of the usual suspects, plus a sides menu that includes free-range deviled eggs, pork cracklins, onion rings, and bacon-braised greens.

KITARO
4551 Hwy. K
O'Fallon
636-300-4422
kitarojapan.com
Sleek and contemporary Japanese cuisine

LADY DI'S DINER
630 N. Kingshighway
St. Charles
636-916-4442
ladydisdiner.com
Classic diner breakfast and lunch, including ten-egg omelet and the tornado casserole; cash/check only

....

{ WHEEL COOL }

Is it a bike shop, a coffee bar, a restaurant, a trailhead? Yep. Get it all, from bike tires (and free air!) to breakfast wraps, at the funky **Bike Stop Café** (701 S. Riverside Dr., St. Charles, 636-724-9900, bikestopcafes.com), just a block off the Katy Trail in St. Charles. Hang out and talk shop, join up in the weekly rides, or just tuck into a Field Hippie salad.

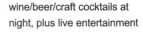

LEWIS & CLARK'S
217 S. Main St.
St. Charles
636-947-3334
lewisandclarksrestaurant.com
Brick-clad, historic setting for American/Mex comfort food, Trailhead beer on tap; balcony seating is tops

MAD DOG & CAT'S
1005 Wolfrum Rd.
Weldon Spring
636-300-9171
maddogandcats.com
Pastas, sandwiches, shrimp scampi, and steak specials at tasteful spot

MISS AIMEE B'S
837 1st Capitol Dr.
St. Charles
636-946-4202
missaimeeb.com
Tearoom with hearty breakfast and lunch options from chicken salad to praline French toast; mooncake is a don't-miss

MOTHER-IN-LAW HOUSE
500 S. Main St.
St. Charles
636-946-9444
motherinlawhouse.com
Historic home fine dining, serving salmon, sole, chicken, and steak dishes

OLD MILLSTREAM INN
912 S. Main St.
St. Charles
636-946-3287
Lovely patio with sandwiches at lunch, plus smoked shrimp, beef tips at dinner, and famous Millfries

PAUL'S DONUTS
1289 Jungermann Rd.
St. Peters
636-447-8836
paulsdonuts.com
Hand-kneaded yeast and cake donuts and two words: donut sundae

PICASSO'S COFFEE HOUSE
101 N. Main St.
St. Charles
636-925-2911
picassoscoffeehouse.com
Locally roasted coffees and bakery goods in the morning,

wine/beer/craft cocktails at night, plus live entertainment

PIO'S
403 1st Capitol Dr.
St. Charles
636-946-2522
piosrestaurant.com
Pastas and pizza, chicken dishes, frog legs, and, in a nod to more than fifty years in business, a "grandkids" menu

ROSCIGLIONE BAKERY
2265 Bluestone Dr.
St. Charles
636-947-6500
rosciglionebakery.com
Fig cookies, date bars, peanut biscotti, and spice balls at authentic Italian bakery

STONE SOUP COTTAGE
5809 Hwy. N
Cottleville
636-244-2233
stonesoupcottage.com
Farmhouse setting for by-reservation, prix-fixe dining on local foodies' must list

VB CHOCOLATE BAR
5326 State Hwy. N
Cottleville
636-352-1139
Husband-and-wife-owned confectionery offers a gourmet experience in chocolate, candies, and even drinks. Small food menu and a lovely patio with fire pits make for an intimate evening out.

SOMETHING TO DRINK

COTTLEVILLE WINE SELLER & BEER GARDEN
5314 Hwy. N
Cottleville
636-244-4453
cottlevillewineseller.com
Plenty of wine choices and light bites

DUCHESNE BAR & GRILL
1001 S. Duchesne Dr.
St. Charles
636-947-0920
dbandg.com
Drinks, karaoke, peel 'n' eat shrimp

MCGURK'S PUBLIC HOUSE
108 South Main St.
O'Fallon
636-978-9640
Guinness, homemade chips and pub food, and nice patio

MOONSHINE BLUES BAR
1200 S. Main St.
St. Charles
636-724-8600
moonshinebluesbar.com
Downstairs from Hendrick's, this joint serves whiskey, and lots of it, along with straight-from-the-barrel moonshine, to complement the live musical entertainment onstage Friday and Saturday nights.

QUINTESSENTIAL
149 N. Main St.
St. Charles
636-443-2211
q-stl.com
Nightclub, live music, and dancing, which also happens to have an ambitious food menu

RENDEZVOUS CAFÉ & WINE BAR
217 S. Main St.
O'Fallon
636-707-1339
Boutique wines, microbrews, coffee drinks, and tapas

TRAILHEAD BREWING COMPANY
921 S. Riverside Dr.
St. Charles
636-946-2739
trailheadbrewing.com
Craft brewer right on the Katy Trail, with people-watching patio

WINERY OF THE LITTLE HILLS
501 S. Main St.
St. Charles
636-946-9339
littlehillswinery.com
Huge by-the-glass selection, full food menu; we recommend the warm Little Hills Alpenglow for a winter holiday treat

FESTIVITIES

FESTIVAL OF THE LITTLE HILLS
Third weekend in August
Main Street and Frontier Park
St. Charles
636-940-0095
festivalofthelittlehills.com
Large, family-oriented festival of crafts from all over the country; live music, food, and drink

HERITAGE & FREEDOM FEST
Fourth of July weekend
O'Fallon
heritageandfreedomfest.com
Parade, carnival/midway/rides area, plus stage for national musical acts and nightly fireworks shows

MOSAICS FESTIVAL FOR THE ARTS
September
Main Street
St. Charles
stcharlesmosaics.org
Juried fine art show, plus live entertainment and children's art village

OKTOBERFEST
September
Frontier Park
St. Charles
saintcharlesoktoberfest.com
German music, food, "wiener takes it all" dachshund races, 5K, kids' activities and bier, bier, bier

SANTA PARADE
Thanksgiving through Christmas
Main Street
St. Charles
stcharleschristmas.com
Part of the larger Christmas Traditions celebration (with costumed carolers, fife and drum corps, carriage rides, and more), the forty-Santa parade includes such characters as Frontier Santa, Civil War Santa, Pere Noel, and many more. Kids will love collecting the trading cards from each!

{ ENSHRINED }

The modernist **Shrine of St. Rose Philippine Duchesne** (619 N. Second St., St. Charles, 636-946-6127, duchesneshrine.org) was erected in the 1960s to honor the life and work of the pioneer educator and missionary to the Indians from the Society of the Sacred Heart. Mother Duchesne founded the first free school west of the Mississippi River and was canonized in 1988 by Pope John Paul II. Interestingly, the shrine remains unfinished according to its original plan, a fact you can see in its architecture and exterior surface.

RECREATION

EXERCISE

ADRENALINE ZONE/ DEMOLITION BALL
1875 Old Hwy. 94 South
St. Charles
636-940-7700
db-az.com
Multilevel laser tag and demolition ball (billed as hockey + polo + football + basketball, in bumper cars), plus arcade games, foosball

BOSCHERTOWN GO-KARTS
3500 N. Hwy. 94
St. Charles
636-946-4848
boschertowngokarts.com
Go karts, sprint karts, and even double-seaters for younger riders to accompany parents

BRUNSWICK ZONE XL
8070 Veterans Memorial Pkwy.
St. Peters
636-474-2695
bowlbrunswick.com
Entertainment plex of bowling, laser tag, arcade amusements

GREAT SKATE
130 Boone Hills Dr.
St. Peters
636-441-2530
greatskaterollerrink.com
Roller rink like you remember!

KLONDIKE PARK
4600 Hwy. 94
Augusta
636-949-7535
Rustic cabin and tent camping among challenging county park hiking/biking trails

{ SHOE IN }

Do you know your ringers from your leaners? You bet your horseshoes that the folks at the **National Horseshoe Pitchers Hall of Fame & Museum** (100 Bluestem Way, Wentzville, quailridgehorseshoeclub.com) do, and more importantly, they can explain it to you. Once you've got the intellectual grasp of the game's finer points, pick up some shoes and let 'em fly on the indoor courts.

At just a hair over six hundred acres, **Indian Camp Creek Park** (Dietrich Rd., one mile west of Hwy. 61, parks.sccmo.org) is the county's largest. Fitting, then, that the four-foot-tall Bob Cassilly–designed frogs and a twenty-two-foot-high aluminum windmill should be prominent features of the eco-friendly play area here. Everything's bigger in St. Charles County! (Don't tell Texas.) Beyond sheer size, your brood will delight in the sand dig, fossilized animal tracks, ten miles of multiuse trails, slides, tire swing, and boardwalk-enclosed fishing pond.

RENAUD SPIRIT CENTER

2650 Tri-Sports Circle
O'Fallon
636-474-2732
renaudspiritcenter.com
City-owned community center includes
Alligator's Creek outdoor water park.

ST. PETERS REC-PLEX

5200 Mexico Rd.
St. Peters
636-939-2386
stpetersmo.net
Community center features multiple ice-
skating rinks, adult drop-in ice hockey,
indoor pools, and more.

WAPELHORST AQUATIC CENTER

1874 Muegge Rd.
St. Charles
636-949-3372 (in season)
stcharlesparks.com
Outdoor water park offers innertube rap-
ids, kids' play area, underground waterslide, and a five-story speed waterslide.

{ KID ZONE }

Watch eyes bug out at **Riverside
Sweets**' (416 S. Main St., St.
Charles, 636-724-4131) array of
fresh fudge (in tons of flavors),
penny candy, peanut brittle,
popcorn caramel apples, and
so much more, all made on-site.
Great stop for a hand-dipped ice
cream cone to savor as you stroll
the Main Street cobblestone.

{ KID ZONE }

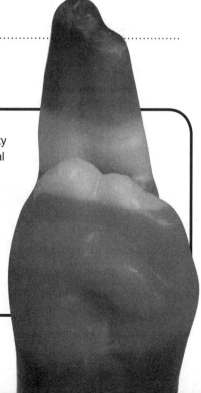

Little people put their grubby hands plenty
of places, so why not channel that natural
urge? At the literally hands-on art studio
My Handyworks (104 S. Main St., St.
Charles, 636-724-7337, myhandyworks.
com), hand (and foot) prints, along with
wax hand models, can be the basis of
cool wall art, room murals, gift-able art
objects, and more. Plenty of other art
and craft projects to choose from.

BOTTLENECK BLUES BAR
One Ameristar Blvd.
St. Charles
636-940-4300
ameristar.com/st_charles.aspx
Casino take on down-and-dirty Delta blues club, hosts occasional big-name national acts, plus homegrown talent

FOUNDRY ART CENTRE
520 N. Main Ctr.
St. Charles
636-255-0270
foundryartcentre.org
Cultural and artistic hub for fine arts performances, exhibition, classes, and working artists' studio spaces (many open to the public on periodic basis)

RIVER CITY RASCALS
900 T. R. Hughes Blvd.
O'Fallon
636-240-2287
rivercityrascals.com
Get up close and personal at the minor-league baseball games of this Frontier League team

J. SCHEIDEGGER CENTER FOR THE ARTS
2300 W. Clay St.
St. Charles
636-949-4433
lindenwoodcenter.com
Exquisite new venue at Lindenwood University

houses twelve-hundred-seat, Broadway-style theatre, flexible black box space and art gallery, with numerous national touring shows on the calendar.

ST. ANDREWS CINEMA
2025 Golfway St.
St. Charles
636-947-1133
standrews3.com
Dollar movies, dollar hot dogs; with five bucks, you're a king!

ST. CHARLES COUNTY HERITAGE MUSEUM & CENTENNIAL TRAIL
Near the intersection of Hwy. 364 (Page Extension) and Hwy. 94
St. Charles
636-949-7535
stccparks.org
Archaeologial, agricultural, and cultural exhibits explore the history and settlement of the area; 2.2-mile asphalt trail links to Katy Trail.

WELDON SPRING SITE REMEDIAL ACTION PROJECT MUSEUM
7295 Hwy. 94 S.
St. Charles
636-300-2600
lm.doe.gov/weldon/Sites.aspx
It's hard to beat the moniker bestowed upon this facility by the excellent local exploration site "Craves, Caves, and Graves" (.com): Beth dubbed it the "nuclear waste adventure trail" (for which she gives a hat tip to RoadsideAmerica.com). Stirs the imagination, does it not? So, lace up your lead sneakers and head on out to this vast former wasteland, site of explosives manufacturing in the 1940s and radioactive waste storage thereafter. Cleanup efforts have been under way for decades, and then some enterprising agency decided to bury it all and plop an explanatory museum on top. (pictured below)

{ CHIMNEY DREAMS }

In the center of historic **Fort Zumwalt Park** (1000 Jessup Ln., ofallon.mo.us) stood a limestone chimney, lone sentinel and only remaining sign of the family fort that stood on the property and provided shelter for ten families during the Indian raids in the War of 1812. The city of O'Fallon has begun rebuilding the fort home around it and will use the facility to display the artifacts excavated from the site and tell the story of early settlers.

SHOPPORTUNITIES

The dominant retail scene in the area is found along the cobblestones of **Main Street St. Charles**. Although its reputation as a Red Hatted "woman of a certain age" paradise is intact, interspersed you'll find shops carving out a slightly different niche. Even if it's not your cup of tea, the strolling is pleasant, the ambience is charming, and you're never far from an ice cream stop!

CALISA HOME DECOR
3354 Mid Rivers Mall Dr.
St. Peters
636-970-0069
calisahomedecor.com
Consignment of like-new furniture and home accessory items

CANINE COOKIES & CREAM DOG BAKERY
822 S. Main St.
St. Charles
636-443-2266
All-natural gourmet goodies for your pup, including dog ice cream and cakes

DI OLIVAS OIL & VINEGARS
617 S. Main St.
St. Charles
636-724-8282
diolivas.com
Olive oils from around the world, plus vinegars, spices, gourmet gifts

DORSEY'S CORNER STORE
1328 N. 2nd St.
St. Charles
636-328-6849
Small market of fresh produce, gourmet mixes, local eggs, and vintage kitchen gear

FAST LANE CLASSIC CARS
427 Little Hills Industrial Blvd.
St. Charles
636-940-9969
fastlanecars.com
Pristine showroom of classic and muscle cars, plus collectible/gift shop

FIGUERO'S GOURMET SPECIALTIES
524 S. Main St.
St. Charles
636-947-9847
figueros.com
Potential dude respite along Main Street, with a staggering sixteen hundred hot sauces/rubs/jerk spice mixes

FIRST CAPITOL TRADING POST
207 S. Main St.
St. Charles
636-946-2883
firstcapitoltrading.com
Disney, Swarovski, Lladro, Christopher Radko, and many other collectibles

THE FLOWER PETALER

620 S. Main St.

St. Charles

636-946-3048

flowerpetaler.net

Fresh flowers, botanical arrangements and accents, garden decor, jewelry, artwork, and gifts

FRIPERIE

610 S. Main St.

St. Charles

636-947-7980

Accessory heaven, from scarves to handbags

HARDWARE OF THE PAST

405 N. Main St.

St. Charles

636-724-3771

hardwareofthepast.com

Have an old house? Or want to capture that magic? Get antique reproduction locks, doorknobs, casters here, plus entire drawers/furniture replacement elements

HOLIDAY HOUSE

612 S. Main St.

St. Charles

636-946-3048

Love Christmas (and others?) Dress your house from top to bottom here

J. NOTO FINE ITALIAN CONFECTIONS

336 S. Main St.

St. Charles

636-949-0800

jnoto.com

Delectable truffles, cookies, pastries, seasonal sweets

JOHN DENGLER TOBACCONIST

700 S. Main St.

St. Charles

636-946-6899

johndenglertobacconist.com

Pipes, loose tobacco blends, cigars, and accessories

KNIT & CABOODLE

423 S. Main St.

St. Charles

636-916-0060

knitandcaboodle.com

Thousands of yarns (including locally spun and dyed) and classes

MAIN STREET BOOKS

307 S. Main St.

St. Charles

636-949-0105

mainstreetbooks.net

Historic building chock full of good reads from local histories to best-selling page-turners, plus great kids' selection

THE MEADOWS AT LAKE ST. LOUIS
20 Meadows Circle Dr., Suite 224
Lake Saint Louis
636-695-2626
themeadowsatlsl.com
Outdoor lifestyle center includes Banana Republic, Talbots, Clarkson Jewelers, and state's only Von Maur department store

NATIVE TRADITIONS GALLERY
310 S. Main St.
St. Charles
636-947-0170
Native American art, pottery

OOH LA LA BOUTIQUES
340 S. Main St.
St. Charles
636-940-2020
Women's clothing and accessories, and down-the-block kids' store, too

PROVENANCE SOAPWORKS
311 S. Main St.
St. Charles
636-577-1972
facebook.com/ProvenanceSoaps
Handmade soaps, bath salts, bath bombs, and oils

{ FOR THE BIRDS }

A world-class addition to the outdoorsy/natural environment treasures of the northern part of the region (see also "Naturalist's NoCo" on p. 165), the **Audubon Center at Riverlands** (301 Riverlands Way, West Alton, 636-899-0090, riverlands.audubon.org) brings to stunning life the vitality and diversity of the migratory bird population in, around, and over the confluence of the Mississippi and Missouri Rivers. For starters, yeah, it's that Audubon (the National Audubon Society, named for John James Audubon, famed naturalist and painter of birds). So the science and information is top-notch and well vetted. The center itself is a family-friendly and engaging spot, a place to see bald eagles, herons, egrets, trumpeter swans, and songbirds of all descriptions. Every season brings new opportunities and new species to discover.

METRO EAST

ALTON ★ COLLINSVILLE ★ BELLEVILLE ★ BRUSSELS
★ CAHOKIA ★ COLUMBIA ★ EAST ST. LOUIS ★
EDWARDSVILLE ★ ELSAH ★ FAIRMONT CITY ★ FAIRVIEW
HEIGHTS ★ GLEN CARBON ★ GODFREY ★ GRAFTON ★
GRANITE CITY ★ HARTFORD ★ MADISON ★ MARYVILLE ★
MILLSTADT ★ O'FALLON ★ PONTOON BEACH ★ SAUGET

....

HISTORY

Mound City is a St. Louis moniker. Mississippian Indians known as the
Mound Builders built more than one hundred mounds at Cahokia, near
Collinsville, centuries ago. Archaeological digs reveal that a sophisticated
society of close to one hundred thousand people once lived here.
Why Mississippian Mound Builders abandoned their city is a mystery.
What is clear is that Cahokia Mounds is one of North America's largest
archaeological sites, which has been designated a World Heritage Site by
the cultural organization UNESCO as well as a National Historic Landmark.

Today, dozens of towns comprise the eastern portion of the metro area.
Here is a sampling of the rich modern heritage of this region. **East St. Louis**
earned a reputation as a jazz, blues, and rock musical melting pot, with Miles
Davis and Ike and Tina Turner leading the way. Three of the Metro East's
most prominent towns—**Belleville**, **Collinsville**, and **Edwardsville**—are rich
in history and intact historic homes that provide a peek into nineteenth-century life. Belleville was the site of the last of the famed 1858 Lincoln-Douglas
debates. Art on the Square in Belleville is perennially ranked a top U.S. art
fair. Collinsville produces much of the world's horseradish and is home to the
world's largest catsup bottle, a water tower built in 1949 by the now-defunct
Brooks Catsup Company. Edwardsville is one of Illinois's oldest cities.
Southern Illinois University–Edwardsville, a vibrant downtown, and historic
homes have landed Edwardsville on small-town "best places to live" lists.

Running parallel to the mighty Mississippi River from Pere Marquette
State Park to the Lewis and Clark State Historic Site is the Meeting of the

205

Rivers Scenic Route and Sam Vadalabene Bike Trail. Along this beautiful byway are river towns that are worth a visit any time of year.

Illinois's first prison was built in **Alton** and saw Civil War duty, housing nearly twelve thousand Confederate POWs. Today, Alton greets antique seekers and eagle watchers with equal enthusiasm. Enjoy a river cruise, a fall foliage drive, or from December through February, a bald eagle–watching excursion along the Mississippi's Great River Road.

The quaint village of **Elsah** is home to Principia, a private college listed on the National Register of Historic Places. **Godfrey**'s namesake and founder, Benjamin Godfrey, was rumored to have sailed with pirate Jean Lafitte. Nearby Rocky Fork was once a refuge for runaway slaves who moved on from there via the Underground Railroad. Just upriver, **Grafton** is a town that suffered extensive flood damage in 1993, but today visitors might find that difficult to believe. Grafton has re-emerged as a popular tourist destination for wine tasting, boating, bikers (both motor and non), eagle watching, and autumn foliage drives. **Hartford** is home to the Lewis and Clark State Historic Site. The Meeting of the Rivers Confluence Tower offers a spectacular view of the area and the Mississippi River.

Columbia and **Waterloo**'s immigrant heritage is Germanic. The Dreamland Palace just outside Waterloo is one of the few remaining German eating establishments in the metro area. The Waterloo German Band, led by Harry Wolf, a former music teacher from Belleville, continues to delight fans of oompah music.

On the short list of other Metro East places to check out: Maryville, Maeystown, Millstadt, Wood River, Glen Carbon, and Fairmont City, where the highest point in the village is actually atop an Indian mound. And if the horses are running, those who like to play the ponies will enjoy Fairmount Park.

{ IF THEY AIN'T GOT IT, YOU DON'T NEED IT }

If it's a show, fair, expo, or themed gathering of a certain size, and it's happening in the area, chances are it's happening at the **Belle-Clair Fairgrounds and Expo Center** (200 S. Belt East, Belleville, 618-235-0666, bcfairgrounds.net). From the annual St. Clair County Fair (August) and the St. Louis Antique Festival (April) to stock car racing on Friday nights (April–September at the speedway) and flea markets every second weekend of the month, it's difficult to imagine a demographic without an event here. It's also home to several large holiday craft shows, including Kay Weber's Belleville Art and Craft Fair (Thanksgiving weekend) and Jann Severit Promotions' Country Treasures Craft Shows (third weekend in October and second weekend in December). "Sure," you might say, "but what about the roller derby girls?" Yep, teams of the Confluence Crush league face off here, too.

FOOD AND DRINK

A BITE TO EAT

222 ARTISAN BAKERY
222 N. Main St.
Edwardsville
618-659-1122
222bakery.com
Breads and fancy pastries

**ANDRIA'S COUNTRY-
SIDE RESTAURANT**
7415 State Rte. 143
Edwardsville
618-656-0281
andriascountryside.com
Fine dining (steaks, pastas, seafood) in historic home setting

**ANNIE'S FROZEN
CUSTARD**
245 S. Buchanan St.
Edwardsville
618-656-0289
anniesfrozencustard.com
Edwardsville's homegrown frozen custard stand

BELLA MILANO'S
1063 S. State Rte. 157
Edwardsville
618-659-2100
bellamilanos.com
Italian dishes like eggplant parm, homemade toasted ravioli, pasta three ways for the indecisive

BIGELO'S BISTRO
140 N. Main St.
Edwardsville
618-655-1471
bigelosbistro.com
Casual bistro with a dozen craft brews on tap

**BOBBY'S FROZEN
CUSTARD**
2525 N. Center St.
Maryville
618-345-3002
bobbysfrozencustard.com
Weekly custard special flavor, and frequent live bands on weekends

{ **KID ZONE** }

Turn up the steps to the second floor of the **Collinsville Library** (408 W. Main St., 618-344-1112, collinsvillelibrary.org) and enter an enchanting children's library (complete with Arthur, the Mouse and his cookie, Alice in Wonderland, and more to lead the way) where kids can sprawl, play, read, paint, giggle, and generally be kids. Entirely separate from the hush-hush crowd, this is a hidden gem for families needing a change of scenery from their living rooms.

If your children give you a blank stare—or worse, say "the store"—when asked where peaches come from, it's time to load those city slickers up and head out to **Eckert's** (618-233-0513, eckerts.com) farms, with locations in Belleville (951 S. Green Mount Rd.), Millstadt (2719 Eckert Orchard Ln.), and Grafton (20995 Eckert Orchard Rd.). Pick-your-own orchards (apples, blackberries, peaches, pumpkins) and cut-your-own Christmas trees provide the kind of family snapshots you thought only existed in *Martha Stewart Living*, and the farms also have an assortment of animal encounters, pig races, slides, wagon rides, funnel cakes, and all the homespun fun you can imagine. Check website for location particulars and the latest ripening schedules.

BULLY'S SMOKEHOUSE
1280 Columbia Ctr.
Columbia
618-281-2880
bullyssmokehouse.com
Award-winning, hickory-smoked BBQ pork, beef, and ribs

CASTELLI'S RESTAURANT AT 255
3400 Fosterburg Rd.
Alton
618-462-4620
castellis255.com
Fried chicken all day long, plus gizzards, t-ravs, and more at this fam-friendly legend

CLEVELAND-HEATH
106 N. Main St.
Edwardsville
618-307-4830
clevelandheath.com
Foodie revolutionaries on the East Side, serving gourmet comfort bites from deviled eggs and Korean-style short ribs to Vietnamese noodle soup

THE CUP
1057 Century Dr.
Edwardsville
618-656-2287
cravethecup.com
Cute-as-a-cupcake bakery

DON & PENNY'S
306 State St.
Alton
618-465-9823
Your basic bar/pizza/Italian/Creole joint

DUKE BAKERY
819 Henry St.
Alton
618-462-2922

5407-C Godfrey Rd.
Godfrey
618-467-2922

3202 Nameoki Rd.
Granite City
618-877-9500
dukebakeryinc.com
Old-school classics, awesome donuts, and meringue pies

FAZZI'S
1813 Vandalia St.
Collinsville
618-344-5440
fazzis.com
Greek specialties like
gyros, saganaki, baklava

FIN INN
1500 W. Main St.
Grafton
618-786-2030
fininn.com
Fish and frog legs on the
menu, and on the move in
wall-to-wall aquariums

**GENTELIN'S ON
BROADWAY**
122 E. Broadway
Alton
618-465-6080
gentelinsonbroadway.com
Upscale food and decor
with New American bent

**J. FIRE'S MARKET
BISTRO**
725 N. Market St.
Waterloo
618-939-7233
jfires.com
Wood-fired pizzas, Cajun
dishes in a historic brick
farmhouse

**JOSEPHINE'S TEA
ROOMS**
6109 Godfrey Rd.
Godfrey
618-466-7792
josephinestearooms-
andgiftshops.com
Sandwiches, salads,
and stuffed tomatoes
for the Red Hatted

KRUTA BAKERY
300 Saint Louis Rd.
Collinsville
618-344-1115
Stollen, cream puffs,
and darling sugar cookies

MISSISSIPPI HALF-STEP
420 E. Main St.
Grafton
618-786-2722
mississippihalfstep.com
Comfortable riverside
room for tasty lunch,
dinner, and eagle-season
Sunday breakfast

MY JUST DESSERTS
31 E. Broadway
Alton
618-462-5881
myjustdesserts.org
Pie. Lunch if you must,
but pie. Pie above all.

{ MARKET DAYS }

Saturdays at the courthouse may not sound like much fun, until you realize it's
Land of Goshen Community Market (618-307-6045, goshenmarket.org) day:
more than sixty vendors selling everything from farm-fresh produce and jams
to fresh-baked treats and handwoven baskets. A "Market Sprouts" program
gets little kids involved in the action, and live music fills the air—8 A.M. to noon,
next to the Madison County courthouse, which is located at 155 N. Main St.,
Edwardsville.

ORIENTAL SPOON KOREAN CUISINE
229 Harvard Dr.
Edwardsville
618-655-9633
orientalspoon.net
Authentic Korean faves like bulgogi, bibimbap, and kimchi

PAPA VITO'S PIZZA
318 E. Washington St.
Belleville
618-277-6200
mypapavitos.com
Wings, calzones, salads, and of course, pizzas: the extra here is the purportedly haunted building they're in!

PEEL WOOD-FIRED PIZZA
921 S. Arbor Vitae #101
Edwardsville
618-659-8561
peelpizza.com
Crowds flock to this trendy pizza café; great salads and dessert pizza, too

PIE PANTRY
310 E. Main St. #1
Belleville
618-277-4140
thepiepantry.com
Comfort food and pie

PITCHERS SPORTS PUB & PIZZERIA
104 W. Main St.
Belleville
618-233-4800
pitcherspubandpizza.com
Big space, big screens, big menu of apps/beer/pizza—big fun for the big game

PRINCIVALLI'S CAFÉ
602 E. Third St.
Alton
618-465-3255
princivallis.com
Apps, pizzas, sandwiches, and pastas, all with Italian accents

RAMON'S EL DORADO
1711 Saint Louis Rd.
Collinsville
618-344-6435
Classic Mexican dishes, plus stellar guac and 'ritas, mariachi music

RAVANELLI'S
3 American Village
Granite City
618-877-8000

26 Collinsport Dr.
Collinsville
618-343-9000

1214 Central Park Dr.
O'Fallon
618-589-3628

ravanellis.com
Brick-oven-cooked pastas and pizzas, plus steaks, fried chicken

SACRED GROUNDS
233 N. Main St.
Edwardsville
618-692-4150
Vegetarian-friendly coffee shop

SEVEN
7 S. High St.
Belleville
618-277-6700
sevensushibar.com
Popular downtown spot for drinks, dinner, and frequent live music

TONY'S THIRD ST. CAFÉ
312 Piasa St.
Alton
618-462-8384
tonysrestaurant.com
Not to be confused with another famous Italian Tony, this one's known for pepperloin steak

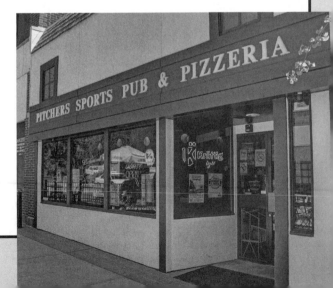

SOMETHING TO DRINK

BIG DADDY'S
313 E. Main St.
Belleville
618-257-0315

132 N. Main St.
Edwardsville
618-656-9706
bigdaddystl.com
Party bar for the party
crowd, surprisingly
good food

BOSSANOVA
112 W. Third St.
Alton
618-462-1175
altonbossa.com
James Bond–inspired
martini menu and worldly
menu make for a hot spot
on the river bluffs

CUTTERS
239 Carlyle Ave.
Belleville
618-235-7642
Tons of space and tons
of food

ENCORE WINE BAR
253 N. Main St.
Edwardsville
618-606-3458
Adjacent to the Wildey
Theatre, great for
post-show libation

FAST EDDIE'S BON-AIR
1530 E. 4th St.
Alton
618-462-5532
fasteddiesbonair.com
Coldest beer and meat on
a stick, no minors allowed

FRIDAY'S SOUTH
624 S. Illinois St.
Belleville
618-233-1724
Corner bar; live music and
bar food

106 E. Main St.
Collinsville
618-223-1017
Pizza on Main Street

GLOBAL BREW
112 S. Buchanan St.
Edwardsville
618-307-5858
globalbrewtaps.com
Hundreds of brews from
all over the globe

LAURIE'S PLACE
228 N. Main St.
Edwardsville
618-656-2175
lauriesplacebar.com
Margaritaville-meets-
your-backyard decor,
frequent live music and
hoppin' patio

{ WATERWORLD }

The **Gateway Geyser** (in the Malcolm W.
Martin Memorial Park, 185 W. Trendley
Ave., 618-346-4905, meprd.org), across the
river from the Arch in East St. Louis, has
the claim of being, at an Arch-mirroring 630
feet, the tallest fountain in the United States
(and second in the world only to a Saudi
Arabian behemoth).

The old **Lincoln School** (1210 N. Main St.) in Edwardsville was the city's African American school from 1912 to 1951, and although today it sits boarded up, eye-popping murals on its exterior are a testament both to its past (with notable alums and historical themes represented) and to its hopeful future, if building owner Mannie Jackson (a star, and now owner, with the Harlem Globetrotters who attended Lincoln) can bring his renovation dreams to fruition.

PIASA WINERY
225 W. Main St.
Grafton
618-786-9463
piasawinery.com
Local producer of Norton, Chardonel, Chambourcin, served on a sizeable riverfront deck

ROPER'S REGAL BEAGLE SPORTS BAR & GRILL
3045 Godfrey Rd.
Godfrey
618-466-2112
ropersregalbeagle.com
Beer (twenty-one taps), TVs, and gameday fun

STAGGER INN AGAIN
104 E. Vandalia St.
Edwardsville
618-656-4221
Cheap beer, live music, and local color

WINE TAP
223 E. Main St.
Belleville
618-239-9463
thewinetapbelleville.com
Copious glass and bottle offerings and light, eclectic bites to savor on the patio

{ MONUMENTAL NOTABLES }

What do abolitionist **Elijah P. Lovejoy** (Alton Cemetery at Monument Avenue, downtown Alton), world's tallest man **Robert Wadlow** (2800 block of College Ave., Upper Alton), and Shoshone guide **Sacagawea** (on the campus of Lewis and Clark Community College, Godfrey) have in common? All are immortalized in the Metro East in statuary form— impressive monuments, indeed, to three who left such lasting impressions.

RECREATION

The Illinois towns across the Mississippi are frequently touted as family-friendly, down-home, neighborly places, so it's not surprising to find a gaggle of community amenities, high-quality outdoor diversions, and enough fairs, festivals, and events to fill anyone's calendar.

EXERCISE

ARLINGTON GREENS
200 Arlington Dr.
Granite City
618-931-5232
arlingtongreens.com
18-hole public facility, par 72, and recently renovated

BIG MUDDY ADVENTURES
1164 Moorlands Dr.
St. Louis
314-610-4241
2muddy.com
Guided and outfitted canoe trips, including full-moon and canoe camping excursions, on the Missouri and Mississippi Rivers

CENTERFIELD PARK
5620 Old Collinsville Rd.
Fairview Heights
618-624-7074
centerfieldpark.net
Mini-golf, batting cages, and bumper boats

GRAFTON CANOE & KAYAK
12 E. Water St. #2
Grafton
618-786-2192
graftoncanoeandkayak.com
They rent those, plus bikes, pontoon boats, waverunners, and a tipi

THE NATURE INSTITUTE
2213 S. Levis Ln.
Godfrey
618-466-9930
thenatureinstitute.org
Guided bird migration hikes, prairie burns, and kids' camps, all with the aim of environmental education and conservation

RAGING RIVERS WATERPARK
100 Palisades Pky.
Grafton
618-786-2345
ragingrivers.com
Big fun directly overlooking the Mississippi, with wave pools, body flumes, lazy river

{ RUSTIC ON THE RIVER }

A jewel at the northern stretch of the Great River Road, **Pere Marquette State Park** (Route 100, Grafton, 618-786-3323, greatriverroad.com/pere) serves as a worthy destination for a few hours (Sunday brunch in the historic 1930s-era lodge) or a few days (with horse stables, riding/hiking trails, and fishing). The park and its naturalists are a great resource during the overwintering bald eagle season, too, so bring binoculars and make a day of it! Finally, make sure the kids see the giant chess set at the lodge.

Among other distinctions, Alton is known as "one of the most haunted cities in America," and local entrepreneurs would love to show you why. Check out Alton Hauntings for walking and extended bus tours of locales like the old penitentiary and the **McPike Mansion** (2018 Alby St., 618-462-3348, mcpikemansion. com), or **Mineral Springs Haunted Tours** (301 E. Broadway, 618-465-3200, mineralspringshauntedtours.com) for walking tours of the former Mineral Springs Hotel and adjacent Alton Cemetery. Halloween, as you might guess, is a popular time.

SAM VADALABENE BIKE TRAIL
(Piasa Park on Hwy. 100) to Pere Marquette State Park (at Lodge Turnout on Hwy. 100)
Alton
Hugging the Great River Road and the mighty Mississippi for twenty miles

SPLASH CITY
10 Gateway Dr.
Collinsville
618-346-4571
splashcity.org
Tons of water-park features for kids and a popular surf/bodyboarding feature

TWO RIVERS NATIONAL WILDLIFE REFUGE
1 Hagen Blvd., Brussels
618-883-2524
fws.gov/refuge/two_rivers/
Migratory bird sanctuary administered by the Fisheries and Wildlife Service, this

9,000-acre site encompasses wetlands, open water, bottomland forests, and prairies and includes walking trails and flat-top levee viewing points, great for spotting beavers, herons, turtles, frogs and dragonflies, among other species.

WATERSHED NATURE CENTER
1591 Tower Rd.
Edwardsville
618-692-7578
watershednaturecenter.com
Forty-six acres of trails and wetlands for hiking, birding, and contemplation

WILD TRAK BIKES
1001 E. Broadway
Alton
618-462-2574
wildtrakbikesracing.com
Rentals and gear for treks up the Vadalabene Trail

ARTS, ENTERTAINMENT, & EDUCATION

1820 COLONEL BENJAMIN STEPHENSON HOUSE
409 S. Buchanan St.
Edwardsville
618-692-1818
stephensonhouse.org
Federal-style brick home devoted to preservation of early history of the Illinois Territory

CHILDREN'S MUSEUM OF EDWARDSVILLE
722 Holyoake Rd.
Edwardsville
618-692-2094
edwardsvillechildrensmuseum.org
Rambling old house with tons of exhibits and nooks for kids to explore

CIGAR INN JAZZ CLUB
119 W. Main St., Suite A
Belleville
618-233-4000
cigarinn.net
Stogies and jazz in loungey atmosphere

FAIRMOUNT PARK
9301 Collinsville Rd.
Collinsville
618-345-4300
fairmountpark.com
Play the ponies (thoroughbred and harness racing)

GATEWAY GRIZZLIES
2301 Grizzlie Bear Blvd., Sauget
618-337-3000
gatewaygrizzlies.com
Minor league baseball action in the Frontier League, a game at the GCS Ballpark is a kid-friendly, affordable way to pass a summer afternoon. If you need a challenge of your own while watching pro athletes show their stuff on the field, take on "Baseball's Best Burger" at the concession stand: a bacon cheeseburger served up on a grilled Krispy Kreme donut bun.

{ **DID YOU SEE WHAT PIASA?** }

The fearsome **Piasa bird** of lore was a man-eating, winged monster enshrined in tales of the prehistoric Illini people and first recorded in petroglyph form. Explorers Jacques Marquette and Louis Joliet wrote of seeing renderings of the bird in their 1673 travels. Today, the creature takes painted shape along the river bluffs, about a mile up the Great River Road from Alton.

GATEWAY MOTORSPORTS PARK
700 Raceway Blvd.
Madison
618-215-8888
gatewaymsp.com
1.25-mile oval with differentiated degrees of banking in each corner, host to NASCAR and NHRA events

HISTORIC MUSEUM OF TORTURE DEVICES
301 E. Broadway St.
Alton
618-465-3200
Gruesome collection of instruments of torture used throughout human history, not for the faint of heart

JACOBY ARTS CENTER
627 E. Broadway
Alton
618-462-5222
jacobyartscenter.org
Arts and community center hosting juried exhibitions, performances, and classes for adults and kids

KATHERINE DUNHAM CENTERS FOR ARTS AND HUMANITIES
1005 Pennsylvania Ave.
East St. Louis
618-795-5970
kdcah.org
World-renowned dancer's cultural center showcases her work (via costumes, programs, and artifacts from her anthropological studies) and her collections (African and Caribbean folk and contemporary art), by appointment only

LEWIS & CLARK STATE HISTORIC SITE AND CONFLUENCE TOWER
435 Confluence Tower Dr.
Hartford
618-251-9101

Immerse yourself in the departure point for the unprecedented voyage of Lewis and Clark at their winter camp (now home to many exhibits and a full-scale keelboat model), or 150 feet above the confluence of the great rivers they explored

LINCOLN THEATRE
103 E. Main St.
Belleville
618-233-0123
lincolntheatre-belleville.com
1920s-era vaudeville house now shows first-run movies, with live organ music on weekends, plus stage shows.

NATIONAL GREAT RIVERS MUSEUM AND MELVIN PRICE LOCKS & DAM
#1 Lock and Dam Way
East Alton
877-462-6979
Hands-on and interactive, presenting the full story of the Mississippi River, from cultural and historical importance to the logistics of getting all those barges through

POP'S
401 Monsanto Ave.
Sauget
618-274-6720
popsrocks.com
Well, it rocks. And you can stay all night, if you're so inclined, after an ear-ringing concert or after your other bar closes.

SCHMIDT ART CENTER
2500 Carlyle Ave.
Belleville
618-222-5278
schmidtart.swic.edu
Contemporary art gallery and programs on the campus of Southwestern Illinois College

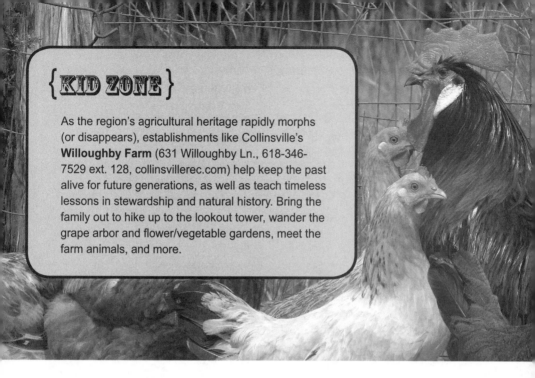

{ KID ZONE }

As the region's agricultural heritage rapidly morphs (or disappears), establishments like Collinsville's **Willoughby Farm** (631 Willoughby Ln., 618-346-7529 ext. 128, collinsvillerec.com) help keep the past alive for future generations, as well as teach timeless lessons in stewardship and natural history. Bring the family out to hike up to the lookout tower, wander the grape arbor and flower/vegetable gardens, meet the farm animals, and more.

TRI-CITY SPEEDWAY
5100 Nameoki Rd.
Granite City
618-931-7836
tricityspeedway.net
Features a three-eitghth-mile dirt oval car racing track, with action mostly scheduled for Friday nights

WILDEY THEATRE
252 N. Main St.
Edwardsville
618-307-2053
wildeytheatre.com
Restored Art Deco–style theatre screening classic films and hosting musical performances

WOOD RIVER REFINERY HISTORY MUSEUM
Rte. 111 and Madison St.
Roxana
618-255-3718
wrrhm.org
Esoteric, yes, and run by dedicated volunteers, so expect to be regaled with all manner of trivia on petroleum refining, Shell stations, historic vehicles, and, as the website promises, "who knows what all"

{ ALTON ANTIQUES }

Throughout Alton's streets is a great collection of antique shops, from the **Alton Antique Center** (401 E. Broadway, lower level, 618-463-0888, altonantiquecenter.com) to stops all along Broadway, selling everything from eighteenth-century European furniture to outsider and folk artwork.

FESTIVITIES

ART ON THE SQUARE
May
Belleville
artonthesquare.com
Charming and internationally lauded fine arts festival along fountain-centered Main Street

GREAT RIVERS TOWBOAT FESTIVAL
June
Grafton
(Historic Boatworks on Front St.)
greatriverroad.com
Demystify those ubiquitous boats plying the rivers by taking a tour and participating in a deckhand contest, or just kick back and enjoy the bands. Event held only as river levels permit.

THE INTERNATIONAL HORSERADISH FESTIVAL
First weekend in June
Woodland Park
Collinsville
horseradishfestival.com
Celebrates all things horseradishy, including a Bloody Mary contest, root toss, and food vendors

ITALIANFEST
Third weekend in September
Collinsville
italianfest.net
Bocce tournament, wine garden, parade, and grape stomp

ROUTE 66 FESTIVAL
June
Edwardsville City Park
Edwardsville
cityofedwardsville.com
Embrace the Mother Road via classic car cruises, classic rock bands, and historical displays

WORLD'S LARGEST CATSUP BOTTLE FESTIVAL
July
Collinsville
catsupbottlefestival.com
Music, games, classic car cruise, catsup taste-offs, and the crowning of Sir Catsup and Little Princess Tomato

{ MOUND CITY }

Only the nickname is left for the St. Louis side of things, but in Collinsville, **Cahokia Mounds** (30 Ramey St., 618-346-5160, cahokiamounds.org) offers the real deal: more than seventy prehistoric earthen mounds, built and painstakingly maintained by native peoples in a settlement that was, in its time, the largest Indian site north of Mexico. Its legacy is only recently getting burnished in local minds, but the rest of the world is far ahead of us: UNESCO named it a World Heritage Site, in company with other spots like the Taj Mahal, the Great Wall of China, and the palace of Versailles. The interpretive center's walk-through replica settlement is a great place to start your exploration.

SHOPPORTUNITIES

HOME/GARDEN/BODY/GIFTS

CIRCA BOUTIQUE
128 E. Main St.
Belleville
618-257-0163
ilovecirca.com
Well-edited selection of handmade boutique lines of apparel and accessories; look for the owner's Mellow Mountain goods, too

THE FLOWER BASKET
317 W. Main St.
Collinsville
618-344-1117
flowerbasketcollinsville.com
Gracious historic home displays decor, candles, garden goodies

HAPPY UP, INC
6654-A Edwardsville Crossing Dr.
Edwardsville
618-656-9596
happyupinc.com
Independent shop for kids' toys, games, and dolls

JOLLY ROGER SKATEBOARDS
307 N. Illinois St.
Belleville
618-277-7113
jollyrogerskateboards.com
Skater-owned wheel shop

THE LITTLE SHOPPE OF AURAS
458 Tamarach Dr.
Edwardsville
618-251-9646
littleshoppeofauras.com
Native American music, instruments, metaphysical ritual items, plus massage, chakra cleansing, and more

{ KID ZONE }

At **K-10s Model Trains** (19 Schiber Ct., Maryville, 618-288-9720, k-10smodeltrains.com), kids can ogle the locomotives, slot cars, kites, and more for sale in the hobby shop, but what'll really get their horns blowing is the chance to operate the model trains in nearly five thousand square feet of track layout, or watch the remote-control car races out back on the banked dirt track, or launch a kit-built rocket. Times of events vary; see website for schedules.

{ FERRY TALES DO COME TRUE }

Any mode of transport besides the mundane automobile makes travel more exciting, and a trip across the river on the **Grafton Ferry** (7597 N. Highway 94, 636-899-0600) is no exception. Load your car or bike up on either side, and for $15 round-trip (cars), you'll be deposited across Big Muddy about ten minutes later. Seasonal hours, and calling ahead is not a bad idea (many river conditions can make passage impossible).

LOST ARTS & ANTIQUES
254 N. Main St.
Edwardsville
618-656-8844
lostartsandantiques.com
Refurbed finds, local fine arts and crafts

**MILO'S TOBACCO ROAD/MILO'S
CIGARS & MORE**
228A N. Main St.
Edwardsville
618-692-1343
2921 N. Center St.
Maryville
618-288-1343
milostr.com
Cigars, spirits, and beer

{ SACRED SPACE }

The **Shrine of Our Lady of the Snows** (442 S. De Mazenod Dr., 618-397-6700, snows.org) in Belleville is a Catholic complex you could spend a weekend exploring, from the large gift shop and popular restaurant (with eight soups on the lunch buffet!) to an outdoor amphitheater, spiritual-themed kids' playground, and events like the Christmas Way of Lights. Of course, its main purpose is worship, prayer, and spiritual edification.

SOLE SURVIVOR
25 E. Main St.
Belleville
618-234-0214
solesurvivorleather.com
Leather shoes, bags, and custom-tooled
belts

WHAT TO WEAR
921 S. Arbor Vitae
Edwardsville
618-655-0222
whattowearboutique.com
Of-the-moment looks for guys and gals,
from denim to dressy

ARTSY

BY DESIGN
136 Front St.
Alton
618-433-1400
lillianbydesign.com
Custom and handmade clothing,
accessories by local designers

COMMUNITY CONCRETE STATUARY
300 Shamrock St.
East Alton
618-259-8270
communityconcretestatuary.com
Thousands of made-on-site choices in
the concrete garden statuary genre

KNIT ONE, WEAVE TOO
303 N. Main St.
Edwardsville
618-692-6950
k1w2.com
Yarn and knitting/weaving accessories

MISSISSIPPI MUD POTTERY
310 E. Broadway
Alton
618-462-7573
mississippimudpottery.com
Substantial and chic tableware,
vases, and more

MOJO'S MUSIC
144 N. Main St.
Edwardsville
618-655-1600
mojosmusic.com
Guitars and amps for all levels

PATCHWORK PLUS
62 Ferguson Ave.
Wood River
618-251-9788
patchworkplus.net
Quilting supplies and classes

THE QUILTED GARDEN
1310 N. Main St.
Edwardsville
618-656-6538
quiltedgarden.com
Fabric, frames, notions, and
classes for quilters

SWING CITY MUSIC
1811 Vandalia
Collinsville
618-345-6700
244 S. Buchanan

Edwardsville
618-656-5656
swingcitymusic.com
Instruments, including band rentals,
lessons, and sheet music

COMESTIBLES

CHEF'S SHOPPE
2212 Troy Rd.
Edwardsville
618-659-9840
chefsshoppe.com
Fine cookware, knives, gadgets, and a host of gourmet mixes, spices, and ingredients

COLLINSVILLE FARMERS MARKET
128 Saint Louis Rd.
618-344-0222

1303 Vandalia St.
618-344-0223
Fresh local produce, seeds, plants, dressings/spice mixes at two locations

CRUSHED GRAPES
1500 Troy Rd.
Edwardsville
618-659-3530
crushedgrapesltd.com
Wine, beer, coffee, and cheese from all over

DAVE'S HOMEBREW & GOURMET TOO
122 E. Main St.
Belleville
618-277-2550
daveshomebrewgourmet.com
Beer and wine-making supplies, plus nonstop friendly advice and an assortment of natural home and body goods

GREEN EARTH GROCERY
441 S. Buchanan St.
Edwardsville
618-656-3375
greenearthgrocer.com
Health food/supplement store and deli

SPIRITO'S ITALIAN GROCERY
228 W. Main St.
Collinsvile
618-344-3256
Olives and sauces, oils and cheese, for your own cucina (takeaway sandwiches are a hit, too)

BOOKS/TUNES

AFTERWORDS BOOKS
232 Buchanan St.
Edwardsville
618-655-0355
afterwordsbookstore.com
Used books and enthusiastic reading recommendations

HOMETOWN COMICS
110 E. Vandalia St.
Edwardsville
618-655-0707
hometowncomics.com
Comics, graphic novels, manga, and action figures

{PICKIN' AND PAYIN'}

Pack rats and treasure hunters, put the fourth weekend of each month from April to October on your calendars, when the massive **Grafton Riverside Flea Market** (next to the Loading Dock Bar and Grill, 400 Front St., 618-786-3494) takes over the Boatworks building with antiques, crafts, food, and such.

OUTSTATE

A HANDFUL OF OUR FAVORITE DIVERSIONS WITHIN A FEW HOURS' DRIVE OF ST. LOUIS

Although the density of urban and near-urban neighborhoods makes them rich in interesting bars, restaurants, shopping, museums, and other amenities, there is a plethora of getaways within just two or three hours' drive of St. Louis that add great character to our region and make for a drive-worthy day strip when you need a change of scenery. Small river towns, world-class wine-producing districts, natural wonders, and more are within easy reach.

DAY TRIP DESTINATIONS

CLARKSVILLE

Home to a cornucopia of craftspeople and artisans, with shops lining Main Street in media from woodworking to weaving, this Mississippi River town also boasts spectacular winter eagle watching and an award-winning inn/farm-to-table restaurant, Overlook Farm. Approximately seventy-five miles northwest of St. Louis. *clarksvillemo.us*

JEFFERSON CITY

The state's capital is a must-do: the capitol itself, domed and topped by a bronze statue of the Roman goddess of agriculture, is classical revivalism at its finest. Other spots around town worth a look include: tours of the Missouri State Penitentiary (ten years old+, reservations required, 866-998-6998, missouripentours.com); the Cole County Historical Museum (573-635-1850, colecohistsoc.org); the Missouri State Museum (inside the capitol; 573-751-2854, mostateparks.com/park/missouri-state-museum); and Old Munichburg, a historic German neighborhood on the city's south side, boasting authentic restaurants, shops, and festivals (573-635-6524, oldmunich-burg.com). Approximately 130 miles west of St. Louis. *visitjeffersoncity.com*

KIMMSWICK

This compact riverside town on the Mississippi is home to all manner of shopping (think collectibles like Boyds Bears, Precious Moments, Madame Alexander; hand-made gifty items like soy candles, personalized dough ornaments, table lace; and

antiques galore). Highlights include Mississippi Mud Gallery for pottery and glass art, and breakfast/lunch/most definitely dessert at the Blue Owl. Approximately twenty miles south of St. Louis. *gokimmswick.com*

NEW HAVEN

On the Missouri River and along the train tracks, you'll find one modest block of bustle, but what a block it is! Several charming B&Bs overlook downtown, the river, and its levee-top walking trail, while the single-screen Walt Theatre offers weekend shows of first-run flicks. The nonprofit Riverfront Cultural Society brings in area bands for hoppin' live shows, in addition to hosting music and cultural events, yoga classes, and a weekly farmers' market in season. And at Astral Glass Studio the whole family can watch glass creations being born. Approximately fifty miles west of St. Louis. *newhavenmo.com*

WASHINGTON

Take the westbound Amtrak from St. Louis, and you'll find plenty within walking distance of the Washington station: charming shops, several dining options (including the renowned American Bounty Restaurant and Cowan's for mile-high pies), and the must-see Corncob Pipe Museum. Artist Gary Lucy has a studio here, and the town's newest attraction is the Missouri Photojournalism Hall of Fame. Plenty of charming, small-town annual events, including the massive Town and Country Fair held the first week of August. Approximately fifty miles west of St. Louis. *washmo.org*

BLACK MADONNA SHRINE

Franciscan missionary Bronislaus Luszcz, a 1927 Polish immigrant to Missouri, venerated Mary and undertook to create representations and shrines to her in his adopted country, which would echo the many homages found in his homeland. Over decades, he painstakingly handcrafted seven devotional grottos from Missouri tiff rock, which are now scattered throughout the shrine site. Various adornments, including costume jewelry, seashells, and decorative rocks, were brought or sent to Brother

WINE HAVENS

AUGUSTA

The closest concentration of wineries to St. Louis makes for a full day of tasting, and that's if you keep up a decent pace. The list includes Chandler Hill Vineyards, Yellow Farmhouse Winery, Sugar Creek Winery, Montelle Winery, Mount Pleasant Estates, Augusta Winery, Louis P. Balducci Vineyards, Noboleis Vineyards & Winery, and Blumenhof Vineyards & Winery. If you can only make one, we recommend Montelle: stunning, shady patio, cozy indoor fireplace for the cooler months, free weekend entertainment, yummy food, and of course, excellent wines. Of interest to beer drinkers, the nearby Augusta Brewing Company produces a full slate of craft beers (and their own root beer!). Approximately forty-five miles west of St. Louis, off Highway 94. *augusta-missouri.com*

HERMANN

The earliest German settlers of this town high above the Missouri River chose the spot, it's said, because the vistas reminded them so much of their home regions. Picturesque and friendly, the area is home to Bias Winery, Bommarito Estate Almond Tree Winery, Hermannhof Winery, OakGlenn Winery, Adam Puchta Winery, Röbller Winery, and Stone Hill Winery. Special events fill the calendar year-round; some of our favorites avoid the high season entirely and instead give you something special to look forward to in February (Chocolate Wine Trail) or July (Berries & BBQ Wine Trail). Tin Mill Brewing Company turns out fantastic microbrews in a historic (you guessed it!) tin mill, using imported German hops, barley, and copper brewing kettles. Approximately seventy-five miles west of St. Louis, off Highway 100. *visithermann.com*

STE. GENEVIEVE

Winding roads through some of the earliest settled areas of the state provide charming views along the way to Cave Vineyard, Charleville Vineyard & Microbrewery, Chaumette Vineyards & Winery, Crown Valley, Sainte Genevieve Winery, Sand Creek Vineyard, and Twin Oaks & Winery. Plenty of variety here in terms of setting and wine styles. We especially love Chaumette (for its patio atop a rolling hill, farm-gourmet Grapevine Grill, and luxe overnight accommodations at the villa/spa complex); the sprawling Crown Valley empire, with a winery, brewery/distillery, champagne house, numerous lodging options, and, oddly, a tiger-rescue sanctuary with tours and educational programs; and the stroll down to Saltpeter Cave from Cave Vineyard. Approximately fifty miles south of St. Louis, off Interstate 55. *ste-genevieve.com*

Bronislaus, and he incorporated them into his scenes. Approximately thirty-five miles west of St. Louis. *franciscancaring.org/blackmadonnashri.html*

CRYSTAL CITY UNDERGROUND

So you've always wanted to ride a barge through an underground former sand-mine network? One of the state's newest tourist attractions has you covered. Or perhaps you'd prefer to kayak or canoe on the 150-acre lake (again, entirely underground)? Or play disc golf, or sand volleyball, or see a comedy show, or attend a concert? Yup. The, uh, cave's roof is the limit on the fun that can be had here. And just to complete the picture, there's a bar. Approximately thirty-five miles south of St. Louis, in Crystal City. *crystalcityunderground.com*

DANIEL BOONE HOME & BOONESFIELD VILLAGE

Homestead of the legendary Kentucky frontiersman (and much of his family) from 1803 until his death in 1820, this living history museum makes the Louisiana Purchase/ early Missouri statehood period come alive with restored, furnished structures including a chapel, school house, general store, and gristmill. Frequent special events. Approximately thirty-five miles west of St. Louis. *lindenwood.edu/boone*

ECO ZIPLINE TOURS

Ever wanted to fly through the forest's canopy like a spider monkey (or Diego, Animal Rescuer)? Here's your chance: two courses (one for noncommittal and faint of heart, the other for the hardcore) cover more than a mile of cables strung high above the ground of New Florence. Minimal walking in between stop platforms means folks of many ages and abilities can zip together (kids as young as three can join in). Check the website for pictures of people zipping around mid-Missouri's trees if you're having a hard time envisioning yourself playing treetop adventurer! Approximately eighty miles northwest of St. Louis. *ecoziplinetours.com*

MERAMEC CAVERNS

If you went there as a kid, you may find the cheese factor has been toned down a bit in recent years, and the five-story cavern is still a spectacular sight. Guided tours run about eighty minutes long, so consider that if you have small children; you may end up carrying or distracting them if patience wanes. Explore the rest of the offerings, too, from a Meramec River cruise on a canopy-covered riverboat to the newest attraction, the Caveman Zip Line, which offers a ninety-minute forest canopy tour, for ages ten and up/between 80 and 270 pounds. Approximately sixty miles west of St. Louis, off Interstate 44. *americascave.com*

PURINA FARMS

Your kids will be in hog (and cat and dog and goat) heaven, with free-range access to all kinds of charismatic animals (the dog agility shows are a hoot), plus a barn and hayloft play area. Grab lunch from the snack bar and, by all means, check out the gift shop if you have a true animal lover on your list. Approximately thirty-eight miles west of St. Louis. *purina.com/purina-farms/purinafarms.aspx*

WARM SPRINGS RANCH

Capitalizing, perhaps, on all the Clydesdale-love generated by their last few Super Bowl commercials, the folks at Anheuser-Busch realized there was more demand for the iconic horses than was being met just by the stables on the brewery tour. Enter this Boonville ranch, where a mare/stallion hookup-and-foaling barn and multiple pastoral pastures let visitors see where the magic starts. Baby Clydesdales! Could the photo possibilities be cuter? Ninety-minute guided tours include the breeding facility, close-up looks at the harness and tackle the horses wear at events, an antique beer wagon, the custom trailers that ferry horses to parades and the like, and Budweiser beer at the

OUTDOOR ADVENTURES

ELEPHANT ROCKS/JOHNSON'S SHUT-INS

Frolic among enormous, red, 1.5-billion-year-old granite boulders, and then head fifteen miles down the road to frolic in "nature's waterpark," the river-smoothed gorges and chutes carved over millennia into the hard igneous rock. These two parks provide photo opportunities like no other in the state and are bound to impress even the most jaded digital-age kid. Approximately one hundred miles southwest of St. Louis. *mostateparks.com/park/elephant-rocks-state-park* *mostateparks.com/park/johnsons-shut-ins-state-park*

HAWN STATE PARK

Perhaps the most frequently mentioned state park by St. Louisans looking to get out of town and back to nature. Outstanding hiking trails lead to canyon-rimmed valleys, through forests, along streams, and among striking indigenous rock formations. Birders delight in the multitude of species found and heard here, and pretty Pickle Creek is a favorite for exploration, providing cool respite on hot days. Approximately sixty-five miles south of St. Louis. *mostateparks.com/park/hawn-state-park*

KATY TRAIL

Named "Best Bike Trail in the Midwest" by AAA (and often designated as such by its more than three hundred thousand annual visitors), the rails-to-trails project, longest in the country at 240 miles (and also among the longest state parks), mostly hugs the Missouri River as it traverses landscapes from forests to farm pastures. Naturally, that means all kinds of options for cyclists and hikers. For proximity and pretty river views, we recommend the ten-mile stretch between Weldon Spring and Greens Bottom trailheads. And you'll do no better for exhaustive trip planning than the resources at *bikekatytrail.com.*

ONONDAGA CAVE STATE PARK

A shining example of why we're called "the Cave State," this natural area offers both above-ground delights (a panoramic view of the Meramec River) and underground wonders (sheer, towering stalagmites, active flowstones, seriously weird rock formations). Two caves at the site—Onondaga and Cathedral—are available to tour. The Cathedral Cave tour is a lantern tour. Check the website for dates, times, and prices. Approximately 85 miles southwest of St. Louis, in Leasburg. (pictured on page 223) *mostateparks.com/park/onondaga-cave-state-park*

end. A Clydesdale-themed souvenir shop caps it all off. Reservations required. Approximately 140 miles west of St. Louis, in Boonville. *warmspringsranch.com*

MASTODON STATE HISTORIC SITE

You've perhaps seen the sign from the highway as you hurtle past on southbound adventures, but if you haven't stopped, you're missing something nearly mammoth: remains of the American mastodon (dubbed "the Missouri Leviathan" by its earliest excavators in the 1830s), found in the hugely significant, Pleistocene-era Kimmswick bone bed of fossils. Check out the ice age in Missouri, and marvel at the human/mastodon coexistence that happened here, briefly, more than ten thousand years ago. Hiking trails and wildflowers are popular draws, too. Approximately twenty miles south of St. Louis. *mostateparks.com/park/mastodon-state-historic-site*

MERAMEC STATE PARK

It's an action-packed paean to the glory of the Meramec River, with floating, canoeing, fishing (in one of the state's most fish-packed spots), hiking, and more. Get your feet wet, literally, on a spelunking adventure into Fisher Cave, or ogle the massive aquariums inside the visitor center. Facilities include a dining lodge. Approximately sixty-five miles southwest of St. Louis. *mostateparks.com/park/meramec-state-park*

SHAW NATURE RESERVE

The far-flung conservation laboratory owned by the Missouri Botanical Garden offers more than fourteen miles of scenic hiking trails overlooking the Meramec River, plus diverse acreage that's home to everything from a conifer forest to a boardwalk-traversed wetland. Approximately thirty-five miles southwest of St. Louis. *shawnature.org*

RIVER FLOATS

The tradition of floating (canoeing for the athletic, rafting for the adventurous, and innertubing for the true lazy river rat) is a time-honored and tradition-imbued one in Missourah. Some folks have been floating in the same spots, with the same gear/stupid jokes/canned beer they've been enjoying for decades, but don't let that intimidate you if you're a novice. Outfitters along some amazingly beautiful streams and rivers can rent or sell you everything you need, and then they'll throw you on a school bus, haul you, your gear, and your cooler upstream, and drop you in! Bear in mind, these are large areas that draw the mass of humanity, so it's entirely possible you'll see nudity, drunken behavior, or other offensive acts, though avoiding the summer holiday weekends can cut your risk. [Side note: If you want to engage in said offensive behaviors, holiday weekends are your time to shine!] On our short list of sweet spots: **Akers Ferry** (573-858-3224, currentrivercanoe.com, Current and Jacks Fork Rivers); **Bass Resort** (573-786-8517, bassresort, Courtois, Huzzah, and Meramec Rivers); **Twin Rivers Canoe Rentals** (314-226-7369, floateureka.com, Meramec River, and the closest float to St. Louis); **Forest 44 Canoe Rental** (314-255-7091, forest44canoerental, Meramec River); **Cherokee Landing** (573-358-2805, cherokeelanding.com, Big River); **Bearcat Getaway** (573-637-2264, bearcatgetaway.com, Black River).

INDEX